pulse

HOME IS NOWHERE

MJ Mngadi

Translated from isiZulu by Nakanjani G Sibiya

OXFORD
UNIVERSITY PRESS

SOUTH AFRICA

OXFORD
UNIVERSITY PRESS

Oxford University Press is a department of the University of Oxford.
It furthers the University's objective of excellence in research, scholarship,
and education by publishing worldwide. Oxford is a registered trade mark of
Oxford University Press in the UK and in certain other countries.

Published in South Africa by
Oxford University Press Southern Africa (Pty) Limited

Vasco Boulevard, Goodwood, N1 City, P O Box 12119, Cape Town,
South Africa

Asikho Ndawo Bakithi was originally published in isiZulu in 1996. This translation is
published by arrangement with Shuter & Shooter Publishers.

The moral rights of the translator have been asserted.

First published 2018

Home is Nowhere

ISBN 978 0 19 075361 0 (print)
ISBN 978 0 19 073792 4 (ebook)

First impression 2018

Typeset in Utopia Std 10.5pt on 15.5pt
Printed on 70gsm woodfree paper

Acknowledgements
Co-ordinator at the Centre for Multilingualism and Diversities Research, UWC: Antjie Krog
Publisher: Helga Schaberg
Project manager: Liz Sparg
Editor: Mary Reynolds
Book and cover designer: Judith Cross
Typesetter: Aptara Inc.
Printed and bound by: Academic Press

We are grateful to the following for permission to reproduce photographs: Shutterstock/
Laurin Rinder/315572780 (cover); OUPSA/Admire Kanhenga (p.iv and p.301). The lines on
p.113 from the original isiZulu poem "Laba bantu bayahlupheka" (These people are suffering)
by DSL Phungula from the anthology *Iqoqo lezinkondlo* published by Shuter & Shooter,
1957, are used in translation by kind permission of Shuter & Shooter.

The authors and publisher gratefully acknowledge permission to reproduce copyright
material in this book. Every effort has been made to trace copyright holders, but if any
copyright infringements have been made, the publisher would be grateful for information
that would enable any omissions or errors to be corrected in subsequent impressions.

THIS BOOK FORMS part of a series of eight texts and a larger translation endeavour undertaken by the Centre for Multilingualism and Diversities Research (CMDR) at the University of the Western Cape (UWC). The texts translated for this series have been identified time and again by scholars of literature in southern Africa as classics in their original languages. The translators were selected for their translation experience and knowledge of a particular indigenous language. Funding was provided by the National Institute for the Humanities and Social Sciences (NIHSS) as part of their Catalytic Research Programme. The project seeks to stimulate debate by inserting literary texts into contemporary public spheres, providing opportunities to refigure their significance and prompting epistemic changes within multidisciplinary research.

This book is more recent than the others of this project but it taps into a shamefully neglected theme with international reach: how do ordinary families manage in the face of such insurmountable odds?

Every generation translates for itself. Within the broad scope of several translation theories and the fact that every person translates differently from the next, it is hoped that these texts will generate further deliberations, translations and retranslations.

NATIONAL INSTITUTE
FOR THE HUMANITIES
AND SOCIAL SCIENCES

UNIVERSITY *of the*
WESTERN CAPE

Centre for Multilingualism
and Diversities Research

MJ Mngadi (1949–)

Matthew Jabulani Mngadi was born in February 1949 in Pietermaritzburg soon after his mother had fled violent racial conflict in Durban. His father worked as a police officer and lived in the police barracks. Mngadi's mother loved reading, and often read novels to her children. Encouragement from an isiZulu teacher who singled him out for the excellence of one of his essays had a profound impact on him. He began to publish short stories in the children's magazine *Wamba*. Mngadi worked in government offices – writing when he could – until his retirement in 2013. He has written and published eight novels and three collections of short stories. His novel *Imiyalezo* was declared a South African Classic by the Department of Arts and Culture in conjunction with the National Library of South Africa. Four of his books, *Asikho ndawo Bakithi (Home is Nowhere)*, *Ifa Ngukufa*, *Iziboshwa Zothando* and *Bayeza Abanqobi* won awards soon after their publication. The awards included the JL Dube–Via Afrika Award for Prose, the BW Vilakazi–Shuter & Shooter Award, the M-Net Book Prize and its award for Overall winner in the Nguni Languages section. Mngadi also won the De Jager–Haum Literary Competition and the Usiba Writers' Guild Kenneth Bhengu Aktua Award for Prolific Writing. In 2009 he received the South African Literary Awards (SALA) award for lifetime achievement in literature.

Main characters

Dubazana family
Dubazana (also called **Zwelisha**): husband of MaZondi
MaZondi (also called **Thuleleni**): wife of Dubazana
Makhosazana: daughter of Dubazana and his wife, MaZondi;
   mother of Sibonelo
Nkosana: son of Dubazana and his wife, MaZondi
Sibonelo (Exemplary-one): son of Makhosazana

Thabekhulu family
Thabekhulu (also called **Thabizolo** by his parents): husband of
   MaDlamini
MaDlamini: wife of Thabekhulu
Thabethule: son of Thabekhulu and his wife, MaDlamini
Thabisile: daughter of Thabekhulu and his wife, MaDlamini

Mxolisi (One-who-seeks-forgiveness): son of Thabekhulu and
   MaZondi

Landlords and landladies
Silangwe: the first landlord
Nyokana (Small-snake): the second landlord (also called
   Phathaphatha, which means "Touch-touch"; he is a habitual
   fondler)
MaMlambo: a landlady

Mr Donda: a school principal
Bhekizizwe Zulu: a political activist, community leader and lawyer
Njayiphume (Dog-kicker): a leader of the shack-land criminals;
   Sibonelo's father

HOME IS NOWHERE

MJ Mngadi

Preface

Dear reader

After spending a long time writing this book, I set aside three days (from Wednesday the 20th to Friday the 22nd of January this year) during which I would finish it.

I tried my best to stick to my schedule for the three days and wrote until my eyes and hands became tired. I vowed that Friday was going to be the final day. It is a few minutes to ten in the morning and I am almost done. In front of me is a church hymnbook, which I have opened at a hymn that will be sung by the character who is going to face his final day. As minutes draw close to the hour of ten, my typewriter is pouring out words as I describe how the character stands forlorn and helpless as he waits to be killed. Just as I describe the priest's car as it approaches the scene, weighed down by its prayer-women passengers, there is a knock at the door. The visitors are local prayer-women, clad in full prayer uniform. Astounded, I stop typing and listen to the women as they sing with my two daughters.

Tears flood my eyes. The women don't enquire about my whereabouts since they assume that I am at work. As they sing, I remain transfixed in my study, kneel down and pray silently. Their actions have touched me in so many ways. It's the first time they have set foot here since I finished building this house some five years ago. Also, as far as I know, the day on which they visit households is a Thursday. And here they are today, on their first visit. They arrive on a Friday morning when my soul is on them, so to say.

They sing and pray; pray and sing. They lament people who set alight, necklace others and destroy by fire the nation's property and hard work. It seems as though they have arrived here having read what I was attempting to write; hence their focus on many aspects of my story.

I am deeply touched when they remind my daughters that God gave me a writing talent and that it was through my writings that He wanted to convey a message. They sing and pray for me. Alas, alone and in silence, I feel tears fall. They sing and pray for more than an hour. As they say their goodbyes, they sing the same song that is on the page that I had opened and which the character in my story was going to sing before he is killed.

To the four prayer-women who knocked at this house, this very moment: Mrs Zulu, Mrs Mchunu, Mrs Sithole and Mrs Magagula: your arrival today indicates to me that God knows before we are aware as to where on a certain day we will be, doing what, with whom; and what will happen to us. It tells me that whatever we attempt to do is not done by us, and we don't do it for ourselves. It tells me that, just as you also mentioned it yourselves, God speaks through His people, in the same way that He spoke through you. Should this work get published and become a success, my wish is that your pictures appear in it, in the full uniform that you arrived wearing today.

The whole of today, all who look at my eyes ask me why I have been crying. I wind up this story now and end it singing, just as you entered and left in song.

Oh God, Mighty Hand that constantly performs great things!

To the late Mrs Mchunu, may she rest in peace.

Matthew Jabulani Mngadi
Friday, 22 January 1993

1

It feels as if his body no longer belongs to him. It feels emaciated, weary and stripped by the burdens that life throws at him. Even as he plods up the steps to the house in Mlazi where he lives as a tenant, Zwelisha Dubazana moves slowly, sweating heavily on this scorchingly hot day.

Zwelisha was born on a farm near Vryheid forty years ago where the onerous farm laws dissipated his energy from a very young age. As a mere teenager he, with his family, was evicted from the farm. Their belongings were thrown out on the road after he refused to continue serving six months without pay. This incident turned his family into perennial nomads. His father wandered from place to place until one of the landlords in Kuphumuleni in Ladysmith offered them a place, while he, young as he was, decided to look for a job in Durban.

His body has good reasons to feel sluggish and sodden with pain. With his arrival in Durban, the world around him shrank further. He could not be in the city without a permit. Wandering around looking for a job, he was arrested countless times and deported back to Vryheid, the magisterial district stamped on his pass book. The police who escorted him would leave him at the court in Vryheid to fend for himself, but he would be back in Durban at the same time as those who had dumped him, if not ahead of them. This happened so often that he was eventually sentenced and served years in the Bethal prison where prisoners laboured themselves to death on its potato farm: Emazambaneni, the Place of Potatoes.

Now it is a dejected Zwelisha sitting in his rented room: his mind vacuous, his cheeks buried in his hands. His life feels hopeless as the past keeps on rushing back to him. When he was released from the Place of Potatoes, the home his father had secured in Kuphumuleni was also a thing of the past. The government had forcibly relocated the people of Kuphumuleni to a township in Zakheni. His father, Bheseni, who could not imagine himself living in a township, packed their things before the arrival of the removal trucks and found a local chief at Mangwaneni who took them in to settle and build a home.

Zwelisha then decided for a second time to return to Durban. Weary of the rampant police harassment, he followed the advice of others to look for a job as a servant for whites in suburban homes. After all, one could only be granted a special permit to be employed in factories after working as a domestic help for two years. Indeed, as soon as he had served as what whites referred to as a kitchen boy for two years, he secured a job at a motor assembly plant in Jacobs. But this special permit did not allow him to be a fully official Durban resident. He could only become one after working for the same employer for ten years or after working for different employers for fifteen years.

As he sits exhausted in the room he rents from the Silangwes, he keeps counting, and, in exasperation, stamps the floor with his foot as he confirms the number of years left before he reaches the fifteen-year mark. Only then will he qualify to apply for a house in one of the nearby townships – for which he could spend an eternity waiting. He had already worked at a motor foundry for seven years when he was retrenched. Therefore, qualifying was still eight years away. Meanwhile, he has married a young woman from the Zondi family of Nkumba, with whom he has fathered a son and daughter, right here in the countless rented rooms they have occupied over the years. It seems obvious that

Makhosazana and Nkosana will grow up in rented rooms, where their father seems destined to be a perpetual tenant.

Indeed, on this Saturday he feels the throbbing pains that overwhelm his anxious soul and serve as a reminder that in this country he is an alien in all the places where he is supposed to be a resident. He was a total stranger in the town of Vryheid and in the village of the chief under whom, according to his pass, he was supposed to be a subject. He was still in prison when his family was removed from Ladysmith, and these changes were not yet reflected on his pass, so in Durban he became a homeless drifter.

He takes a glance at his wristwatch and shakes his head. It's exactly one o'clock. At two o'clock he is supposed to attend a community meeting at Mbalasi Primary School. A newly elected councillor has called a meeting to discuss the housing crisis in the community. Since early in the day, people have been flocking to the hall in droves, eager to hear what strategies the new councillor has and how his plans differ from those of his predecessor, who failed to deliver in his six-year office term. Despite the sweltering heat, Dubazana goes out and heads to the school perched on a nearby hill.

As usual, the meeting does not start at the appointed time. It is only at half past two that there is a prayer and the deliberations begin in earnest after the committee secretary explains that the purpose of the meeting is to alleviate a plethora of problems engulfing the township. The hall is overflowing. People seem to be participating in a hand-raising competition, thus keeping the secretary on his toes. The comments are generally off-point, as if deliberately, and marked by a collective failure of speakers to nail the seemingly elusive topic.

"Honourable Chairperson, the purpose of this meeting defies clarity. Could you please elucidate the exact issues that we have convened to discuss here, or if there are any new things that we are going to be told here?" Mthembu, asking the question, is a short, thickset man, extremely dark in complexion. His raven black hair, with a few strands of grey, is brushed back, resulting in his having a fine resemblance to a hammerhead stork.

The chairperson of the meeting, Mr Mavimbela, and the newly appointed councillor, Mr Zithulele Silas Bethule, are both bald men of medium height and both are seventy-two years of age. Despite the extreme heat in the hall, they are both wearing suits, waistcoats and matching grey scarfs. They continuously wipe their faces and bald heads which are glittering with sweat.

"Mvelase," says the chairperson, addressing Mthembu by his clan name, "the new councillor, honourable Bethule, has brought us all here to discuss and find a solution that we can use to end the problems that overwhelm many families, such as alcohol abuse by women and men, and other evils that destroy families. One may count, amongst others, the premarital cohabiting of teenagers, the increasing number of babies born out of wedlock, and so on. We need to hear from you, residents, what your opinions are, because some of these evils are caused by us parents. Women have taken so much to the bottle simply because men have become weaklings. Our Councillor Bethule," he turns and slightly tilts his head as he looks at him, "is sitting here, in silence. He does not want to say anything because he still wants to hear what all of you have to say so that he can deal with your afflictions directly. So engage with us, or do you suggest that we found some associations for women where they will guide and advise each other on the different challenges they face? For the youth, different entertainment activities can be established so that they can stay away from alcohol and cohabiting." He thanks the audience, sits down and shuffles in his chair.

Another hand is raised.

"Let us hear your contribution, sir."

The chairperson points at a tall man who stands up, as if reluctant: "What I am observing here, Chairperson, and about which I feel the Word urging me to comment, is that all our people as a collective are lost; they are estranged from Jesus!" He sinks his shoulder, opens a bag and takes out a Bible which he waves above his head and roars, only to lower it within seconds, banging it angrily with the other hand, saying, "Owu! Oh! This is what torments them! They are short of hope! They are obsessed with the wealth and joys of this perishing world! They do not want to forsake worldly things and strive for a new world that beckons with everlasting honey!"

"We will attend church services tomorrow!" interjects Lawrence Mthembu. "This is a community meeting, not a congregational revival gathering. Sit down and stop talking nonsense!"

"My fellow brothers, could you please listen! Lend me an ear!" This man, whose surname is Sangweni, spreads his hands out in exasperation, lowers his shoulders and gives the gathering a piercing look as if silently asking the audience why they keep silent while a fellow resident strays. His finger lingers as he points at Mthembu, "You and your breed of rascals will be burned alive! Had I not been a God-fearing person, I would have uttered some profanities." He sits down, then suddenly jumps up as if the seat burns him, and walks off wearily yet haughtily, his rather generous buttocks protruding as he staggers towards the exit.

"It is high time that meetings like this one come to an end, and may there be more revivals and prayers for the lost ones," he mumbles aloud, spreads his hands and walks out with an air of finality in his steps.

Another hand shoots up, calling for attention. The person stands up, scratching his head: "The theme of the meeting is rather unclear, honourable Chairperson. The gathering meanders around the topic and audience members end up at loggerheads with each other without resolving anything. I am not trying to preach, but would request that before we dwell on the community or a desolate nation, and other issues, we scrutinise individual needs first, without any racial bias."

"Poor us!" Mthembu moans again. "We are flooded with preachers today! Kindly leave us, young man, and follow the man with the Bible to preach with him in revival meetings."

"The Bible has not done anything wrong," continues the young man who introduces himself as Bhekizizwe Zulu. "Over and above the good lessons it contains, it is a book with a wealth of histories that any leader should familiarise himself with, along with other books that are similar to it, so that he can be aware of things that have happened in the past, and how challenges were overcome in the past."

The meeting suddenly takes a united turn, with everyone listening intently and some starting to nod their heads in silent assent. Bhekizizwe continues: "It is said that in the beginning God created heaven and earth, after which He created day and night. After creating the firmament, He separated the earth from the sea and then added grass and vegetation. He then created the birds along with the land and sea creatures. After He had created all this, He created man in His image, to emulate Him and rule over the world. Our case, however, is a hopeless one. We live a life that is in sharp contrast to God's grand design.

"Firstly, there is the scarcity of housing. There is abject poverty. The shortage of these basic necessities has created homelessness. Let us ask ourselves what to do when conditions are like this. Firstly, evading the matter won't bring solutions, nor will swearing at each other or using bandages to hide the cancerous conditions that have taken over our lives. Let us begin with the housing dilemma. When I consider the promises made by the honourable Councillor for the election campaigns, one of them was that he would build us houses. A noble wish indeed. But will it come to fruition?"

Bhekizizwe proceeds: "Another speaker here in the hall quite eloquently referred to ancient Babylon. Unfortunately, all the honourable speaker could discern in Babylon was sin and depravity. He neglected to mention that in ancient times, social development in communities, politics, civilisation and commerce gave birth to great cities such as Rome, Athens in Greece, Babylon, that was mentioned earlier, and Carthage in Africa. I believe that some of Babylon's troubles arose from an influx of people into a city that lacked the proper infrastructure befitting a city of its size. We have, right here in Durban, experienced another Babylon that was called Mkhumbane. We are still going to see many more Babylons mushrooming around us if the laws of the country continue to stipulate that millions of blacks in this country should be settled on arid patches of land amounting to a paltry 13 percent of the entire country, if those who hog vast stretches of farmlands continue to evict blacks living there. Misery will keep escalating if the government insists on deporting people back to the magisterial areas that are stamped on their passes, not considering whether the person was initially evicted from a farm in the very same magisterial area, and if the government continues to load people into trucks after forcibly uprooting them from their own lands. As a result, families disintegrate, and the few who used to own homes end up destitute. Some are dragged from their homes in rural areas and dumped in cities – the very same cities from which the government evicts them, deporting them back to their homelands.

"The respectable Mr Bethule promises to end all of this misery. I wonder how *he* hopes to end it? As far as my meagre knowledge goes, the government here in South Africa is divided into three structures: at the top is the national government; immediately below it are four provincial governments, and right at the bottom are municipalities, the city governments. Unfortunately, the honourable Mr Bethule belongs to the municipal government, which, in turn, is directly controlled by the national government. A solution will only be reached the day that we handle affairs democratically; the day the government realises that it is a government that belongs to the people in their numbers, not a government that bosses people around." This Bhekizizwe says and sits down.

"I bet my last cent that, for this man," whispers one of the two men whose eyes have been fixed on Bhekizizwe, "today is the final day. He will be jailed. To a government that is not a servant of the people, but instead does a disservice to them, speaking the truth is taboo. You simply die for speaking the truth. Anyway, let us be quiet, my fellow man."

As if another thought has just hit him, Bhekizizwe gets up again and simply continues: "Now that the situation has deteriorated beyond salvaging, the housing dilemma will haunt the nation until those responsible sit down, put their heads together and seek a collective solution. Only time will tell as to when that solution will see the light of day. But the way I see it, we seem to be running out of time and a wildfire has already been set off. The reserves in the form of townships are overflowing ominously. In fact, they are on the brink of bursting now. By the time the fire that I say has been set off has been transformed into burning embers, even those who kindled it will be scared to walk past it, let alone sit around it. My opinion is that discrimination should end, and let us hasten to disarm the lurking two-legged time-bomb. I mean a bomb in the form of the multitudes of children who are born of parents who claim that their birth was a mistake." Bhekizizwe finally sits down.

The meeting is eventually adjourned, deadlocked and without a solid conclusion. If the solution is to put an end to discrimination, how many people are willing to put their lives on the line for this? As the people disperse and go back home, none of them wants to comment on dismantling discrimination. They cannot really trust each other – who knows who might be a police informer? – and some have started labelling others as sell-outs and traitors. Bhekizizwe, who is obviously at risk of being imprisoned at any time, is being isolated as if he has a deadly infectious disease, and associating with him will be an open invitation to being hurled into jail with him. He has become a loner. It is only Zwelisha Dubazana who summons some courage and joins him, walking back.

"You spoke so well about the challenges we face, my fellow brother, and it was as if you were reading aloud an extract from the story of my miserable life." Dubazana speaks as they walk together, pouring out anecdotes about the farms on which he was born and grew up, his deportation, the eviction of his family from Ladysmith and how he got married without owning a home, with a slim chance of ever owning one.

"This is exactly my point, my beloved brother. On the one hand, they restrict you by not allowing you to register for housing. On the other hand, they are not building any houses. They should allow you to register so that it becomes easier to ascertain the extent of the present and future housing needs. Also, the building of townships has been put on hold indefinitely, so the existing ones are now like thick masses of unwashed, tangled hair full of lice – they are slums. I repeat what I said: if things continue in this way, the Babylon about which one reads in the Bible will soon be a reality."

They are standing next to Silangwe's house, saying their goodbyes, when a rather elegant, sleek black car emerges and comes to a sudden stop next to them. It seems overloaded with a bunch of men, some white, some black. While Zwelisha is still surprised by this, the back doors fly open and out storm two black men, clad in black from shoe to suit, including spectacles, shirts and even hats.

"We are from the Special Branch, Bhekizizwe. We would like to question you on the evil you have been spreading around to innocent people, inciting them to revolt against the government."

"I did not say they should revolt against the government, all I said was that they should revolt against discrimination."

"Oh, we have a little hothead here! People like you are hurled into a bottomless abyss to cool off." At lightning speed they bundle him into the car and it speeds away, spewing a cloud of smoke as its tyres screech on the tar road, as if in revenge. Dubazana remains dead still and solemnly watches the car until it disappears into the distance, leaving him scared, loose-jointed. His whole body is shaking as he mounts the steps, swathed in a sense of fear and exasperation that will keep him trembling even inside the miniature room that he is renting.

2

It is a late Saturday afternoon. The lanky, wire-thin Dubazana, light skinned and curly haired, jumps off the train at the station in Zwelethu and sets out with a leisurely stride, feeling young. He has been working overtime and is on his way home, wearing his brand new multi-coloured jersey, while on his shoulder a bag dangles, stuffed with treats and food he has bought for his family. The house where he is renting a room is not too far from the station, so he prefers walking home. But as soon as he can see the house, his mood plunges, and a terrible feeling comes over him: renting a room in someone else's house, the thought of it, makes him stagger. As he approaches Silangwe's house, his eyes see only chaos and confusion. A crowd is gathering in the yard where a fierce fight is raging. Swear words and insults fly through the air; two fighters are throttling each other, and onlookers try to intervene by pulling them apart, only to see them chasing each other again seconds later. A scraggy woman is being held back by the onlookers. She wields a big stick with which she clearly wants to beat a young woman who is frantically trying to hide behind whoever is within reach.

Amid the crowd that has been attracted by this fight, there is a man whose actions surprise the onlookers. Light skinned, with a round face, a rotund, clumsy figure and a big ugly mouth; his small piercing eyes resemble those of a wild cat. He wears a yellowish coat with thick baggy pockets, and his cap is slightly slanted to the side. He does not intervene, nor is he saying a word; he simply paces up and down the yard. Now his hands are deep in his pockets, then he puts them behind him and shakes his head, then he folds them on his stomach, throwing a menacing glance at the women threatening each other, then curses aloud into the air and moves up and down the yard all over again.

As he gets close to Silangwe's house, Dubazana immediately recognises the young woman who is being chased around the yard. She has a presence, this thirty-seven-year-old woman, tall and slim-figured with shapely legs that are always shiny and spotless. Indeed, it's his wife, MaZondi. He quickens his pace and is almost running up the steps to the house when he is greeted by the horrible spectacle of his fifteen-year-old daughter belting her lungs out every time the stick threatens to fall on her mother's shoulders.

Wielding the stick, the rake-thin woman spits fire: "It was a grave mistake to take you in as tenants in my house! You filthy impoverished riff-raff! I felt pity for you because you were desperate!" To Dubazana she yells, "I thought you were a husband to this despicable wife. It never crossed my mind that you brought a slut here who would steal my husband!"

"Could you please calm down and tell me what has happened?" Dubazana asks in a low, tired voice, filled with foreboding. The owner of the house, Silangwe, wearing his skew cap and leaning against the fence, gives them all a penetrating look, opening his mouth wide for a long while. Those caring to look see his huge tongue sticking to his palate before he slowly lets it hang out as he curses and snorts under his breath. But his wife, who seems all over the place now, turns on him: "You have the guts to stand here grunting and behaving like a pig! Is there a sane man who has an affair with another man's wife, while the husband is around, and worst of all, while I, who am your wife, am around?"

After a cold, knife-like stare and another unhurried grunt, the one who has been called a pig seconds earlier, indeed looks like one as he insolently scans the faraway horizon, showing no interest in commenting.

MaNcanana beats her chest repeatedly and pushes it forward: "This is my house! I swear that this worthless wife will not spend another night here. If you want to go to the housing office and read those thick official documents, you will see that it is *my* name that appears as Silangwe's rightful wife, not the name of this wretched wife of yours."

She threateningly moves towards a retreating Dubazana. "Move away from me, I want to beat your corrupt woman!"

Dubazana, who now has opened his arms wide, trying to protect his wife, also gets a few beatings on the head amidst the shouting: "Suka! Move away before I take my frustrations out on you!"

"Please, tell me what happened."

"Even if I do tell you, what will you do? You have turned into a weak bewitched man, under the evil spells of this wife of yours who is having an affair with Silangwe!"

"I am not having an affair with Mr Silangwe!" MaZondi protests, denying the accusations in a soft voice. Any movement startles her. "*He's* the one who just held my hand. And Mama, I believe that you also heard me telling him to stop."

"Thula! Why have I suddenly become your mother, don't we share a man any more? I would be a useless, forsaken woman if I were your mother who had soiled her bowels by giving birth to the despicable child that you are."

"Go inside, my children, do not pay attention to this crazy woman," says Silangwe, looking at them with shifty eyes.

"Into whose house are you telling them to enter? *My* house?" MaNcanana stamps her foot down and walks around frantically. "Over my dead body will that happen. You have been taking me for granted far too long." Suddenly she runs into the house and those outside hear the clattering sound of breaking furniture and dishes. Then MaNcanana comes flying out and with clanging sounds throws the Dubazana pots over the fence onto the road. She disappears again and comes out with the Primus stoves that, with surprising strength, she now sends soaring over the fence into the street. Dubazana is still petrified with shock as MaNcanana goes to the gate and turns a suitcase upside down, scattering all its contents in the street.

"Wenzani MaNcanana? You are doing what?" asks Silangwe with his head tilted to the side.

"What do you mean, what am I doing? Can't you see for yourself?"

"Are you not aware that you are insulting me, making me enemies with my son here if you insist that I am making passes at his wife?"

"The issue about the hand is comparatively trivial. Do you want me to disclose everything?"

Silangwe grunts to himself, embarrassed, and shuffles to the back of the house.

"You two," says MaNcanana, pointing the stick at Dubazana and his wife, "get inside the room, pack all your remaining rags, take them out with you before I set them alight and smash your heads open. Do me a favour and save me before I am accused of murder and sentenced to death by hanging."

Disconsolate and overwhelmed by a depressing sadness, Dubazana enters the room, his embarrassed wife in tow. Without saying a word to each other, they carry the bed and wardrobe out to the front gate.

"Listen carefully, you two with your dubious marital status – whether married or cohabiting unlawfully: take all your rags off my premises."

"Bear with us please, Mama," Dubazana begs. "I still have to ask the neighbours to lend me a hand." With heavy legs he goes to a neighbour's yard. No sooner has he entered than MaGumede, the neighbour's wife, waves him back, her flabby arms flying in the air. "Emuva!"

"Mama, I have come to ask Sibiya to help me carry things."

"Is it Sibiya's responsibility to help the husbands of immoral wives? You find us living peacefully and then you come and sow evil among us!"

Dubazana finds himself in a confused daze. Then Mr Ndlela, another neighbour, who is also of middle age, takes pity on him and helps him lift the furniture over the fence, leaving it leaning against the wall of his house.

"Dubazana, I will keep your belongings here for a few days. You need to search for a place to stay and you'd better do it quickly before the rain drenches everything."

Dubazana gives his thanks and stands transfixed on Ndlela's lawn for a long time, in the rain which has now started to fall. To say that he is confused is an understatement. After what seems like a lifetime, he drags himself back to the Silangwes, takes the suitcases, gathers the discarded clothes and places them all on the other side of the road. He has no energy to talk and just beckons his wife and puts some of the luggage on her head. He picks up a suitcase with one hand, takes the hand of his fourteen-year-old son, Nkosana, with his other hand, and so continues their journey as luggage-laden wanderers.

Soaked by the rain, Dubazana and his family comb the neighbourhood for accommodation until they eventually bump into Mbonambi, a colleague of Dubazana who is the same age as he is. The misery of the Dubazanas is obvious to Mbonambi, who lives with his wife and their children – the mother, daughters, sons and grandchildren, all sleeping together, bundled into one room.

If they are willing, Dubazana and his family can sleep under a table in the kitchen. All of them are silent. Dubazana's heart is throbbing, his mind occupied by images of his disintegrating family. His imagination is beginning to persuade him to ask his wife as to what was true and what was fabrication back there. As the night progresses he begins to have no doubt that they are sleeping under Mbonambi's table because of his wife's loose morals.

As soon as daylight breaks, they quickly wash their faces, ask to leave their children for a little while and go out hunting for a room to rent. They go in and out from house to house but no one has time to attend to them. It is a Sunday and most people are still recovering from the previous day's festivities. Some are getting ready for church services, parties and gatherings at drinking spots. The sun becomes warm, then hot, and finally scorching while they are still walking the streets. They begin to feel hungry and weak, but neither of them suggests going to a tearoom. Each has enough trouble and anger to fill a hungry stomach.

"You see, MaZondi, sometimes I think about our situation and feel that it would have been a lot better if you were my sister," Dubazana finally says in exhaustion, sitting down at the bus stop shelter. His wife, dragging herself along, sits down and looks at her husband with soft, brown eyes.

With a calm voice she asks, "Why would I have to be your sister?"

"If you were my sister, and had committed some immoral act, it would have been easier to love you and offer advice without shunning you, since you would have been my flesh and blood."

"What have I done?"

"Don't you know what you've done?" Dubazana gives her an angry look. "You have the guts to frown at me and ask questions instead of feeling ashamed! Are you aware that we are in this mess because of you?" He looks at her and then suddenly feels flames of love when his eyes lock with hers. His heart is unexpectedly softened by MaZondi's naturally curly hair peeping from under a multi-coloured sishweshwe head wrap, and the dark, slender face adorned with small incisions that always characterise members of the Zondi clan. She has a pointed nose and dimpled cheeks that cave in smoothly when she laughs and lips that look succulent as if evenly glossed with honey. In her teens, she was renowned for having suitors fight over her and cast spells on her or on one another.

MaZondi takes a moment to calm down, then responds to Dubazana, "Father of Makhosazana, most of you men are ridiculous and sometimes say things without giving much thought to what you say."

"What should I be thinking? That you are fooling around with Silangwe and gambling with my life?"

"That is exactly the point I am making, Makhosazana's father. We as women still have a huge responsibility for teaching our sons who will be boyfriends and husbands one day."

"What will you teach them?"

"That whenever they see or think about a woman, they should see a human being who is a creature of God and who knows the difference between good and bad; to despise destructive things and strive for constructive ones. We have to teach you, show you by our actions, so that you know that a woman has pride in her body and has no regrets about being female. I am asking you, too, my husband, please do not join those naïve men by accusing me of such things. You know very well that when you arrived in Nkumba there were many men who had tried for a long time, but failed to win my heart. When we got married, it became clear to us that it was our good fortune to be together. But since I have agreed to marry you, you think that I am a loose woman?"

The feelings of heartache and temper that had overwhelmed Dubazana slowly dissipate, making him also calm down.

"Silangwe didn't hold you by the hand?"

"He did hold me, but I was fighting against it to show him that I would never agree to what he was doing."

"When did he start making passes at you?"

"A long time ago, but I did not want to start a fight between the two of you and that is why I have been repeatedly nagging you to find another place for us to stay so that by the time I revealed this, we would be living elsewhere. Makhosazana's father, have I not said that before?"

She looks fondly at her husband, as if urging him to gaze at her soft eyes, and she shows no hint of any guilty conscience that might be devouring her. Her sweet, melodious voice fills his heart with a soothing feeling, like a remedy that washes away all the pains from a wound.

"And, father of Makhosazana, since we have nowhere to go, people will now take advantage of our plight and try to pull us apart. Some consider you a suitable man for them, while others assume that I may love them to secure shelter in their homes. But if our love can be strong, like concrete that gets its firmness from the rain, no one will be able to tear us apart."

There had been a distance between them as they sat, but the allusion to the hardening of concrete makes them shuffle closer to each other.

"The truth is that I love you, MaZondi. Although we are homeless in Durban, a day without your company would be unbearable, and I can't even let you go and stay with my family at Mangweni while I look for accommodation in a nearby hostel."

"Sithandwa sami, my love, that would mark the end of our love. Life in the hostels has had a major role in damaging the relationships between black women and men. I became a part of your life when I married you, and I can't afford to lose you. Father of Makhosazana and Nkosana, maybe I have never told you this before, because we don't have a roof over our heads and we can't afford privacy. But since our predicament has landed us here, all we can do is unburden our hearts and talk about our love under the roof of this bus stop shelter."

"What is this secret that you want to share with me, Thuleleni?"

"I want to tell you that ever since I fell in love with you, there have been five pillars in my heart that support the flame that kindles the love in our marriage. What are the pillars that I am talking about? The first is looking at you. Even though we are troubled, looking at you makes me feel as though I have drunk from the fountain of life. I drank from this fountain the first time I saw you. The day I die, like Jesus, who cried out from thirst when he was crucified, the last drink I will cry out for will be you. The second pillar is when we touch. When you hold my arms, when you hug me, I love the softness of your hand as you caress me. The third is the ear. Your voice is like music that I would recognise even if we were lost, deep in the forest. There are songs I hear that remind me of you. Even the singing of birds reminds me of the times when we were a younger couple under a tree. The fourth pillar is your scent. Have you ever loved someone so much that even when they are away, you can still smell their presence? And the fifth and last pillar is simply the pleasure of intimacy. What should I do? Should I be like those women whose husbands are in the hostels – those women for whom the pleasure of all those feelings is buried and lost in the hostels?"

"There's one thing you've forgotten," Dubazana adds while looking at her and smiling, because he feels the same way about her, "and that is your writing. When we still wrote to each other a lot, it was your letters to me that would comfort me. Even if I woke up in the middle of the night, I would read them, and in the days that followed, I would read them over and over again. To this very day, it is your writings that, to me, are pillars."

"That's true! I had the same feeling about your letters. Even when you sent me celebration cards, I appreciated them more if the message was in your handwriting."

There under the bus stop shelter they draw even closer to each other, embrace, and thereby wilt the weed that was sown in their marriage by the Silangwes. When they get up, they suddenly feel stronger, and even the scorching sun is more bearable. Their hands interlock while they continue their search.

Eventually, just when they are losing all hope, somebody comes to their rescue and suggests that they approach a Mr Nyokana, who lives near Mnyandu train station. Although it feels as if the sun is almost burning into their skulls, they pull each other along to where they have been told to go.

3

They disembark from the train at Mnyandu station, holding hands as they walk down the steps to the basement, passing through an exit that leads them to the road. The sun's heat is so unbearable that it feels as if it no longer shines from the sky but is right here on earth. Even the mist enveloping the area seems like smoke from the sun itself. A shortcut takes them to the house number they are looking for.

They find themselves in front of the gate of a house that looks the same as all the other four-roomed township homes, with one glaring difference: most of the neighbouring houses are plastered and colourfully painted, and some even have big windows, beautiful doors and electricity. A few of these small houses have also been extended, but not the house that they stand in front of. The condition of Nyokana's home is easily readable from the yard, which is full of tall grass, bits of paper, car tyres, and the shell of an old car resting on its belly with deflated tyres. Not even a child is playing in the yard.

"Why does it feel as though we are walking into a snare far worse than the one we come from?" Dubazana mutters as he opens the gate, closes it behind them and announces their arrival.

Unfortunately, with the noise coming from his broken Primus stove that spits flames and does not burn properly, the person inside the house cannot hear them. Wet with sweat, he kneels, prodding the stove with a needle, making it flare up again. The smell from paraffin smoke fills the room. He pauses, shakes his head and walks around aimlessly in the house. Only then does he hear the people who have stopped at the gate to meet him, and who are now knocking at his door. He opens it and grins generously when he invites them inside to be greeted by the paraffin smell.

"Please take a seat on the sofa. I am busy lighting the Primus and will be back right now." The man, who is in his fifties, with a small head like that of a mamba and the eyes of a cat, briefly looks at them and then leaves.

However, the moment they sit down on the sofa, it caves in and they seem to sink away with their feet flying up in the air. Dubazana grabs the side of the sofa, gets up, lifts his wife and then they both sit precariously with only one buttock each on the sofa, just as they had been told to do earlier. Although they feel as though they have almost broken their spinal cords, they nevertheless notice that the house itself is clean and the lino floor covering has been polished and shines brightly. The two sofas, one of which they are sitting on, and four chairs, also sunken in, surround a round coffee table. A steel cupboard and a big hi-fi stereo lean against the door. Hanging on the wall are photos of the master of the house, who is still in the other room, cursing the flaring Primus stove.

When he finally returns, he pulls a chair from the table and sits down.

"Our surname in this house is Nyokana, the place of Phathaphatha." After exchanging greetings and introductions, the Dubazanas explain their predicament. Their request is followed by what is common among landlords: complaints about tenants' bad behaviour. "Some bring their kids along, and make this place dirty. In some cases a person is desperate when he arrives here, but as soon as you take pity on him and take him in, he suddenly behaves like he is the head of the house and starts waking up in the morning, strolling around the house in pyjamas. Another has the guts to buy a car, while you as a landlord don't even own one. I wonder how he expects you to feel about him?"

And he goes on and on about what a clean person he is. The reason the floor is shining so brightly is because he cleans it all himself, on all fours, polishing it. But he is hoping to get relief since he is to be married soon and already has a fiancée at his home in a rural area. While busy explaining, complaining, he realises that the stove has suddenly become silent. He excuses himself and returns to the task of pricking it and watching it flare up.

The stove flickers a bit, but nothing more, so he returns and sits down, sweating. He mentions that he has had tenants before but they caused him so much headache that he had to let them go. Stamping his foot on the floor, he says, "And I swore that I would never have tenants again!"

But the couple in front of him beg him in tears and he succumbs and agrees to temporary accommodation to determine their suitability as tenants. He leads the way and shows them a clean, freshly painted empty room.

"I suggest you pay for it right now lest a smooth talker comes along and persuades me to give him the room."

He paces the floor arrogantly as he takes the money. Nodding his miniature head, perched on his long neck, he tells them that they can move in any time. It is with mixed feelings that the two bid him goodbye, and their minds are so preoccupied that they do not even feel the venom of the sun outside. On their way back, they immediately look for a delivery van and are lucky to find one. They go first to the Silangwes, but find none of the food they left there the previous day – not a bit of sugar, nor even a mealie pip. Then they load their things at the Ndlelas' home into the van, and go to the Mbonambis to thank them and fetch their children. By the end of the day they are installed at Phathaphatha's place.

"Isn't it remarkable that at a home with such an unusual name no one bothers to explain to us whether Phathaphatha is the clan name or surname," Dubazana mutters to himself as they try to arrange things comfortably in the room.

Soon after they have unpacked and are pondering the dilemma of their empty stomachs, the owner of the house knocks on the door and asks to see them. They meekly follow him and all perch precariously on the sofas for a briefing on the house rules.

"I am not sure about the arrangements you had at the places where you have been tenants previously. However, as you might be aware, each and every household has its own set of rules. The same applies here in this house. In my case, when a person is my tenant, I don't treat them as a tenant. I treat them as a sibling. Therefore, I have found a brother and a sister in you, the Dubazanas."

"We are very glad to hear that, my brother. As the saying rightly goes, a true brother is found amongst strangers," says Dubazana, anticipating more.

"The manner in which we conduct ourselves in this house is like this: let us start with the room that you will be occupying. The cleanliness that you see in it is solely because cooking never happens in the rooms. There is a kitchen for that. Secondly, in this house, we don't tolerate separate cooking. We share the cooking, with the exception of cases when pork or fish are served – food items that we, as Nyokanas, don't eat."

Although Dubazana decides to say nothing, he finds himself emotionally disturbed by the idea of sharing the cooking. If they are expected to share cooking chores, when is this wifeless person going to cook?

"Dubazana, I know that one cannot owe a stomach its dues, and I make sure that I feed my stomach without any delay. I will therefore not be troublesome to you guys, but will bring you the money for food personally, long before you even ask for it. Are there any complaints in this regard?" He once again pierces them with his small, fearsome, wild-cat eyes.

The Dubazanas suddenly feel, poor as they are, that all they can do is look at him in bewilderment.

"And madam, one other thing that I strongly dislike, but which is unfortunately usually done by you women, is that while every one of us here pays, there are still discrepancies in how plates are dished up. You find that the wife dishes out huge pieces of drumstick to her husband, but when it comes to oneself, who is not her husband, some lousy chicken neck or winglet arrives on one's plate. Personally, I absolutely detest that." The way he says it makes it clear that the issue of huge chunks of drumsticks really upsets him.

"It is precisely because of this that I ask that we, as one family, don't have meals in our separate rooms, but instead sit here together at the table when we eat. Do we understand each other?"

"Nyokana, it is a bit difficult to promise that we will always be able to sit together at the table to have meals. We work very hard at work. By the time we arrive back home, we are so tired that sitting down is almost impossible."

"Dubazana, it is obvious that you have accustomed yourself to the habit of eating alone like a snake. Here at the Nyokanas you will have to get used to eating with a fork and knife, seated like a real person." He leads them to the kitchen, but when they enter, trickles of soot on the walls greet them. Black traces of smoke escape from the Primus stove. The kitchen is sparsely furnished: a table with the Primus, next to the window is the sink, and against the other wall leans a cupboard. On opening it, Nyokana says, "This is where all the food should be stored; not in the bedroom where it will breed cockroaches."

Dubazana mildly shakes his head while looking at the cupboard that Nyokana has left open: not a sign of food! On one shelf are two saucepans, a small kettle and a few utensils. Nyokana opens the cupboard even wider on a growing number of empty shelves. Nowhere is even the slightest sign of an empty packet that may have once contained sugar or maize meal. But wait: on one shelf, when Nyokana reveals it, a single item emerges in the form of a cockroach lying on its back, wriggling from hunger. A little further from it, fellow cockroaches lie motionless. Unfortunately, they have passed away.

"Don't worry yourself about the flickering stove, I will fix it." Nyokana mentions this as he looks at it, vomiting its red flames, flickering on and off while it boils a neighbour's chicken that has fallen victim to his spring-trap.

After an elaborate briefing on the house rules, the family retires to their bedroom in a daze. The enormous challenges they have to face from this afternoon are very clear and bright to them.

Since the Dubazanas have nothing to cook for the evening, they think of how to cautiously approach the landlord for some money to share in the expenses. Didn't he warn them beforehand that he was always aware of his obligations and didn't have to be reminded?

"Let's knock at his bedroom straight away, because if we allow him to have his way, it will be a recurring habit and we'll forever be footing his bill," Dubazana says while they are quietly discussing the issue in the bedroom. They agree and Dubazana heads for Nyokana's bedroom and knocks. He starts timidly, but gradually knocks harder and louder. All in vain. There is no response from inside.

"Perhaps he went out," suggests MaZondi, totally unaware that Nyokana is feasting on the neighbour's chicken in the main bedroom. He gulps down the meat, putting the bones aside for later attention.

Giving up, the Dubazanas go out to buy some food and start cooking, with MaZondi using her own Primus stove. No sooner does she start than the house warms up in appreciation of a woman's natural homely flair. Even the household cockroach that lay comatose on its back seems to suddenly spring back to life, prancing up and down, exploring the packets of maize meal and sugar.

When the food is ready, the children get theirs to eat in the kitchen, while their father and mother sit down at the dining room table. No one but Nyokana knows how he hears that they have started eating. His bedroom door opens, and he emerges, yawning, his mouth wide open like a python's.

"Stupid me! I felt drowsy and fell asleep before I could pay you the money for food," he scolds and rebukes himself. "Anyway, there is nothing to be done now. Tomorrow is another day." He goes out, washes his face under the tap, returns and takes his place at the table, reaching for and uncovering his plate. It is laden with rice and chicken meat, the soft white part of the breast. He casts a quick glance at Dubazana's plate and sees big pieces of mouth-watering meat. He shakes his head and whistles in disbelief, ignoring the fact that his own stomach is already laden with a full fatty hen that he consumed earlier – head, feet and all!

All the while the Dubazanas fix their eyes on their plates.

They started eating earlier than Nyokana and are surprised when he unexpectedly says, "I don't feel full, my sister."

They stare at him as he sucks his fingers like a hungry child, staring at them with his piercing cat-like eyes.

"Makhosazana's mother, is there by any chance some food left in the pots?"

MaZondi gets up, cleans out the pots and returns with the last of the food to the table. Nyokana thanks her and literally devours everything, finishing the second helping before the Dubazanas have finished their own initial share. He looks at them with pleading eyes, but they keep their eyes on their plates, ignoring him.

"It is obvious that I'll sleep hungry tonight. I feel we'll have to sever our relationship if this annoying tendency to cook measly meals persists." He leaves them and goes straight to the pots to dish up for himself. From there they hear him cursing, "And these stupid modern saucepans don't even leave a charred crust of phuthu at the bottom that one can eat." He goes back to his bedroom and locks the door. While MaZondi washes all the dishes, dries them and packs them away, the smell of dagga envelopes the house.

By the time the Dubazanas go to sleep it is quite clear to them that they cannot stay long with Nyokana since they simply cannot afford to feed a bottomless stomach on their meagre finances. Dubazana leaves for work early in the morning while the children set off to the faraway school they enrolled in at the beginning of the year, when their parents could not have known that this month would find them at their sixth house as tenants.

With the rest of the family gone for the day, MaZondi is stuck with a dilemma. Phathaphatha's actions the previous evening gave clear signals that he does not regard MaZondi as a tenant's wife but rather as *his* wife. Quite soon after her husband has left, she finds him standing in her room, ordering her to warm water for his bathing, put it in a wash basin and take it to the bathroom. As soon as MaZondi has done that, he demands his preferred breakfast: a fried egg and liver. But Phathaphatha does not even bother to feel in his pockets for money to give to MaZondi to buy food. Even though she tries her best and uses her last cent, it feels as though the food ends up in a bottomless pit. Nyokana finishes everything on the plate and immediately complains about still being desperately hungry. After breakfast he goes straight to his bedroom and draws so hard on his dagga that it seems as if he holds a grudge against it. Cleaning her room, MaZondi wonders whether the dagga triggers his hunting instincts because he soon leaves the house and walks around the yard; before long, she can hear a hen pleading for its life as, cackling, it runs back to the safety of the neighbour's yard.

"Yesterday, I lost my guinea-fowl coloured hen. And now the other one is running for its life. God only knows how long I will have to keep an eye on that hawk with whiskers!" Despite the terrible dread and anger inside her, MaZondi cannot help laughing to herself when she hears the neighbour's wife who is loudly complaining from her house.

By the end of the first day that MaZondi spends at home alone with Nyokana, she is absolutely fed up, feeling as though she is being treated like a house slave. Dubazana, already burdened by the never-ending problems at work, finds his wife in tears when he returns.

"Dubazana, you are my beloved husband. You suffer on my behalf and you do your best to feed and take care of me. And you never cause me the distress that I've suffered at the hands of the monster of this house. He doesn't pay a single cent, but he forcefully demanded food the whole day. As you've noticed, his appetite is abnormal and I'm sure that we'll be penniless by the end of the month. Besides that, this man is ..."

"And why do you stop mid-sentence? What is he like?"

"I mean, if I look at him I don't think it's safe to be left alone with him during the day." She stops herself before blurting out that she has already had to brush him off several times when he tried to hold her hand.

"Oh my!" groans Dubazana. "Does this mean we have to move again?"

"We are definitely moving if that's a safer option than being locked inside with a mamba the whole day. You know as well as I how things are in lodging places. I have also been forced, on several occasions, to leave at short notice when women tried to take you away from me."

With a sinking heart that suddenly changes the way he missed his wife earlier, and the love and the jokes he meant to share with her, Dubazana throws himself on the bed, a million thoughts criss-crossing through his head like lightning. Confused too, his wife busies herself with the Primus stove.

By sunset, the family is relieved to find no sign of the house owner, but at midnight he knocks at their bedroom complaining of hunger. Dubazana, in turn, shouts from the inside, telling him where the food is. Nyokana shouts back that he needs his food to be warmed up.

"My wife is already asleep! She is tired too!"

"What makes her tired, since she doesn't work?"

"Even I, as her husband, never wake her up at midnight to warm up my food."

"That is none of my business! You should lay down the rules in your own house! In *my* house I have rules that even a fly that flies around here must abide by!"

"Of course, in your house, as you rightfully say. I am also referring to *my* wife, not our wife. Secondly, I am not staying here for free. I pay."

"Oh, so you see, this is how tenants are! When they are outside the gate, at your mercy, they are always shy and choose their words carefully. Once they are inside the gate, their tongues become sharp." He remains silent for some time until they assume he has left. After a while, they hear him saying, "I can see

34

that you think you are clever. You will soon realise how stupid you are." He goes to the kitchen and takes the cold food, finishing everything while groaning and complaining that his share of the meal is a lousy morsel.

This night Dubazana tosses and turns without any sleep, trying to figure, yet again, a way out of a mess. He wakes up, having barely slept, and goes to work accompanied by his problems, scared to leave his wife with this poisonous snake. He tries to work today, but for his co-workers, he is a difficult colleague. He keeps staring at empty spaces and only reacts when one of them directly intervenes.

Still angered by Nyokana's actions, Dubazana knocks off from work. Not wanting to discuss food with Nyokana when he arrives back home at midnight again, Dubazana goes to the butchery and buys some pork which his wife cooks for supper. They eat and go to bed.

Nyokana takes his time coming home and announces his return by knocking at their door while yawning hungrily.

"We decided to cook pork tonight, my brother," shouts Dubazana without much energy in his voice.

Nyokana is silent for a long time, and then says, "Oh, you cook that to spite me."

"Our understanding is that pork is also a worthy meal."

"You did this deliberately, Dubazana, because you guys know very well that I don't eat pork," he barks angrily. "Why didn't you tell me that you were going to cook pork so that I could find myself something to eat in time?"

"You were already gone when I arrived with the pork."

"You know what, I really regret suggesting that we share the cooking. What am I supposed to eat now?"

"It seems that we won't be able to intervene in your hunger plight right now, since the only food we have left is canned fish that we'll cook tomorrow, seeing that we don't have any money left."

"Let's just spare ourselves the talking since we only irritate each other." Nyokana enters his bedroom, curses to himself, sleep defying him.

When he gets up the next morning he is depending on MaZondi to cook for him, but has to give up as she says that she has nothing to prepare for him except fish. He goes to a shopping centre and buys himself meat at a shisanyama braai place, and asks them to braai it for him. There he eats to his heart's content before going back home where he locks himself in the bedroom and smokes dagga until he falls asleep.

He does not bother them at midnight on Wednesday since they have told him that they are serving fish for supper. They tell him the same on Thursday. On Friday, Dubazana brings beef home, which they fry and cook while Nyokana is away. They put away his food for him before retiring to sleep.

The family is fast asleep when the kitchen door is suddenly kicked open, off its loose makeshift lock, at about eleven o'clock. Dubazana hears it and panics. He is still fumbling around for a match when their bedroom door flies wide open, followed by flashing torchlights.

"Don't even start anything! Imali! Sheshisa! Money! Hurry up!" Someone slaps Dubazana while fist blows rain down on him.

"Stop screaming, you stupid woman!" They shut MaZondi's mouth with a fist.

Dubazana, seeing knife blades glittering in the rays of torch lights, takes an envelope and pleads for mercy as he gives it to them. A dirty hand snatches it, opens it and counts the money.

"There is some money missing in this envelope. Where is the rest?"

"My brother, as you can see: only ten rand is missing and I used that to buy meat for my family. I was still going to do groceries tomorrow."

"Never ever use your money until we have arrived and given you permission!" And the man stabs him in the shoulder with a sharp knife. "Take this bad-luck money and buy food for the kids in the morning!" He hands over a brownish one-cent coin and orders his companions, "Boys, do the work!"

Those called boys push the Dubazanas aside and start working with admirable speed, opening wardrobes, pulling out suitcases, loading things and leaving what they do not need. They ransack the room and strip the Dubazanas of their possessions. They even take their blankets and show Dubazana their appreciation by slapping him across the face once they are on their way out, leaving him in darkness, dizzy from the smack.

The room is quiet for a very long time. The Dubazanas are too scared even to light the candles, let alone try to close the kitchen door. Their minds seem to have deserted them. But as soon as Dubazana's senses start registering things, he searches for matches and lights a candle. Only then can they see how the hooligans have stabbed him. They go to the kitchen and inspect the door. It is not broken and the pathetic lock can still be nailed back.

"We may as well leave it open since the thugs took all my money," says Dubazana, inadvertently wiping tears off his eye-lids. He fixes the door and they return to the bedroom to digest their plight.

"At least they spared our souls, and for that we must be grateful. You may still be able to earn back the money we lost."

"There is no soul that was spared, my dearest. The fact that they slapped me in front of you and beat you up while I watched helplessly – all this in front of our children, and robbed me of my whole week's earnings – is like death to my soul. That is how things are, MaZondi. Losing your dignity destroys your soul. Our children will always remember the time when we were slapped and kicked around in front of them."

The room goes silent as they sit, downcast, as if mourning a death in the family.

"The fact that we were robbed while indoors makes me suspect Nyokana. What made these thugs go straight to our room and ignore Nyokana's door? How did they know that he wasn't inside?"

"That's a good question, indeed," his wife nods in agreement. "It's obvious that the lock on the door is loose so that his tricks can be successfully executed."

They are still discussing the robbery when they suddenly hear a key unlock the dining room door. Nyokana enters, locks the door and heads for his bedroom. After a while, he emerges and calls out to the Dubazanas, complaining of hunger.

"I wonder if you guys cooked pork for supper again?"

"Not at all, honourable landlord. We bought beef today but are not sure if the thugs left any in the pots, given that we are in trouble as we speak. There was a break-in: they took all our belongings and left us moneyless."

"You had a break-in?"

"Of course."

"Who is this demeaning me, bringing bad luck to my house? I can't believe this." He paces down the passage, goes to the kitchen but suddenly turns back. "Don't play tricks with me. How can you say there was a break-in while there is no evidence of any scuffle marks showing that the man who is a tenant in this house fought back?"

"How could I fight back when they were already inside and armed to the teeth?"

"Those people are not holy spirits. They couldn't have sidestepped the kitchen and dining room and headed straight to your bedroom. How did they do it? Did they break a window and enter?"

"They kicked the kitchen door open."

"The kitchen door? Don't take me for a fool, please. The kitchen door is locked, even as we speak. It is intact and without the slightest hint that anybody has tampered with it."

"I personally fixed it just before you came in."

On hearing this, Nyokana laughs. "Seemingly, the tenant is more important than the landlord in this house."

"I think you miss the point. I never said that you are insignificant."

"I am saying this because you tell me that your room was broken into. But mine was left untouched. Seemingly, the thugs felt that I was poor and not worth the effort. But one never knows with tenants. Perhaps you are pulling this trick so you can hog the meat and claim that the thugs took it." He returns to the kitchen where the Dubazanas have said the meat was. The plates are empty. The thugs had fought over the meat, licked the plates clean and left them spotless.

"It's fine, be stingy with your food, but my turn will come one day." Fuming, he goes to his bedroom and locks himself inside. Dubazana goes to the kitchen and stares in disbelief at the plates standing empty and spotless. Then he knocks on Nyokana's bedroom door, asking him to come and inspect the extent of the theft and injuries so that he may be a witness when Dubazana reports the matter to the police.

"This is yet another insult to my dignity. As far as I am aware, it is the landlord who is supposed to report to the police. But evidently, this has suddenly become Dubazana's house." This is followed by the head-splitting stench of dagga smoke. "The doors to *my* house were kicked open, yet you don't suggest that the two of us report the matter together. Leave me alone! I have lost all interest in the matter!"

Dubazana throws himself on the bed, his heart drumming against his chest as if there are flashes of thunder inside him. And at dawn, thunder roars as if in solidarity with his throbbing head. A fierce storm is breaking loose, punctuated by deep rumblings and blinding green lightning.

4

"You see, my sister, I won't let you starve. But this husband of yours, who makes you cook pork and fish with the intention of letting me starve, will not even get a titbit." This is said by Phathaphatha at midday on Saturday on his return from the butchery where he has roasted the meat that he is now clutching. He puts another packet in front of MaZondi that he has already sprinkled with love potion.

"Ngiyabonga kakhulu, Nyokana, thank you very much. But I'm going to keep it for Dubazana since I hardly have any appetite when he is hungry."

"Do you hear what you are saying?" He stares at her with wild-cat eyes. "Are you saying you lose your appetite when *he* is hungry?"

"You heard me correctly. I only have an appetite once he has had something to eat. It's even worse now since the recent robbery; his soul is crushed while mine is as good as dead."

"Please don't disappoint me now. I brought you this meat out of love. Could you please eat it immediately?" He looks sternly at her with his intense, penetrating eyes.

"As I've already said, my brother, I will starve when he starves and die where death finds him. That is my marital obligation. My husband and I share both the scarcity and abundance of whatever we eat, learn, smell and taste. We share the joys and the miseries, the famine and glut."

Nyokana shakes his head, "Oh, I can see that he's done a fine job in making you imbibe his potent love potions."

"I'd shake his hand in appreciation if I learnt that he used a love potion to make me cherish our marriage to the grave. Fortunately, he is my marriage."

Phathaphatha, who has been hoping that MaZondi's hunger will make her vulnerable, feels deeply disappointed. "Fine, but please take the meat and give it to that beloved idol of yours."

Dubazana returns in the afternoon, having withdrawn the little remaining money he has in the bank to buy meat for his children. MaZondi cooks it and serves the family. Phathaphatha, who clearly cannot stand seeing a married couple happy, stares at the Dubazanas with envious eyes. He is much pained by MaZondi's decision to reject the meat that he bought her with what had been stolen from her husband.

The week in which Dubazana starts to work at six in the morning, knocking off at two in the afternoon, also starts off with Phathaphatha still demanding a plate of food from them. Their plight is exacerbated during the week by the arrival of a woman who is more or less the same age as MaZondi, but thinner in build. She arrives at midday on a Thursday, soon after the landlord's departure, and introduces herself as MaDuze, Nyokana's fiancée. While she and MaZondi are still busy chatting, she mentions that she is not feeling well, excuses herself and retires to the main bedroom.

MaDuze's arrival has meant some respite from Nyokana's advances, but it is an additional burden in the form of an extra mouth to feed. Nyokana still does not bother to pay anything, yet demands food from MaZondi despite being aware that the Dubazanas have been robbed of their money. Using pork and fish to get round his non-payment no longer works, because they fear that Nyokana will retaliate by robbing them of their belongings again.

Ten days after MaDuze's arrival, there is discord between her and her boyfriend. At midday on a Monday he locks her inside the bedroom. Two full days pass and on Thursday she begins calling out from inside her jail.

"Yini, what has happened, my sister?" MaZondi asks as she clings to the wall from where the voice comes.

"My dear, it is this thug of a man. Please check outside whether he is back so I can tell you something."

MaZondi goes out, looks on every side, and returns. "No, I can't see him yet. Tell me then, why are you locked inside?"

"I'm being chased away, my dear. This rascal of a man is telling me to go away and doesn't want me to talk to you lest I spoil his chances with you by disclosing all his closely kept secrets."

"Why would you spoil his chances? I don't have anything to do with him!"

"Please don't mention this discussion to him because I am as good as dead if he should hear about it. I could pour out more stories if I knew you could keep secrets."

"Please tell me, I swear, I won't tell a soul."

MaDuze begins to weep, "You see, daughter of the Zondis, it scares me to hear him talk like this; it's become obvious that you are experiencing what once befell me. That is how Nyokana operates when he embarks on a mission to destroy another man's family. This is exactly what he did to me. You won't believe that, pathetic though I look, I was once married to the Chilizas. It was out of desperation that I arrived here, looking for accommodation, just as you people did. I found him living with another woman that he referred to as his fiancée, in the same fashion as what is happening to me now.

"He then spread rumours that we were lovers. Such lies eventually reached my husband's ears. After that he would fondle me with a hand smeared with umuthi since he's an expert in medicinal charms. Unfortunately for the poor soul that I am," she sobs, "when he continued holding me with this hand, I started feeling weak and faint, and would look at him with endless affection. After I had agreed to be his lover, not even knowing what I was agreeing to, he killed my husband before the week was through, in the same way that he'd killed the husband of the woman with whom he'd been living when we became lovers. He chased her away and squandered the husband's entire pension fund. He is now chasing me away to prepare the same fate for your husband." She cries. "Has he fondled your hand yet?"

"I can't count the number of times I've had to withdraw my hand from his clutch."

"There's no doubt that your ancestors have favoured you. You seem immune to the charms with which he's captured many a woman's heart, killing their husbands in the process."

"We should run away from this place before a catastrophe strikes. I really can't afford to have my husband killed. Over my dead body!"

"You would do yourself a big favour. We are dealing with a beast here and I'm in constant fear for your husband."

"Is he threatening him already?"

"He feels that your husband and I are stumbling blocks to his aspirations. I know very well that he will soon succeed in throwing me out and prepare to anoint you."

"What do you mean by anointing me?"

"I mean anointing you for widowhood."

"This is a bad omen indeed!" MaZondi almost faints on hearing MaDuze's emphasis on the word "anointing".

"Before you go, my sister, please give me a piece of bread through the window. I'm starving to death. The food you gave us this morning was snatched away from my hand by this monster."

Overwhelmed by sadness, MaZondi dishes up some food, passes it to MaDuze through the window and goes back to her room, still shaking from shock and fear. The recent robbery attests to what MaDuze has said. The only solution is to get alternative accommodation immediately. But where would they get it at short notice, since rooms are so difficult to find?

The following weekend, the couple determinedly hit the streets, room–hunting, but in vain. The following Tuesday, MaZondi is struck by a fear that makes her feel as if her skirt is going to fall to the ground when she realises that MaDuze has suddenly disappeared. Now she is really terrified to be with Nyokana during the day. His eyes look blood-soaked and he is deliberately shying away from looking her in the eye. Things are made worse by the fact that this week Dubazana is working from two in the afternoon until eleven at night. Realising that the house is becoming an obvious snare, she and her children run to find refuge in the old car standing in the yard. There they hide until Dubazana arrives back from work.

At about five o'clock on a Wednesday afternoon, she goes to the shops to do some shopping. When she ascends the steps, a middle-aged woman of about her mother's age approaches her and asks to have a word with her. She stops and looks at her, but suddenly casts her eyes down when she realises that the woman is wearing a miserable, faded multi-flowered dress with several holes in it. On her head she has a beret that was once black but is now faded and greyish. She wears black, torn shoes.

After briefly exchanging greetings, the woman explains why she wants to talk to her.

"You see my child, you don't know me and that's how I want it. I have long been waiting for you to come to the shops here." She looks at MaZondi. Wrinkles circle her soft eyes which exude kindness and familiarity, hunger and grief. "I was scared to death, worrying that the sun was already setting and I hadn't seen you. My child, I am here to tell you that you must leave that house at once, right now. Don't sleep there because if you do, you will be wearing mourning clothes by tomorrow."

MaZondi takes a deep, heavy breath: "Why do they want to kill my husband?"

The woman frowns. "They will kill him because of you. You may not be aware of this, but being a tenant exposes one to many sink-holes. Some holes harbour black mambas, in some there are mongooses and jackals and in others you find all sorts of other things. Regarding your landlord, the term scoundrel does not even befit him. He is worse than that: a monster, a killer, a robber, a rapist. He robs men and kills them. He robs, rapes and kills female strangers. A married woman like you, who is unfortunate enough to be his tenant, will find her husband killed. Then he takes his pension money and throws the woman out once the money is finished.

"We have been silent but we could have whispered you a warning ages ago. Unfortunately, you are not gregarious and hardly venture out into other people's houses. And besides that, Nyokana would kill any person that he finds talking to his tenants."

"Hawu, Mdali wamazulu nomhlaba! Oh, Creator of the heavens and earth!"

"Nyokana has an army of thugs and uses umuthi to win cases. Even in the High Court he is always acquitted. You have to believe me, as difficult as it is. He recruits our children to his regiment in numbers. I was lucky to hear about the plot against your husband from my boy who recently defected from Nyokana's criminals. As we speak, this monster is hunting him down. He chased away the widow whose husband he had killed – all in preparation for you."

"Hu," MaZondi breathes heavily, "but can't you help me and accommodate me tonight?"

"That won't do, my child. That would be suicidal to me and my family, because it would be obvious that I'm the one who's alerted you to Nyokana. We are already enemies since my son's defection." The woman fearfully glances around. "Let me leave you, my daughter, otherwise you will remember my features and haul me to the witness box in a criminal case that will kill me one day."

She turns away and disappears in a cloud of misery, leaving MaZondi alone and wailing to herself, "Oh my God ... oh my God ...!"

It suddenly becomes totally dark to MaZondi although it is still daytime. She decides not to go into the shop. Dubazana is on a late shift this week. She fears that if he returns to the house at night, there is a certainty that he will be killed. She hurries back to Nyokana's house. What propels her to walk as if she is flying is the sudden sight of hearses all over the place, doing their deliveries, since it is a Friday. To her, it feels as if one of them already has Dubazana's remains from the mortuary.

As soon as she arrives at Nyokana's home, she packs whatever she can and waits for sunset. It is already dark outside when she emerges from the house, dragging her bags, driving her children forward and hitting the road. They are heading for Zibunge, where Dubazana works. She is going to tell him everything, and they can sleep at the factory gates if no other options are available.

She is terrified, feeling Nyokana hot on their heels and looking for them in the dark. She avoids all the street lights because walking past them makes her feel exposed. They take shortcuts to the station and it is with relief that she feels the train start moving. Tears well up in her eyes when Mlazi begins to fade, flickering with lights that are dimmed by smoke that licks the sky.

She sees flames engulfing parts of the township but it is not clear if they emanate from burning grass or tyres. Mlazi eventually disappears as the journey continues and soon they can see the city beckoning with its bright and welcoming lights.

She disembarks at Zibunge and frantically drives her children towards the tyre factory. On reaching the gate she is crying as she asks the security guards for her husband. When they make excuses, explaining that she can only see him at certain times, she floods them with tears, so they have no option but to call Dubazana. He walks towards them, facing the night that gives him no assurance of where they are all going to sleep. His mind wanders aimlessly while his wife tells him what she has been told by the woman at the shops. No solution for this dilemma comes to his mind.

"All I am saying, my love, is that I would rather sleep on the street with my children than make them orphans or become a widow. Oh my God, what would become of me?" Now she floods him with tears.

"Please, Makhosazana's mother, don't cry." He pulls her a distance away from the children. "Who else besides you could have rescued me? I'm so grateful. I live for you and you live for me." He holds her by the chin, draws her face closer and kisses her. He feels even more in love with her.

"What I don't know is where we'll sleep until sunrise. If I leave you here now and go back, where will I find you when I knock off tonight, and it's Friday, of all days?"

Indeed, as it is already eight o'clock, thugs, who have shed their humanity and become wild animals, are combing the streets. Dubazana leaves his family at the gate with the security guards, and, somewhat bewildered, goes to the foreman to beg him for permission to leave early. Since he has already been paid, they let him go. He takes off his uniform, and, after a quick shower, changes into his clothes. Meeting them at the gate, he now has to lead his family out into the street. Indecision overwhelms him at the bus stop. He does not know whether to take a bus to town or one that is going back to Mlazi.

With thugs swarming around, the Dubazanas are blind with panic as they get on a bus to Gijima. They do not take seats because, in haste, they decide to disembark opposite King Edward Hospital. But here they meet with more fire! Thugs are pickpocketing everybody in sight, even confiscating medication from patients on their way from the hospital. Dubazana thinks on his feet and crosses the street, taking his family straight to the hospital. They go to the reception area where he tells the clerks that his wife and son are ill and need to be in hospital. The clerks look somewhat amazed by this, but register them, take payment and show them benches where they can wait.

On this night the Dubazanas are seeing a different side of Durban: the continuous arrival of ambulances wailing incessantly; private cars blocking the entrances; carrying in of people who have been stabbed, chopped or dismembered as if there is a concerted effort to inflict as much hatred and cruelty on humankind as possible. Nurses have to be on their toes, pulling stretchers from every side. Some patients die on stretchers even before the doctors can attend to them.

Dubazana stares at it all, overwhelmed with fear, and shakes his head in disbelief. "This is how we would have landed here if I hadn't decided that we should find shelter inside the hospital. Things are treacherous out there! If you, my darling, hadn't risked your life in the night to fetch me from work, perhaps I'd be here right now as a patient. Or perhaps I'd be lying in a police van bundled with corpses on their way to the state mortuary." They draw close and hold hands while their bodies shake all over.

Indeed, in the meantime, Nyokana's thugs have given up combing the streets for Dubazana and gone back to his room. When they find no one there, they vent their anger by stabbing the mattresses and pillows repeatedly.

"This person couldn't have run away without being alerted. We have sell-outs amongst us," says their red-eyed ringleader.

"No, perhaps it's his ancestors who orchestrated his running away. How dare he escape with such a beautiful wife? But I swear, we will meet one day and he will pay dearly for all of this." Nyokana is restless and paces the floor despite it being one o'clock in the morning. Perhaps his restlessness is caused by the blood of the victims who are groaning and moaning in pain at the hospital. Some of those who are on stretchers and those who have died have had to endure the deadly weapons that Nyokana and his gang carry.

In the hospital, Dubazana's children are now fast asleep: Nkosana with his head on his father's lap, and Makhosazana leaning against her mother, who in turn is leaning against her husband, dozing off. MaZondi falls asleep at dawn and Dubazana, who has not slept the whole night, watches over them. The injured keep arriving throughout the night until sunrise. Then, in the morning, those injured arrive who have been picked up by the police in the streets. Others have been robbed this very morning on their way to work. At seven in the morning the Dubazanas leave the hospital without having been attended to by a doctor.

At the bus stop, they still do not know what to do. Which direction should they take? They sit in the bus shelter contemplating their fate. Sleep is still heavy on their eyelids and the noise of the passing traffic lulls them back to sleep. Soon they are nodding their heads, their foreheads banging against each other. The children then move to the grass next to the shelter and they sleep as though they were sleeping at home. The parents sleep while seated, with mouths wide open, saliva dripping.

After a long time, Dubazana wakes up and sees a woman in her late fifties. She is tall, and her clothes hang loose from her body. She looks at him with red swollen eyes and protruding veins; her face is reddish, inflamed and emaciated.

"Kwenzenjani? What's up? Why are you sleeping like this with children at a bus stop?"

"It's the misery of life, I mean ..." He is not sure whether to address her as mother or sister.

"My brother, there is too much misery in this world. Are you homeless?" Dubazana nods his head. While MaZondi is in deep sleep, Dubazana talks for a long time with the woman who has introduced herself as MaMlambo, married to Mlangeni. She sounds sympathetic towards their plight. Fortunately, a tenant who has been renting a room from her has just recently vacated the place.

"When I look at you, I can tell that you are humane. Perhaps I will find decent tenants in you guys. I am sick and tired of people who come with all sorts of evil." Then she mentions a plethora of evils that tenants commit.

"Surely my ancestors are travelling with me!" This sings in Dubazana's heart as he praises his ancestors for offering him a ford to cross this flooded river.

"Wake them up so we can catch the next bus."

He shakes his family awake and introduces MaMlambo to his wife. MaZondi smiles gratefully in appreciation of MaMlambo's generosity, but feels a little resentful that her husband has concluded negotiations with MaMlambo while she was still asleep. The bus arrives, they all jump into it, and off they go to face yet a new set of rules in a new house – yet another among their countless rented homes.

5

They disembark near Mfongosi, take a brick-paved road and pass some young boys playing, pushing old car tyres. Next to this road, a brand new car is burning, probably stolen and set alight the previous night. MaMlambo leads them along and takes a turn that leads to a house that does not have even a scrap of fence. Where one expects the entrance to the yard to be, stands a young man of about twenty-eight, red-eyed and staring at a fire that he is making with old pieces of cardboard and sorghum beer containers that he has clearly picked up around the house.

"This is my grandson," says MaMlambo pointing at the young man. "Did you sleep well, Myboy?"

"We did, Granny," Myboy replies.

"That's good, my dear."

Entering through a kitchen, they walk into a four-roomed house that is unplastered and unpainted, here and there sporting drawings of what look like small black crucifixes. The inside of the house is a filthy mess. Dirty dishes and plates litter the floor, the tables and the Primus stoves.

"Wonder of wonders!" MaMlambo screams, arms akimbo. "To think that there are grown up girls in this house!" she fumes.

Still berating her household, she leads the Dubazanas to the lounge where their eyes meet three young women sleeping on the floor. Startled by this entrance, the women look at the family lazily, with slow, bloodshot eyes. They are sharing the floor with several empty beer bottles. Since this morning, it seems three beer bottles have been bought and now stand cold in front of them, sweating from the ice, to be used to take care of the hangovers.

As Dubazana looks at all this, his body sinks, and his heart is immersed in pain. For him now, the whole country seems hopeless. Life in general is chaotic and people console themselves through alcoholic suicide. It occurs to Dubazana that the designers of townships for blacks deliberately promote this, since in all the townships that are built, he has observed a mushrooming of bottle stores. There are bottle stores in all sections of the townships, yet not a single library or recreational facility.

"Oh my God, why do you bring people while we're enjoying our sleep, Mama?" one of the women mutters, rubbing her eyes and looking sleepily at her mother.

"You are supposed to have woken up ages ago, Thandabani."

The one she calls Thandabani – Who-do-you-love – is about thirty-eight. Drinking has done a fine job of shrinking and withering her. She gives Dubazana a swift appraisal with her tired eyes, smiles and flutters her eyes downwards.

"Thandabani, Funani and you, Lindeni," she calls them all by name and turns to Dubazana and his wife. "This is Mister Dubazana and his wife, MaZondi."

Funani – What-do-you-want – is thirty-seven and Lindeni – What-are-you-waiting-for – is thirty-five. Their mother explains how she met the Dubazanas at the bus station near the hospital, recounts their plight and says that she is going to give them a room that has recently been vacated by Makhathini. "May I therefore ask that you Dubazanas sit outside on the bench while your sisters prepare your room?" Her eyes focus on the beer bottles that are still sweating.

"Mama, why do you wait? Are you not going to take a sip and wash down the ailments that made you go to hospital?" Lindeni extends a glass of beer to her.

"But how can she drink before taking the medication she brought from hospital?" This must be Funani. With lightning swiftness, their mother gives them all a rebuking eye. The effect is immediate and the arm and glass are withdrawn.

The Dubazanas are given a bench outside, their eyes burning and longing for nothing else but sleep. The women finally get up and busy themselves tidying up the house. However, as the Dubazanas wait in the shade, they are looking at the three shacks in MaMlambo's yard, slanting and made of mud. A swarm of children, young girls and young men keep going in and out of the shacks. A cursory look at some shows that they are emaciated from starvation, and hungry even now, with no one caring whether they sit outside or sleep.

As nomadic tenants familiar with passing through many peoples' households, the Dubazanas know what that misery is going to mean to their own children: they will be sharing their meals.

Dubazana, who is now afraid of collecting his belongings from Nyokana, hires a car and goes there, accompanied by a police van. He finds his wardrobe, his bed with a stabbed mattress, another stabbed bed, stabbed pillows, a few pots and a Primus stove. Nyokana has confiscated most of the items, giving the lame excuse that Dubazana had left his house unattended, which resulted in a break-in. Dubazana takes whatever he can find and puts it in his new room, paying the rent soon after. As soon as MaZondi has made the beds, the children doze off. Dubazana sits by himself, but soon falls asleep too.

But at around two in the morning, sleep leaves him completely. He goes out of his room to use the toilet. When he is in the passage, MaMlambo, who is wide awake, sees him and beckons him to her bedroom. He stands dumbfounded, afraid to enter.

"What's wrong? Why are you hesitant? Step inside. Don't forget that in this house you are not a son-in-law who has to avoid his mother-in-law's bedroom. Instead, you are a son that I begot at King Edward Hospital this morning," she says, sitting on a bed that has a beautiful maroon cover. There is a beer bottle on a small cupboard at the head of the bed.

"Step inside, my son, into the head office and receive the new rules of this house." It becomes obvious that the rules of the house are given from the bedroom and he has to abide and enter.

"Sit here next to me, my dear," she mumbles and points to a spot close to her. Dubazana sits down timidly.

"Do you drink, my boy?"

He shakes his head in dissent.

"I thought I had given birth to a son, but it seems I begot a shy one, a mouse." She sways in his direction. "For your information, Dubazana, there is no man as head of the family in this house. Some hawks snatched him away and he left me, using my drinking as an excuse. I live by myself with my daughters who have populated this house with children. Though Mlangeni has left us to fend for ourselves, your arrival has brought us a family head. You are the one who is going to take care of us now."

"MaMlambo, I hear you very well."

"Oh, by the way, you men generally associate my surname with uMamlambo, the notorious snake that causes tornados? I may be MaMlambo but I ask that you call me by my name. My name is Thoko, but I wouldn't mind if you called me Thiza."

"I hear you, sister Thiza."

"Wow, that's my newly born baby!" She looks at him with slightly closed eyes, refills the glass, drinks and grimaces. "Such a handsome son-in-law." She licks her lips, opens her eyes, nodding her head backwards and forwards. "By the way, my son-in-law, I haven't told you the rules of the house yet, have I?"

While he is enduring the flirting, another daughter whom he did not see when they arrived, suddenly appears in the doorway. She shakes her head and scolds her mother.

"Don't make yourself enemies with his wife so soon after their arrival here. Come with me, my brother."

"Ntozami, don't interfere in the affairs of *my* house. I am still busy enlightening this boy on the rules of the house."

"Never mind, you'll tell him later. Come with me, my brother." She forcefully takes Dubazana by the arm and goes out with him, leaving her mother slanting her head, saying, "You always walk over me and take the lion's share."

The Dubazanas have arrived at the Mlangenis at a bad time. The whole household is on a drinking spree. The mother of the house, her daughters and grandchildren all drink. In the lounge where Ntozami – My-one – makes him sit, there are drinks everywhere. There are young women, wives and young men who are drinking. Some have slumped on the sofas; some are leaning against each other, fast asleep. Others are dancing to music from a record player.

Ntozami is about thirty years old and light in complexion; her eyes and figure look like those of a person who does not touch the bottle. She makes Dubazana sit next to her, then gets up, washes a glass and pours from the chaser that the others are using to soften the sting of their drinks.

"Even if you don't drink, my dear, how long will you hibernate in your room?" she says, and offers him the drink.

"The guy hasn't even settled down here and you are already making room for him?" asks Thandabani, swaying, her eyes refusing to open.

"If I can get emotional support from him, I don't see anything wrong with making room. After all, a lady can also make a move on a guy." She sits next to him again, and they both feast their eyes on one another's attractiveness.

The giant that resides in the bottle finally defeats those who have been fighting him, and one by one they fall asleep, which leaves Dubazana and Ntozami all by themselves, stealing glances at each other.

"This is how lonesome it becomes in this house if you don't drink," explains Ntozami.

Realising that their sitting like this alone may get him into trouble with his wife, Dubazana excuses himself and goes back to his room. With nothing else to do, Ntozami whiles the time away by sipping the dregs that the others have left in their glasses. Eventually, she too, leans against them, deep in sleep.

The main door of the house remains open the whole night while children from the shanty outbuildings flock in and out until sunrise.

On the day of the drinking spree, nobody in the Mlangeni household has touched the cooking pots. The Dubazanas would have felt uneasy cooking while others did not, and so ate bread and polony for supper.

On Sunday mornings, everybody at the Mlangenis walks around haggardly. The worst off are the swarm of children who sleep in the outbuildings, with no one taking care of them. As soon as the sun comes out, they hit the streets to fend for themselves. This is how it also is this Sunday: they are all over the street on empty stomachs, heading for the shops to cause chaos.

At ten in the morning, MaMlambo, with red, swollen eyes, walks into MaZondi who stands nervously in the kitchen. She greets her and asks her to fetch her husband so that she can brief them on the house rules. She has no recollection of summoning him to her bedroom-cum-office the previous night.

As soon as MaZondi fetches Dubazana, the three sit on the sofas in the lounge. The couple listen attentively as the laws of this lawless household are explained to them.

"My dear Dubazanas," MaMlambo kicks off, slanting her head and rubbing her hands, "there isn't much in the form of rules that need telling." She nods her head, punctuating her speech with a hangover-induced hiccup. "I'm not sure about your arrangements with your previous landlords. However, as you know, every household has its own rules." The hiccups wage their war repeatedly.

"First and foremost, no cooking must be done in the bedrooms; allowing that would mean I have to repaint the walls now and then. Firstly, our number is ... eh ... eh ..." The hiccups attack once again, making her burp and hold her mouth. "Poor me, I'm sure these hiccups want to kill me!"

"Just by the way, when hiccups pester like this, they are calling out for something that will cure them," teases Dubazana with a soft laugh.

"You can say that again, my dear. Let me sip some water." She goes into the passage and takes hurried strides to her bedroom where her daughters have already congregated, nursing their individual hangovers. They pour her a glass that she gulps down, and she feels her whole body shiver. She steadies herself and rejoins the Dubazanas.

"I have sipped some water, so let us continue. And where were we, now?"

"You were saying that cooking in the bedrooms is not allowed in this house. The hiccups strangled you while you were about to tell us the second rule," Dubazana refreshes her memory.

"What do you mean, the hiccups strangled me?" She stares at him with tired eyes. The drink she has just slipped down is reviving the previous day's alcohol.

"Don't play tricks with me, my boy. Well, I will ignore this since later I will come to a rule that says the house owner should be respected."

"My sincere apologies, madam."

"And the second rule," she says, between a mixture of hiccups and burps. "The second rule is that no one is regarded as a tenant in this house. All of us become one family. Regarding the pots, we cook together and eat together as a family, sharing every crumb. No one eats in the bedroom by themselves. A good thing about us, which I am sure you will appreciate, is that we are not choosy – there is no type of food that we don't eat."

Dubazana can't help laughing softly.

"My boy, you were desperate when I found you in hospital and now you're laughing at me. Tell me, what do you find funny in this?"

"It's not what you think, honestly. I am not laughing at you as such. It is just that the issue of cooking and sharing meals reminds me of our recent landlord. He insisted that cooking be shared in his house. But he was tight-fisted when it came to buying the food."

"Don't tell me about that bachelor lion who was making passes at your wife. Listen to what I tell you and don't ever defy me, because if you defy *my* rules in the house, I show you the gate. For your information, Mlangeni has to roam the streets because he became stubborn and wouldn't respect my rules. When I say one word, you shouldn't add two words of your own. My point is, as whites rightly indicate, when in Rome, you are supposed to behave as Romans and live according to their rules."

"In order to avoid any conflict, I would like to know from the mother of the house as to the number of plates that one should cook for. Obviously, in our case, there are only four of us."

"Oh my, do you think I can remember all the members of the tribe that populate this house?" She rubs her face as if in deep thought. "Let me fetch the mothers who can do their own counting." She gets up, sways to the bedroom and emerges seconds later, daughters in tow. Sitting down, she orders them to stand in a row in front of them.

"Did you guys meet Thandabani yesterday?" Dubazana nods in agreement. "Thandabani, please tell him how many children you have so that no child can complain of not being given food because the Dubazanas didn't know about them."

"Oh Mama, I have eight children and five grandchildren." On hearing this, Dubazana grunts aloud.

"Why are you groaning now?"

"No, I am just amazed that Thandabani already has five grandchildren though she looks so young."

"But, my brother, the number is high because my two daughters had twins, with the other daughter contributing one child," Thandabani responds.

"And that means your share will be 14 plates?"

"That's true, my brother," Thandabani nods coyly in assent.

"The second one is Funani. Tell him how many kids you have, Funani."

"Mama, my case is better; I have fewer kids. There are only six, including three grandkids, my brother."

"Mm, which means we are talking about six plates."

"Indeed."

"We already have 25 plates, including the mother of the household. I am not sure if there are still more?"

MaMlambo erupts: "Mention yours too, Lindeni!"

Lindeni has five children and one grandchild.

"We have 30 plates now. Do others have anything to add?"

"Say something, Ntozami." Her mother sulks and looks the other way. Ntozami only has six. Of the six, one is pregnant.

Dubazana keeps counting. "We now have a total of 39 plates."

"Swidilami, mention yours, in closure."

Swidilami only has three.

"Which means that the Mlangeni plates amount to 43. All in all, we are a total of 47."

"It is so, Dubazana." She looks at her daughters, "It's fine now, my daughters, you may leave." She returns her gaze to Dubazana. "I'm sure we're done now, Dubazana. Don't worry about the money, we'll share the expenses." The hiccups attack again. "Let me go and sort this out," and she leaves Dubazana and his wife in a cloud of confusion.

In total shock, the Dubazanas follow each other to their room in a daze like mourners and sit side by side on the bed, in solemn silence.

"You know what, my husband? I've lost all energy. Indeed, as long as you're a tenant, you remain nothing. In all the rooms we've rented, we've been exploited. The rent we pay for a room either equals or far exceeds renting the whole house. All landlords insist on sharing the cooking but hardly pay a cent towards expenses, which means all our effort goes into feeding landlords, without one being able to save for one's own accommodation."

"As you rightly say, my wife, if you're constantly on the road and in and out of rented rooms, you end up like a car tyre that wears out and gets dumped thanklessly. But still, whether they like it or not, we'll share whatever we can with them and take our plates and eat in our own rented room."

"Of course, Dubazana, there's nothing else we can do. Anything beyond that will mean that we'll starve to death while we're busy feeding other men's kids."

As the day progresses, MaZondi approaches MaMlambo for her contribution towards food. Bottles seem to stare at those who called themselves parents earlier, and MaZondi is looked at with squinting eyes and given brownish coins, not enough to buy even a loaf of bread. The Dubazanas have to empty their own pockets, and MaZondi goes to the shop to buy eggs, hoping the Mlangenis will be guilt-stricken and contribute more money. She cooks and serves, gives up at the twentieth plate, then goes to their room to eat with her family.

She decides not to bother about who is able to get a share or not. However, soon they hear the noise as parents and children fight over the food. And the plates, in this fight, slip and crash on the floor. From their window they see one boy running towards the outbuilding, a chunk of food in the shape of a huge ball in his mouth, being chased by a crowd of boys. They trip him before attacking him all at once, banging his back. Some hit him in an effort to choke the food out of his mouth. After that, comments from some of the daughters of the household, who are now mumbling incoherently, reach the Dubazanas: their children have ended up fighting due to the stinting hand of the person who dished up.

By the end of the week, Zwelisha, as Dubazana is called, is on the tongue of all the women of the house, as if they have known him for years. In the afternoons they fight over him, begging him to come and play cards with them, something that breaks MaZondi's heart, since she herself does not know how to play cards. Unwittingly, Dubazana has become the focus of rivalry among the women. His wife pleads with him to remain with her inside their room, while the others openly entice him to play cards with them in the dining room. MaMlambo, on the other hand, keeps insisting that he must not address her as MaMlambo, but as "Sis'Thiza".

This could overwhelm Dubazana as the only man, plunged into the midst of women who are all beautiful. During the week, if there is not too much alcohol in the house, the skins of the daughters become normal and it becomes clear to Dubazana that all of them are, indeed, in their own way, stunning. If they could only get men who loved them powerfully enough to save them from the booze, they could be decent wives whom any husband would be proud of.

Dubazana, slightly ashamed of being a cause of conflict between his wife and the family here, tries to please two kings. Still, in the card games, it becomes obvious that the Mlangeni women are fighting among themselves to win him over, especially Ntozami – My-own – and Swidilami – My-sweet-one. Ntozami, in particular, can barely hide her affection for him. Whenever they play, she quickly chooses to partner Dubazana, whom she affectionately calls Zweli. Gradually, yet steadily, he becomes Ntozami's Zweli; and he becomes Zwelami to Swidilami.

"Brother Zweli!" she screams excitedly one night during a card game.

"Ntozami!"

"Go for it, Zweli! Go for it!" she jumps up and holds him close. And when they win, they are so excited that they embrace each other.

And what a woman he embraces! Ntozami is definitely someone with presence. She is of medium height, has a round, full posture, is dark in complexion, her face longish with lovely brown eyes which look fondly at Dubazana, leaving unanswered questions.

Then he hears "Zwelami, My-world!"

"Swidilami!"

"The dance floor is supposed to be shared by all. It is my turn to be your partner now." Swidilami is light skinned, with generous legs and an hourglass figure. All of the sisters have shy, naughty eyes, just like their mother. Dubazana sees much of these eyes during the card games; after all, eyes are a major feature when playing cards.

"My dear Zwelami, go for the kill! Take all the points!"

"I have taken them all, Swidilami."

MaZondi listens to all this from her room, sleep evading her. While the players jump in victory and excitement, her heart is aflame. One night, she feels she has had enough and refuses to restrain herself any longer. While everybody is speaking with their eyes, plotting how to win the game, she stands in the doorway for quite a while, looking at Dubazana and Ntozami. They jump in shock when she suddenly asks for her husband and then retreats to her room.

Sheepishly Dubazana follows and sits down on the bed. His wife sees red.

"Is it your intention to make me a laughing stock? First of all, how come that you, being the father of my children, allow yourself to be called Zweli and Zwelami, names which even I, your wife, am too respectful to use? Secondly, where do you get this habit of calling MaMlambo, who is old enough to be your mother, 'Sis'Thiza'? Is she your sister now? And what matters were you discussing in private that made you know her first name so well?"

"I will explain, Makhosazana's mother."

"Will you explain that you are lovers?" She covers her eyes with her hands and speaks through bitter sobs.

"What can I say when you have the audacity to call your girlfriends, right in front of me, affectionately as Ntozami, My-own, and Swidilami, My-sweet-one? So, how many sweethearts do you have in this house?"

"Makhosazana's mother, you know very well that in this world, only you belong to me, you are my only sweetheart.

Ntozami and Swidilami are merely the names of two girls in this house."

"And again you repeatedly say they are yours and your sweetheart respectively." She weeps until her body shivers. "In all the places we have stayed as tenants I made sure that I protected you, but you collude with my enemies and call them your sweet things."

"Oh my Lord, honestly, Makhosazana's mother, I have never done that. They are neither mine, nor my sweet things. They were named as such, long before I knew them. And I can't suddenly call them Ntozakho, Your-things, and Swidilakho, Your-sweet-one, lest we look even more foolish to them than before."

"I don't mind Ntozami who now calls you Zweli. The worst is this good-for-nothing Swidilami who possessively calls you Zwelami, My-world!"

"You know what, I honestly don't know what to do now."

"Don't be distracted just because you've come to a place full of drunkard girls. As far as I know, you and I support each other through all our miseries. So, please distance yourself from these loose women and, to sustain our marriage, spend time with me in the room that we rent."

In everything he has done, Dubazana has always tried his best to avoid anything that could destroy his marriage. He tries to do as his wife tells him. So after this incident, when the ladies beg him to come and play cards with them, he makes excuses. However, the challenge of how to avoid calling them Ntozami and Swidilami when he addresses them, remains. He wonders to himself what made the Mlangenis give their first three daughters names with question marks, and the last two, nicknames. While he ponders on their names, those with question-like names are the trickiest of the women, as if they were planned this way. In fact, their intention is to hurt, and this time it is his wife who is hurt, his wife whom they think is always sulking out of jealousy. When he calls Thandabani (Who-do-you-love?), the quick response is likely to be "You!"

"Funani! (What-do-you-want?)"

"I want you, my love."

"Lindeni!" Lindeni responds by saying, "I am waiting for you, indeed, sweetheart!"

"Can't you hear your lovers brag in their mother's house simply because they're fighting to ensure that you become the slave who'll feed their flock?" His wife is venting her anger at him in their room. "For sure, in this world, you lose all your dignity if you don't have a home of your own." She weeps.

The issue of names and answers is merely the beginning. Their marriage is to be severely shaken on a Thursday night at eleven as Dubazana arrives back from work. As soon as he knocks at the kitchen door, it opens quickly as if somebody has been waiting for his arrival. A whispering voice tells him to get inside quickly. No sooner has Dubazana entered than the woman hastens to kiss him with soft lips on his cheek and on his own trembling lips, all the while whispering, "I don't know what is happening to me, Zweli. I just have a loneliness that only you can cure."

"Please, Ntozami, don't do this. Run away! Our bedroom door is opening."

"My God, things have really changed in this world. Cats are now running from rats," Ntozami whispers as she pulls a blanket over herself in the dining room. By the time MaZondi enters the kitchen, Dubazana is already locking the door. Holding a candle in one hand, she turns and leads him with its light to their room.

"The night shift is killing us," Dubazana complains as he sits on the bed, licking his lower lip and swallowing.

"How is it? Does it taste sweet in your mouth? You lick, and even close your eyes when you swallow."

Dubazana is taken by surprise and opens his eyes wide, "What taste are you talking about?"

His wife looks at him with eyes fierce as those of a tigress whose cubs have been stolen: "Dubazana, I ask that you speak the truth at least once since we arrived here at MaMlambo's. Who opened the door for you?"

"I thought it was you, because I knocked on this window and then the kitchen door opened." He licks his lower lip again.

"You can't stop licking, big guy. There has always been a place called Manzimtoti, Sweet Waters. I think we should now have one called Ndebezimtoti, Sweet Lips. Dubazana, I plead with you in the name of the Lord to please tell me who it was that kissed you?"

"Who kissed me?" Dubazana frowns, and bites his lip this time.

"Lest you lick all the evidence away," she opens her bag, retrieves a hand mirror and gives it to him, "here, see how you look."

Dubazana takes the mirror and cringes: the lipstick has left a big imprint of lips on his cheek. His mouth, too, is red. It is with this red mouth that he remains agape, looking at himself.

"I don't mind the lips on your cheeks that much. The ones on your chest choke me with pain, because they were put there to affirm a message from the heart." She clears her nose.

"And where do you see that?" Dubazana asks, looking down at his shirt. Everything happened so swiftly and unexpectedly that he had not noticed how and when Ntozami had planted her lips there. On his green shirt, right over his heart, are red lips, and the woman has, as if for emphasis, smeared some more lipstick on his ear.

"There is absolutely no doubt in my mind that this was done by Ntozakho, Your-things, if not by Swidilakho, Your-sweet-one.

If you don't tell me who did it, I will go straight to them, remove their blankets and check their mouths."

"Please, Makhosazana's mother, don't do that," he pleads.

"You favour girls who make me, your wife, a fool. They may have done it to others in the past and got away with it; but they have found their equal in me!" She reaches for the door.

"My wife, please calm down." He pulls her by the arm when she tries to go out. "You know the saying that when one's away from home one becomes vulnerable. You and I are strangers here. I beg you to ignore all this, painful as it is. As for me, even if I knew who did this to me, I wouldn't divulge her name because I know that it's difficult to show restraint. You might end up in a fight and get us evicted in the middle of the night."

"Are you suggesting that I secure this accommodation by sacrificing my dignity and being mocked by all and sundry?"

"That seems to be the norm when you don't have a home, MaZondi. Have you forgotten how Silangwe used to make passes at you, but you had to keep it a secret from me, fearing that it would make us fight and be evicted in the process? The best we can do now is to look for alternative accommodation and await further fleecing." So Dubazana calms his wife down until she subsides, sobbing on their bed.

"This is exactly what I meant earlier, Dubazana, when I said that if you are a tenant, you are devoid of dignity for yourself, your family and whatever else you possess, because everything you have now belongs to the house owners instead of to your own home. Just recently, I had to contend with flirting and you stood to be killed because of me. Today, it is you who is being kissed; I am the enemy of those who thirst to exploit you. Tomorrow it will be our children's turn."

Feeling the words touch him, Dubazana remains silent and deep in thought, biting his lower lip, unaware that he is courting trouble. His wife looks at him and says, "I used to fight with Silangwe whenever he made passes at me. But I sense that perhaps it feels good to be kissed by your beloved Ntozakho and Swidilakho."

"But Makhosazana's mother, how can you say it's nice to be kissed by a girl when you have a wife? That's not fair. I wish you could enter into my heart and feel for yourself how painful it is as I sit here in silence."

"No, that's not the reason. I've been looking at you, you move from the lower lip to the upper lip since it tastes like Swidilakho's sweets. You can say that a dog may even eat mud when away from home, but I don't think the lipstick tastes like mud."

"I had forgotten, my wife. Let me go and wash myself." He gets up but when he opens the door he turns back to his wife, "Please Thuleleni, come with me, lest they pounce on me again."

"Indeed, I'll come with you so that I can see this cheeky woman."

They accompany each other to the toilet. The sound of water from the outside tap pouring into the wash basin while Dubazana washes is audible in the house, and, underneath the blankets, listening to all of this, the Mlangeni girls burst out laughing.

6

During the week, alcohol is a problem at MaMlambo's house. But on weekends, from Friday to midnight on Sunday, it is a scourge. The Dubazanas have observed the warning signs of an impending disaster to which the Mlangenis are oblivious. This is caused by some of the males who drink with the mothers of children whose futures the men are already destroying. On several occasions, MaZondi and Dubazana have seen old men leaning against the outbuilding walls with the young daughters of Thandabani and her sisters. At these times, the grandmother and her daughters have barely been able to see straight. And when the children are making out in the shadows with men who are regarded as their mothers' boyfriends, one can rightly wonder who, in the case of those who are already pregnant, would be named the father.

The Dubazanas' worries soon deepen: their daughter, Makhosazana, already carries firm pointed breasts on her chest. They watch over her strictly and do not allow her to play with the children of the house. Of course, isolating her from others irritates the mothers even more as they interpret it as snobbishly ostracising their children.

The level of drinking at this house has always been high, but it reaches a peak with the arrival of a certain gentleman by the name of Maqhobozela Qumbisa. He drives a brand new silver-grey BMW, with several dents on its body acquired after previous drinking sessions. Qumbisa is introduced to the Dubazanas by MaMlambo, who describes him as a boyfriend who has promised to marry her. According to her, Qumbisa owns a bottle store in Mlazi and has recently divorced his wife.

The grey-haired Maqhobozela – He-who-crunches – is in his sixties and always wears a suit. Despite being dark complexioned, his face already shows signs of alcohol abuse, and is becoming puffed out, with alcohol-ravaged cheeks. He was obviously once a plump man. Now he walks with a sway, his body burdened by suits that are usually wrinkled, suggesting and sometimes confirming that he has slept in them.

Maqhobozela usually arrives at MaMlambo's place in the evenings, as soon as he has closed his business for the night. One can tell from the way the car's boot almost touches the ground, laden with liquor bottles, that it is going to be a wild night. Maqhobozela is usually as tame as a lamb when he gets out of his car, his arrival announcing the start of a drinking marathon, after which – if not during which – his drinking companions will, one by one, end up lying on the floor wasted, having failed to consume all the alcohol. That's when his behaviour transforms, making him grow suddenly, discarding his lamb status. He then becomes a beast, rubbing and shaking his head, dishevelling the well-combed hair that adorned him on his arrival. Endlessly he moans about all the miseries that have befallen him. Instead of comforting each other over their failed marriages, he and MaMlambo throw verbal abuse at one other. Maqhobozela then sits, crestfallen, burying his hands in his cheeks, while he laments his wife MaZamisa, praising her for ensuring that he was always spotlessly well-groomed and never forgetting that he had a stomach that needed feeding. Stung, MaMlambo will retaliate by waxing lyrical about Mlangeni, who, despite being stubborn, is not a weakling reduced to tears by alcohol. Usually, the end will see MaMlambo being carried to her bedroom, leaving the others lying around in the dining room. Indeed, Maqhobozela has stamped his mark at the Mlangenis. From Monday to Monday, alcohol now flows like a river in the rainy season.

With alcohol having the upper hand, any attempt to share cooking chores and expenses turns out to be disastrous. MaZondi ends up cooking and serving meals exclusively for her family – an act that makes her the bane of the mothers of the other children. Sarcastic words intensify: "Who does she think she is? She's arrogant because she has a husband that she assumes belongs only to her. And the husband has become stingy with his money. Mama should evict them and make room for people who will help us feed our kids." All this is said behind the Dubazanas' backs.

One Saturday night, Dubazana is working overtime and only knocks off the following morning. The grey-haired Maqhobozela is, as usual, organising a fierce bout between the household and beer bottles, making participants drink until they lose their minds. It is also on this Saturday night that Makhosazana wakes up and goes to the outside toilet while her mother is still fast asleep. After a while MaZondi wakes up, notices the empty place, panics and begins to look for her daughter. She searches in the toilet. No sign of her. In the lounge she finds male and female drinkers not asleep but seemingly dead. She asks about her daughter and gets snores in response. The doors are left open while everybody sleeps. She walks around the house and outbuildings. Nothing.

"My child can't just disappear like a piece of meat stolen by a dog. Makhosazana!" she calls, nearly hysterical in the dark, scared that her daughter may have walked in her sleep and got lost in the thick darkness. Losing hope, she goes and knocks on MaMlambo's bedroom door. There is no response, just wild snoring. She pushes the door open. She cannot believe her eyes. Maqhobozela is sitting on a chair and on his lap is Makhosazana, who is trembling and in tears. On the floor green notes amounting to a hundred rand lie scattered.

"Hawu Nkosi yami! Oh my Lord! How can an old man like you do this?" MaZondi, out of respect for him, cannot raise her hand and beat him. She just wails and clasps her head with both hands in astonishment.

"No, my sister ... it's not what you think ..." he says, ashamed, and pushes Makhosazana to her feet.

That's when Makhosazana starts crying bitterly. Her mother bundles her in her arms, "What did he do to you, Makhosazana?"

"Mama, he grabbed me as I returned from the toilet." Maqhobozela is soon on his feet, arms behind him, saying, "What bad luck is befalling me here!"

Meanwhile, MaMlambo sleeps the sleep of the dead, snoring loudly and swallowing her saliva. With voices rising in the altercation, those in the dining room and kitchen wake up and assemble in the bedroom.

"What is the matter, Qumbisa?" Thandabani asks, her red eyes heavy with sleep.

"They are fighting me and making false accusations," he says innocently, spreading his hands and pointing at them.

MaZondi resists, "Why do you tell lies at your age, Baba? Why would we accuse you falsely?"

"You are accusing me of something I didn't do."

Lindeni raises her voice in anger, "Qumbisa, tell us what happened."

"Ask them to tell you, then I will explain."

With naked contempt and disgust for MaZondi, Thandabani looks at her: "What are you doing to Qumbisa, who is older than you by many years?"

"We didn't do anything to him. In fact, it is he who betrayed our trust through his abominable acts." MaZondi recounts the story and allows Makhosazana to take them through the events, step by step.

Thandabani's red eyes turn to Qumbisa and become a little softer. "Are they telling the truth, Qumbisa?"

"My daughter, even if I were the most notorious, infamous, corrupt person in the world, she is like a grandchild to me, and how could I ... please don't do this to me and pile shame on me, your guest."

"But here they are, insisting you did it."

Mumbling, Qumbisa denies everything and explains his side of the story. "I went out of this bedroom to pee. When I opened the toilet door to get out, the door opened slightly. First to shock me was that MaZondi showed her tongue at me, wriggling it like a snake. Meanwhile, she was beckoning me to her room. Bantabami, out of deep respect for her as a daughter, I entered, not knowing that I was stabbing myself with my own spear. No sooner had I entered than she showered me with words that shook me. She was all over me, bantabami, asking me why I am so dumb, ignoring her despite all her beauty and wasting my money on stinking drunkards such as you guys. She added that she had heard that I am divorced and have a home all to myself. She said if she could have her way, she would dump her useless, homeless husband and marry me."

"Baba, you are telling lies about me! I never said such a thing," MaZondi cries in exasperation,

"Mntanami, my child, I didn't cut you short when you were foaming at the mouth, pouring out blue lies about me. I showed you respect and allowed you to finish weaving lies about me. And you, out of disrespect, you brush my teeth while I'm still chewing."

"But ..."

"Shh!" That was Funani, telling MaZondi to be quiet, as she would to a fowl. "Shut up, you holiest of the holy, and let us hear more about you."

MaZondi is crying, but Qumbisa is unfazed: "I felt my energy sink when I heard her say that I waste my money on filthy pigs." As he says this he turns and points at the sleeping MaMlambo who responds by snoring noisily and clearing her nose.

"Oh, you pretend to be shy but you dare to take a bull by the horns?" Funani looks at MaZondi with a despising eye.

"Her words were just a prelude," continues Qumbisa, now on a roll. "She seduced me, despite my old age. And then, as if that was not bad enough, she asked me to give her R500, and, when I refused, shook this child awake. When it became obvious that she was bent on besmirching my reputation and dignity, I fled, but couldn't escape them as they were in hot pursuit; and we ended up in this bedroom with her still wanting to get my money by force. She kept scolding me for wasting it on you, whom she kept referring to as pigs. All was in vain: even when I tried to absolve myself by offering her the hundred, she just threw the notes on the floor, as you can see for yourselves."

The MaMlambo girls and their friends, with alcohol still fresh in their blood, of course cannot even begin to think the matter through. They begin pushing MaZondi around, taking turns to tear her apart, and, instead of commenting on Qumbisa's illicit behaviour, repeatedly say that MaZondi insulted them by calling them pigs.

"Let us check if this holy angel of hers has been sexually assaulted as she says," Lindeni suddenly suggests, and with the help, as if on cue, of Thandabani and Funani, the sisters lift Makhosazana like a weightless piece of paper, throw her on the bed and strip her naked. Seconds later they shake their heads in unison. Maqhobozela nods his head and roars with laughter on hearing that he has been acquitted of the accusations.

A stunned MaZondi tries to reach for her daughter's clothes, but Funani and her sisters throw them at her. She catches the clothes in mid-air, pulls her daughter by the arm and hurries past men who spank her rear while they direct taunts and defamatory insults at her.

Although the worm in the form of Maqhobozela fails to inflict any visible damage on Makhosazana, it has left her mind confused, lost, disappointed and angry. Dubazana arrives in the morning and is greeted by a daughter still breathless with crying. He tries in vain to get any idea of what has happened, but the words of both Makhosazana and her mother are drowned in rivers of pain from their shattered hearts. It is only from the Mlangeni girls who find him in the room still asking questions amid tears, that Dubazana hears what has transpired. Beating their chests, the girls say that he has to go to the dining room to be briefed about the shameful deeds committed by his wife and daughter in his absence.

Dubazana and his family all sit on the dining room floor since all the available chairs are occupied by household members and their friends. Makhosazana and her mother tell their side of the story. And the Mlangeni daughters recount what they have heard from Maqhobozela, all the while pointing fingers at MaZondi and repeating all the insults she is alleged to have uttered. Maqhobozela himself is nowhere to be seen, having sneaked out before dawn. However, the house is still littered with the bottles of beer and spirits he brought the previous night. This is what they are still drinking during the discussion.

MaMlambo sits like a stranger on a sofa, deflated, her cheek leaning on a shivering hand. This is all news to her. Though she is silent, she fumes inside. The insults alluding to pigs make her whole body shiver with anger.

"But the child tells a different version from what you are saying. She complains that she was molested by this grandfather," Dubazana explains in a calm voice, suppressing the anger brewing inside him.

Funani finishes the contents of her half-empty Scotch whisky glass, grimaces and glances at Dubazana with her bloodshot eyes. "Dubazana!"

"Yes, Funani?"

"What do you and your wife want from us?" She stares at him for a very long time until tears ooze from her eyes.

"You are not man enough to defy this useless wife of yours. I bet she has used strong love potions to soften and weaken you. Please give her enough money to stop her from cheating other women's men out of their money. I, for one, am sick and tired of her." She dries her tears, but in seconds her eyes are again tear-flooded. "I have heard that she goes around in the neighbourhood telling all and sundry that we are starving mongrels who are fed by her husband. She has even decided to cook on her own simply because we, the starvers, are squandering your money. It would be better if you vacate the premises and leave us alone to our starving."

"She has dished out enough insults to me, and I'm fed up," interjects Lindeni, who has just put down a still frothy beer glass.

"Dubazana, I thought I was renting out a room to a daughter in this home. Little did I know that I was harbouring a rival ..." A fierce hiccup makes MaMlambo pause for breath. "I live with a rival who competes with me to win over people who are trying to build a family with me. Instead of parting ways with Maqhobozela, who is a source of joy for my family, I would rather let go of your family, mfana wami, my boy. So please do me a favour, and leave with your good-for-nothing wife before she and I tear each other apart."

"And leave just like that, Mama, without reporting the matter to the authorities?"

"You can, of course, do that in the comfort of your own house, mfana wami; not while you reside in *my* house!" She rises to her feet, lifts up her skirt in anger and points a swollen finger at Dubazana's eyes, saying, "It is now clear to me that you are a tempter of people's souls with this wife of yours and your stupid daughter who seduces an old man like Maqhobozela. On the day I met you, you complained that it was Nyokana who had pounced on your wife. Now you want to press charges against us, to leave us with damaged reputations while you can see – and know very well – that you harbour a beauty queen who entices men with her looks. This must be an extraordinary, beautiful angel indeed, seeing that all sorts of men, the world over, seem to fight over her. Please do me a favour, leave me innocent and spotless as you found me on these premises. Your being destitute shouldn't be a curse to me."

"Which means I should be like a stone and not feel any pain or affront when my wife is beaten up beyond recognition?"

"I am not the one who beat her up, my child. She was beaten by the insults she hurled at us and by her seduction of another person's lover."

The altercations start all over again. The three daughters with their question-like names and their mother spare MaZondi and her daughter no insult. Dizzy with confusion, Dubazana stands up, holds his wife and daughter by their arms and leads them to their room, locking the door behind him. The mother and daughter cry with such desperation that Dubazana finds himself holding his tears back with his eyelids. Just on the other side of the wall, the pandemonium, laughter and drinking continue in earnest.

Tired from the night shift, Dubazana is dozing off on his bed when he hears, as if in a dream, the voice of a man greeting people. He is let into the house, and Dubazana hears him explain his misery at being homeless. He is asking for accommodation. He also hears Funani laughing like a carefree girl by the riverside:

"You know what, my brother? You are such a lucky guy. I wonder what lucky charms you cast on people!"

"How can you say I am lucky, my sister, when I don't have a roof over my head?"

"I am saying this because the person who was hogging a room here is busy packing as we speak. This will be good riddance, Mama. Let him pay and fetch his belongings."

MaMlambo and her three daughters are supported by their friends in celebrating the latest unexpected developments. With all of them mumbling incoherently, struggling to keep their eyes open, licking their lips, the decision is unanimous that the Dubazanas are to be evicted promptly. Funani, who uses the wall to steady her wobbly steps, summons Dubazana unceremoniously to the dining room. They introduce him to a lanky man of the Qwabe clan who has an untidy bush covering his cheeks. Qwabe and his family are to occupy Dubazana's room with immediate effect. Qwabe confirms this by immediately making an upfront payment in Dubazana's presence. Dubazana's attempts to beg and plead fall on deaf ears.

"Let me go and fetch my things. I'm sure this gentleman will pack while I'm gone."

"I am sure you hear what he says?" MaMlambo asks Dubazana, her head drooping.

"I hear him well."

Dubazana sways as he walks to the room to pack their things, wondering who will rescue him and his family, at least for the impending night.

7

It is a windy Sunday afternoon. The township is enveloped in a
sea of red dust that seems to obscure the sun as it dangles over
the mountains. The clouds are adorned with a veil of red streaks.
MaZondi sits side by side with Makhosazana and the driver in a
derelict bakkie that shakes all over as if it is about to fall apart. She
is deaf to everything that surrounds her and apprehensive that the
bakkie is taking them from the flames of hardship to a furnace of
misery. Dubazana, Nkosana and a teenage boy, who is completely
covered in dirt and wearing a torn shirt, sit at the back, clinging to
the wardrobes, screwing up their eyes against the wind. Everything
that Dubazana sees has misery written all over it.

The driver, a man in his mid-sixties, of medium height, wearing
an overall coat covered with engine oil stains, jumps as he tries
in vain to engage the gears. When at last he manages to put the
vehicle into gear, he clears his throat: "The red dust is killing us.
I, for one, hate the red sun and moon because my grandfather
used to tell me that they are bad omens. Just look at this sun! It
is weeping blood." With a pitch-black face accentuated by the
motor oil, and an uncombed beard with bits of blanket fluff on it,
he stares at his silent passengers. It startles him when MaZondi
and her daughter look at him with tired, inflamed eyes and then
pour out a torrent of tears. MaZondi's eyes are streaked with
misery and violent anger.

The driver's eyes scan the slums across which the bakkie is now
meandering. The houses are made from sorghum beer cartons,

rusted corrugated iron, mud and all sorts of other material. Most of these houses are slanting and congested, their yards filthy. Wretchedness is written over the entire place and on the faces of the adults and naked children who roam the yards, their ribs protruding. Astonishingly, in this congestion of houses, there are no taps, roads or toilets.

The teenage boy sits with Dubazana and has been tasked by his father to direct the vehicle through the maze of shanty houses. When they are about to reach the shack that his father is going to rent out to the Dubazanas, the boy bangs the rusting cab of the bakkie, making a big hole in the process and cutting his hand. Blood drips all over the place as he shakes it. The driver stops and the boy tells him to branch off the road.

The bakkie traverses the grassy footpaths until it comes to a stop in front of a maze of mud shacks. Dubazana and the boy jump off, followed by the driver. The teenager leads them to a yard in which stands a slanting mud lean-to house. It has a rusty corrugated iron roof with holes all over it. The windows on both sides of the skewed doorframe are small and without glass. The makeshift door is not even locked.

The boy, who has introduced himself as Mkhumbane, pushes the door open. Inside it is bare. There are blood puddles; dagga and cigarette butts litter the floor alongside discarded playing cards.

"Oh! How will we survive here if we're greeted by blood as soon as we enter?" Alarmed, Dubazana retreats.

"Don't worry, Baba. This is life in the slums." Mkhumbane is unfazed. "It seems that the local gangsters have found a convenient hideout in this room. But they will leave you alone once you guys occupy it."

"But the lock looks small and easy to break."

"At least you'll have a roof over your heads, even if the lock is unreliable," the driver comments dryly.

Despite all the suffering that permeates the slums, they find comfort in hoping that life will be better than their previous experiences of rented rooms. Since there is neither river nor tap from which they can get water to clean the floor, they offload their possessions from the bakkie, helping each other to put them on the blood-stained floor. The sun is setting when the bakkie rumbles off, leaving them in their clogged dwelling.

They do not cook today. Now even sleep is impossible as people circle the room right through the night, making noises, cursing, swearing and banging the sides with their fists. Dawn finds the family sitting closely together and exhausted with fear and anxiety.

It is their first morning in the slums. When they see their neighbours, whose shack is to their left, they are reluctant to leave their room at all. They are evidently a household of children who have become parents. As the morning becomes warmer, they see three children in the yard: two girls and a boy. All are skinny, emaciated, but potbellied, with dangling tussocks of hair. Their clothes are rags. They are of similar height and it seems as if less than a year separates them. Their parents, a female of about eighteen and a male of about nineteen, are as thin as toothpicks, straining under the weight of oversized heads. Both are unemployed – the products of apartheid machinery and casualties of the struggle against it. Clearly, none of them have had anything to eat since the previous night, and now, this morning, their mouths are white with hunger, and they stare at the Dubazanas with the eyes of starving tigers.

Eventually they see the neighbours to their right. The father is a tall man, fifty years of age or so, darkish in complexion, with quick, mamba-like, unblinking eyes. His hair is dishevelled. His black shirt, trousers and boots make him look even darker. His wife, also dark skinned, is more or less the same age and also tall. She is not wearing anything save for some tattered strips covering her body. Although she sees the Dubazanas, she does not greet them. Her yard teems with teenage boys and girls as well as small children, making one wonder how they all fit in the one room that serves as their home.

After lunchtime on the following Saturday, a crowd of youngsters pays them a visit. The throng comprises a broad mix of boys, girls and some teenagers with a sprinkling of a few elderly men and women. What they all have in common is their near-nakedness, the various weapons they carry, and their red, piercing eyes. They look hungry for food and ready to drink blood. When they appear at the Dubazanas' door, the family says a short prayer, fearing it may be their last.

The groups knock and are asked to enter. They stream in and fill the whole room. Some sit on the bed, squashing three of the Dubazana family onto the corner of the bed. In the meantime Makhosazana has quickly hidden herself under the bed. Dubazana greets them and looks at them, his eyes filled with fearful tears. A tall man resembling their neighbour acknowledges the greeting.

"My fellow man, we have come here not to fight you, but to seek information."

"I hear you." Dubazana inwardly sighs with relief. It seems that the mob has come in peace.

"Introduce yourselves and tell us who you are, where you come from and what your affiliation is," says the tall one, looking at him with such craving eyes that it seems as if he wants to swallow Dubazana alive.

Carefully, Dubazana explains who he is, his origin, his place of work as well as who his wife is and the number of children they have.

"You haven't specified your affiliation yet. If I were addressing a young man in a rural village, I would expect him to specify the regiment to which he belongs."

This confuses Dubazana. He looks around, "Perhaps I am missing your point. Many people have become Christians. So, are you asking me about my religious affiliation?"

"I am not talking about religious crap! Sir, why do you pretend to be a foreigner who doesn't live in this country? You know there are political parties in the country, don't you?"

Dubazana nods, relieved to get the drift of the questioning.

"Do you know that there are two political parties that are currently at war?"

"Yes, I know."

"We are one of the parties. As you see us here in front of you, we are in the struggle for black people's liberation. We have trampled the enemy. Our guns are still smouldering from the gunpowder and our spears drip blood."

Indeed, Dubazana sees blood and more on the instruments lying in front of him. He shivers inside, as he looks at an axe that clearly has the remains of something that looks like brain on it. A bush knife spotted with marrow; is he to understand that these are not an animal's but a human's?

"We can't have someone in our midst and not know their affiliation. Hurry up! Declare yourself!"

"Fellow brothers and sisters, as I have already explained, being destitute has disorganised my mind to such an extent that I haven't had time to affiliate myself to any party. If my memory serves me well, ever since I got married, if I am not at work, I am either room-hunting or relocating to a new place."

"We understand that," one of them interjects, "all of us are slum dwellers since we don't have houses of our own. Nevertheless, we haven't forsaken the struggle for freedom. If you are trying to conceal your affiliation from us, then let us open your heart and read it." Their eyes, as Dubazana now knows, still fresh from looking at the corpses of the victims they have killed during the night, look at him and thirst for his corpse. "What political party did you belong to where you last stayed?"

"My people, I was a tenant in a house owned by women who didn't have time for anything but booze."

"Pho, so why did you leave there?"

"There was some misunderstanding regarding the cooking arrangements."

"Did you share the cooking and were pissed off that they were not paying?"

"Exactly; you seem to know what I have been through," Dubazana eagerly agrees.

"Oh, you are the kind that we abhor and have to eliminate. You are selfish and can't share with others. Oh, now I understand." The tall one keeps nodding his head. "And still you refuse to disclose who you share your sufferings with?"

"I ask to affiliate myself with you."

"Kulungile, it's fine. But first, you will give us the number of the house where you last rented so that we can enquire about your status. You will be part of us once we've confirmed your political membership, because we don't want sell-outs who pretend to be part of us and then betray us instead. Secondly, you will have to understand that this is a war zone. Some of our greatest enemies are the township dwellers across the road, who won't allow us access to their taps. We therefore can't fight for your freedom while you sit back and fold your arms. Do we understand each other?"

Dubazana nods.

"How many kids do you have?"

"Two."

"Where are they?"

"The boy is sitting over there, behind us. The girl was startled when she saw you guys and hid under the bed."

"Tell her to come out!"

Makhosazana crawls out and sits on the bed, leaning against her mother, fear written all over her face.

"Ah, so you have a young girl here! Both she and her mother are desirably chubby and curvy. It's obvious that they sleep in warm blankets and are well fed while we starve and sleep out in the open, fighting for your freedom. Today then, this boy of yours should understand that being a sissy will henceforth be a thing of the past. We organise camps in this neighbourhood. We fight. We will let you know about the next camp date.

"One other thing you should know: don't leave this place until we have come back and told you what we found out about you. Should we catch you trying to move to another place, we will necklace you!" Without saying goodbye, they all get up and leave the family paralysed with fear and horror. Although they are hungry, they suddenly lose all appetite and thirst. Every second is spent awaiting the worst.

On Sunday afternoon the Dubazanas hear ululations outside. It is a call for all males to take up arms and accompany the women with containers to forcibly fetch water from all taps in the township houses that are said to belong to members of another political party. Dubazana, who cannot afford to ask how members of different households could all belong to the same party, takes his sticks to join the others.

"Don't waste our time! Who do you think you will kill with such pathetic things?" A pitch-black, burly man asks furiously, holding a Russian-made gun and shaking his head.

"Please bear with me, my people. I have been in and out being a tenant in other people's houses. You know very well that you can't bring your own weapons to another person's house."

The young man curses: "Phambili! Forward! I wish I could spill your stupid brains with this gun. Take this!" He pulls out a bayonet that he has stuck to the gun-holster and gives it to him.

"I can see that in your heart you harbour all sorts of civilised nonsense induced by an obsession with Jesus. I want this Jesus of yours to jump out of your heart with immediate effect. If I say, 'Kill!' you must kill. These are the slums. You may tell your pastor, if he excommunicates you from church, that you discarded Jesus in the slums." He scowls. "If you don't kill, we will kill you and your whole family."

MaZondi, Makhosazana and the other women and girls gather, carrying water pails, bowls, buckets and even saucepans. The men trail a short distance behind them. It being a Sunday afternoon, the people on the other side are enjoying themselves, and everyone is taken aback when the bucket-carrying women emerge out of the blue.

While the residents are still asking questions of those who are arriving, the taps start running all over the area. The adults there quickly realise that they are being taunted to make them retaliate, so they zip their mouths and some start loading whatever they can into their cars in anticipation of the impending danger.

Unfortunately, the children have not asked their parents how to handle the situation and begin pelting the bucket-carriers with stones, so all hell suddenly breaks loose. Men advance at full speed, and in the blink of an eye they are swarming all over the place. There are screams and wailing from every direction. Gunshots fill the air and attacks with axes, pangas, assegais and knives spill blood within seconds. In total panic, those who can, run for their lives. Unfortunately, some already lie dead with gaping wounds.

"Stab that woman, you fool!" the hulk shouts at Dubazana, pointing the gun in a woman's direction. Light in complexion, plump and aged about forty, she wears earrings, a necklace and a ring, all gold. She staggers as she runs away, holding a baby in her arms.

"Plunge the assegai into her shoulders, you fool!" So Dubazana chases her. Within seconds he is panting behind her shoulders. The poor woman glances at him over her shoulder and wails.

"Ma-yeh! Oh my! Have mercy on my kids, my brother!" She stops, turns and looks at him, tears streaming from her eyes. "Why do you kill though you don't look the part?" She tilts her head, her eyes pleading. "Why do you kill me, a woman? As a woman, am I not like your mother, and like your beloved, and like your sister?"

"I am not the one who wants to kill you. You can hear for yourself that they threaten to kill me if I don't stab you."

"If you died for me, it would be fitting! We women sometimes die when we give birth to boys."

"So why are you standing still? Good Lord, run away so that I can die for you!"

"Ngiyabonga, thank you!" She turns and darts away. "Please pass by my place one day if you survive this," she adds, and gives Dubazana a house number that he cannot hear.

Everything is done in haste. They enter the houses and loot clothes, food, television sets, video players and many other things. Dubazana, after dipping his assegai in the blood of a young man who lies dead, also takes what he can and makes off with the booty like the rest as they retreat back to the slums.

"Did you kill that woman?" the hefty man asks Dubazana when they arrive back home, some of the others already surrounding him.

"I stabbed her. But I don't know if she died."

He glowers at him with bloodshot eyes, "Why didn't you prod her heart to check that she was really dead?"

Close to tears and staring death in the face, Dubazana pleads, "May I please tell the truth, my brothers?"

"What gibberish do you talk now? What truth are you talking about?"

"That woman suddenly turned, looked at me and asked me why I wanted to kill her while she represents our mothers and lovers. When I told her that I am at war and will be killed if I spare her life, her response was: it is good that I die for her since women also die for us when they give birth to us. I couldn't answer her, my brothers, and let her go with the one stab wound that I had already inflicted above her shoulder blade."

"Let me see if your assegai has any blood on it."

Dubazana gives the man the assegai. He sees the blood and stares at his companions. "Guys, what do you want me to do with this man? Would you rather I take this assegai and plunge it into his Jesus heart?"

The men look at each other. A grey-haired man of medium height comes forward. "Let him be, since you can see that he still has some ubuntu. He is not yet familiar with killing. He has love in his heart; and if he has love, he has peace."

"Ntshingwayo, I don't give a damn about all that crap! If I instruct him to kill, he must listen."

"But Njayiphume, it's unfair to expect him to kill at your command, as if he doesn't have his own brain and conscience." The one they call Ntshingwayo shakes his head. "Njayiphume, has it ever occurred to you that the millions of people from various nations and races, including those whose freedom you claim to fight for, all came from a woman's body? You easily say they should be killed, but has it occurred to you that they go through birth pangs and, as that woman said, they could die at any time when they give birth?"

Njayiphume remains silent, his face sullen. After a while he eyes Dubazana: "It is fine, you with the heart of Jesus. One day Satan will visit you and tell you that not all say 'Lord, Lord' in that religion of yours."

He turns away with his gun and sword, leaving his followers complaining, "Looks like this church-goer didn't come to unite, but to cause division."

By the end of that day the Dubazanas' souls are withered and bruised. Never, in their entire lives, have they ever attacked other people's houses, nor, worst of all, plundered their possessions. In the room stands a big stereo radio set that Dubazana felt himself forced to steal. He does not have batteries to make it play. And now it serves as a curse and evidence that may one day land him or his family in jail. Dubazana shivers at the thought that he is now being forced to kill, simply because some people want him to kill his conscience.

What amazed the family during the attack on the township dwellers was how young women and husbands, mature women and men, some of them obviously very dignified, all emerged from these dilapidated shacks. These are clearly people who have managed to survive and cope with the realities of shack life, which means that the Dubazanas can also give it a try. Perhaps their fear is caused by the fact that they are still new to this environment.

The prevailing violence makes them befriend other men and women who are the same age as themselves. They hear them grumble and complain about how blacks are annihilating one another in their quest to overcome their challenges and empower themselves.

At last nightfall descends and they sleep like babies. Dubazana goes to work the following morning and returns in the afternoon.

For a change, they manage to sleep without any disturbance for a few nights. But early on Thursday evening, when it is already dark and Dubazana has just arrived home from work, turmoil confronts them. Someone knocks on the door as if drilling a hole in it.

"Ubani lowo? Who is that?" Dubazana frowns.

"It's me, Njayiphume. Vula! Open at once!"

Dubazana and his wife look at each other before he opens the door, and his eyes fall on Njayiphume, who is in the company of a flock of children: young girls, young boys and young men.

"The camp day I talked about has arrived. Your kids must join us, Dubazana!" Njayiphume yells to intimidate Dubazana, scowling at him and his wife as if trying to read something on their puzzled faces.

"My Lord, but they are too young!" pleads MaZondi.

Livid, Njayiphume glares at her, pointing at the flock, "How old are these ones?" he asks, fixing his torch on them. The Dubazanas look at them in shock. There are even ten-year-old girls.

"But oh my Lord …!" cries MaZondi.

"Thula! Thula!" Njayiphume shouts, brandishing a fist at her. It silences her.

"Are your kids joining us, or do you refuse and face the consequences?" He turns and looks at the group. "We are tired of people who idle around in comfort while we fight for freedom. Sondelani bafana, boys, come closer."

Two boys aged about ten emerge from the dark and enter the room. They block the door, two car tyres in their hands. They look at MaZondi and Dubazana, who are their parents' ages, with the whites of their eyes dark red. They have killed before and are infused with a hunger to kill again; burning a person alive has become a pastime for them. The screams emitted by victims as the flames swallow them are sweet music to their ears and worth dancing to.

Holding tears back with his eyelids, Dubazana looks at his children, who stand behind him wide-eyed. "Join them, my children."

"I am scared, Mama!" Makhosazana begins to scream as if she has gone mad, clutching her mother and cowering behind her. She has heard blood-curdling stories from her friends at school about the horrors and atrocities committed at the camps.

"Are we supposed to plead with you till sunrise? Didn't you hear your father telling you to join us?" Njayiphume reaches out, grabs them by the shoulders and throws them out of the room.

"Dad! Save me, Dad! Please save me!" Makhosazana cries in the dark as the crowd scuttles away.

"They are going to assault my kids, Dubazana. Let me go and die with them!" MaZondi wails hysterically, trying to break free from Dubazana, who struggles to restrain and placate her.

"Please sit down, my sweetheart. Think: if you throw yourself at death, they'll either necklace you straight away or first rape you before killing you." He sinks onto the bed, sits her on his lap and hugs and kisses her, trying to wipe the tears from her eyes with his face.

"My conscience haunts me, Dubazana. It won't allow me to sacrifice my kids. Does being homeless mean I have to lose all my treasures in exchange for accommodation? Not long ago at the Mlangenis I had to endure seeing you being kissed and flirted with simply because turning a blind eye would secure me a room. Terrible, terrible, terrible, that is my life!"

"Mother of my children, we're desperate; we're vulnerable to all the storms and the floods that wreak havoc on our lives. My being silent doesn't mean I'm not hurting. It's the flesh and blood of both of us that has been taken away to be violated. And what can we do about it? This is how the world has turned out to be. Let's just pray that they spare their lives. If we brood on our plight we'll die from heartache and leave our kids as orphans with no one to care for them."

But MaZondi is not to be consoled. She keeps on crying, sometimes too exhausted to make a sound, but sometimes the words pour out, "Dubazana, I am sure you're proud of me because you know that you found in me a virgin with a multitude of suitors. I married you out of love; nobody forced me into doing it. I spoke to my heart, and it accepted that my body and your body belong to our family. Today, some monsters are going to destroy my daughter in the name of freedom, but tomorrow the very same men will be insulting her when she's no longer a virgin." She floods Dubazana with hot tears.

The children have been dragged all the way to a slanting four-roomed lean-to shack. Three teenage couples and their five children are the caretakers. The teenagers also met at the camps, and their children, born of pregnancies that were unplanned and unwanted, are products of those meetings. The original owner of the house, his wife and four daughters all died in a hail of bullets amid allegations that they were sell-outs. Their daughter made them victims by following her heart and falling for a policeman, a taboo in sectors of the community.

It is in this shack that the campers are made to sit down. The new recruits are briefed on the rules. First and foremost, in this political organisation, a girl is not allowed to go out with a policeman, or anyone from another party. This rule can only be side-stepped if she does it on instruction from her handlers to be a decoy to lure a policeman into sympathising with their cause; in this way the police can be made to favour them and turn a blind eye whenever the party commits atrocities.

Secondly, in the struggle for freedom, members cannot do as they please but have to abide by the strict rules that their commanders mete out. Here, a woman is a warrior and belongs to her fellow warriors. No one is expected to object to this rule. However, the most cardinal rule is that no one is allowed to report a matter to the police, not even if a sibling or a parent has been murdered. The party is very strict about this. The victims cannot lay charges because then the police will get involved. The supreme authority rests with kangaroo courts that dispense harsh sentences to those who rush to the police.

During the session the camp inmates receive no formal instruction on politics nor the national economy and how this should be handled. After being subjected to sermons on the camp and party rules, they chant freedom songs and slogans. Thereafter, a list of cases follows, involving alleged sell-outs who receive death sentences in absentia. A decision is made that those unwilling to support the struggle must be hauled before the courts. Then they embark on a house-to-house manhunt for those who are apathetic towards the struggle. Dagga-smoking seems to be the order of the day. When their voices are hoarse from singing, it is lights-out time. In the anonymity of darkness, destruction reigns. The hardened bullies target the new recruits to ensure that they are properly "initiated" into the party. By sunrise they have gone to sleep elsewhere to evade any suspicions.

In the morning, the children are released to their families who have sat through the night in anxiety, anticipating the worst.

"Who is there?" MaZondi hears voices that are hard to recognise.

"It is us, Mama!"

"Abantabami, Nkosi yami! Dear Lord, my kids!" She jumps to the door and almost faints when she sees her daughter's condition.

Dubazana's soul is so crushed that he cannot control himself. He weeps like a child, not knowing where the next breath will come from. He stumbles out, deranged and without any destination in mind. It is still dark on this July morning, and the valley of shacks appears to be ablaze. Those who do not have Primus stoves or paraffin are already outside making fires and preparing to start the day. The place is red with fires and covered with smoke. It does not occur to him that in most of these houses the same tragedy has struck. In fact, to some this has become such a frequent occurrence that they shrug off the disregard for HIV infections in the camps. The disease is tearing the community apart. After a while he retraces his steps and staggers back to the room where he finds everybody: they seem as if they are mourning a death.

"Mama, please may I take a bath?"

"She mustn't bath, mother of my children; we need to have all the evidence when we report the matter to the police," explains Dubazana, afraid even to be specific.

"Report this to the police and you're in deep trouble!" shouts a voice from behind the room. "You have been told repeatedly that this place is out of bounds to police vans. If you don't zip your big mouths, something will come to silence you. And stop weeping as if it's the end of the world. Or is this how you cast bad luck on the camp?" The voice goes silent for a while. "Go to the police then! But you will be tyre-necklaced all the way to your graves!" the voice adds, after what seems like an eternity, making them wonder if the speaker is still lurking outside. Stunned, they weep in silence.

That day Dubazana doesn't go to work. He would not have coped at all, and would very likely have plunged into the traffic, confused, dazed and unable to hear or see anything. Suspecting that countless eyes are now spying on them, they are afraid to take their children to hospital. Despite the fact that he and his wife also need a comforter, they lock themselves in the room and try to console their children, but Makhosazana is beyond consolation. Her father can hardly look at her. He feels guilty because it feels as if he, as a male, had a hand in helping the other males commit their atrocious activities. He cannot put the moment out of his mind: when things had reached a stalemate, he succumbed and allowed the thugs to take his children to the camp. The terrified voice of his daughter, as she pleaded with him the previous night, still rings in his ears: "Dad, please save me!" He failed to intervene on her behalf.

The merciful giant from slumberland intercedes late in the afternoon and takes all of them into a well-deserved sleep. They wake up just as it is beginning to darken outside. A commotion somewhere outside stirs them: people are exclaiming and women screaming. They light a candle and go outside.

"What happened, young lady?" MaZondi asks a woman hardly visible in the dark. Their faces carefully peeking out, the Dubazanas see the world in a cloud of dust.

"It's the cruel world in which we live!" the woman exclaims in fear. She is very young. "Didn't you hear the youth and their handlers walking past here, dancing and chanting?"

"We were fast asleep, my sister. In fact, yesterday we stayed up the whole night waiting for our children who had been abducted to the camp."

"But still, my sister, never allow yourselves to sleep deeply in this neighbourhood. One day you will die in your sleep. They have just passed by, dragging a teenage boy, and they entered Biyase's place. On arriving there, they took Biyase's daughter and hauled her to the courtyard, the land of no return, under the big tree. They were still busy interrogating them when I left. The boy is alleged to be friends with a policeman and the girl is dating the latter. Rumours are they were caught red-handed at Isipingo, chatting, laughing and sharing a fried fish snack. ... How terrible! What has become of this world?" Her eyes widen with fear, but then she strains her ears. "Hhayi bo! Oh no! What are they doing now?"

At that moment a girl runs towards them "Help! Maye babo! Save me, Mama! Put the fire out, Mama!" She is all in flames, literally falling apart with the burning tyre still intact around her neck. It is amazing how the girl can still see her way home amidst the flames. She goes straight to a woman who is wearing black mourning clothes, walking slowly, tired and resting a bag with small packets of maize meal, sugar and offal on her head so that the family can have a morsel to eat in order to sleep. She has good reason to be exhausted: she has been up since dawn, washing, ironing and cooking for her white employer in the suburbs. On seeing the ball of flames running to embrace her, she jumps and pushes it aside, shouting as it flies past her, "Oh my Lord, whose daughter is this on whom such cruelty has been inflicted? I pity her mother!" Still holding her nose to ward off the smell of burning human flesh, she exclaims in horror, "What is this person doing? Why does she go straight to my house, ablaze?"

"It is Thenjiwe, MaSangweni!" Another woman's voice pierces the dark.

"Oh my God, which Thenjiwe?"

"Oh, my dear MaSangweni, the one and only Thenjiwe, your daughter!"

"Dear God, how can it be my Thenjiwe, the only daughter you gave me?" She stares at the room into which Thenjiwe has disappeared. It was black but is now red inside. She tries to turn back but falls down, rises to her feet, only to collapse again.

"Where are you, Lord? Why are you silent, Son of Heaven, while my daughter burns alive?" the mother's voice tears the sky, as her daughter stumbles, rises and stumbles yet again. "But Biyase, why are you silent, wherever you are? And why do you not intercede in this wrath that grips the world, where you've deserted me, leaving me homeless? Oh my!" While she screams, the mother throws herself onto her flaming daughter and the door, already burning, closes. "Maye, ma-yeh! Please rescue us! My daughter and I are burning to death! What a painful death faces us, my daughter! Are we the architects of apartheid, do we deserve such a horrible end?"

The flames engulfing her daughter all the way to the room have licked the clothes against her body, setting them alight. By the time the mother jumps, the fire is already raging. The flames cling to her like a wag-'n-bietjie thorn-bush. With the smoke choking her blind, she is unable to find the door. With amazing swiftness, the fire swallows her. The saddest part is that the mob of youth who were present during her sentencing includes her siblings; they could not object to a decision that was proclaimed unanimous. While their house burns to ashes, the mob is mocking the young man who is alleged to be a sell-out and who is also blazing in his own ball of flames, falling a few metres away from Dubazana.

The mob momentarily forgets the burning young man when the room caves in and collapses on MaSangweni and her daughter. Flames are now all over the place, and the smell of burning human flesh permeates the air. Meanwhile, a certain man has seen MaSangweni drop her bag; he quietly picks it up and heads home to hide it. By the time her charred remains have been smothered, he has emptied the bag's contents to prepare a meal for his children.

When everything has burned to the ground at the Biyase's, with only smoke, charred bones and flesh remaining as proof of what transpired earlier, the mob starts chanting, turns and heads straight to Dubazana's shack. The family has no time to flee when they see the mob. They run inside and await their death.

"MaZondi, should it happen that they set me alight, please help to finish me off and spare me a painful death."

"Dubazana, don't speak like that! How do you know that it is not the ultimatum day for me as well? Whatever happens to me, please look after my children, Dubazana."

Then the room is surrounded and the entrance blocked. Some of the crowd enter and the room is suddenly filled with smoke and the smell of roasted meat. They look at the Dubazanas with eyes that flicker with fire as if they are still reflecting the bodies that have just burned to death. Before they say anything, they blow out the candle.

"You regard yourself as superior to other parents and hide your children and let them laze around indoors, while other parents' children actively take part in the struggle for your freedom," a hoarse voice says in the dark.

Dubazana clears his throat and pleads, "My fellow brothers, I beg for your forgiveness. I was totally unaware that there was a mission that had to be accomplished today."

"Your children were at the camp yesterday and are supposed to have known and informed you."

"My brothers, I thought only Wednesday was mentioned."

"Listen here, man." The speaker slaps Dubazana with a backhand smelling of tyre. "You should be alert. These are the shacks, not the suburbs. The red thing that has just consumed others will soon, on my order, be all over you if you don't wise up." The words are followed by another slap. "Be grateful that I warn you with my hand and a few knife slashes; you are supposed to have died." He slaps him again.

"I appreciate it, my brother."

"Let your kids move and join their peers. We are going."

"Have mercy on them, my dear brother. They're not feeling well," says MaZondi in a pleading voice.

"Hey, do you see this tyre? What's nice about it is that it doesn't discriminate. It looks good on any neck. It fits the young and the old, males and females. If you didn't witness what just happened to the others outside, you will see it first hand, right inside this room."

MaZondi goes silent.

"I can see you are stubborn and think that I'm a weakling like your husband. I will show you how a real man calls the shots. I want you to take your daughter by the arm and present her to me. Shesha! Hurry up!"

"Hawu! Hawu! Mama, please help me. My whole body is sore!"

"What am I supposed to do, mntanami, my child? You can see that they'll kill all of us if we don't abide by their rules!"

"But Mama, you fought for Dad at the Mlangenis when the women wanted to take him away. Why don't you do the same when it's my turn to be taken away?"

"Woman, let me feel her hand in mine, please!"

Panting loudly and weeping, MaZondi bends down and holds Makhosazana, trying to lift her up: "Stand up, my children, join them and save your family." She pulls Makhosazana closer, but she now wriggles and cowers away.

The voice keeps threatening, "Hand to hand, please."

"Here she is," says MaZondi, groping in the dark for her daughter's hand. A coarse hand grips hers. She screams, "No, this is my hand, not my daughter's."

"Hurry up then and give me her hand."

"There you go." The hand releases hers and grabs Makhosazana's.

"Hheyi wena, hey you, you must appreciate that we aren't taking your children by force. You've showed real commitment to the struggle, and offered them to us. Don't worry about your daughter's crying; it takes a while for a calf to get used to the rope around its leg. She'll soon get used to the yoke." He drags Makhosazana to join the rest of the group.

They haul her along, her body aching, past a smouldering tyre, some marrow and flesh. They all swear at the corpse, kick it and canter around it. MaZondi watches them until they disappear from sight, swallowed by the night.

"What an unbearably cruel world," whispers Dubazana. The hurt suffocates MaZondi and not a sound leaves her quivering mouth.

MaSangweni's weeping echoes in her ears, igniting flames in MaZondi's broken heart. She feels that Thenjiwe's torture is similar to Makhosazana's fate. She imagines her daughter in flames, a burning tyre around her neck. Her heart feels dead, her eyes are blurry and her mind completely blank. She searches her pinafore pockets, finds a box of matches and clasps it tightly. She lights a candle and grabs a bottle of paraffin. Dubazana enters when she has already poured the whole bottle onto her body and is trying to strike a match, but it fails to ignite. He throws himself onto her and grabs her by the arms.

"Mother of us all in this family, how do you expect us to survive without you if you do this?"

"Leave me alone, Dubazana, let me kill myself! My conscience is destroying me for handing my daughter over to those bandits." She protests and tries to wriggle away.

"There's not much we can do, my wife; we're caught between a rock and a hard place." He snatches the matchbox from her and throws it away, then pulls her gently by the arm, and sits on the bed with her on his lap. He wipes the tears: "Thuleleni, perhaps it's because you can't open my heart and read from it how much I love you. I live not for myself, but for you and my children." He kisses her. "My belief is that I belong to you all and you belong to me. I am you, you are me. If I lose one of you, I will no longer be myself since part of me will have been taken away. If you want to take your life, my love, that means you don't love us any more, and you want us to suffer pain for which no one will console us. I want to impress this on your mind: you don't belong to yourself but to us, and, homeless though we are, we have a home in you."

He kisses her again and caresses her gently, as someone would a small child. "Imagine the devastation if our children return from the camp's tortures and find their mother dead. They'll accuse me of not stopping you from killing yourself. No, Thuleleni, please calm down, beloved daughter of Nondaba."

MaZondi leans against her husband's shoulder. At last she gets drowsy and falls asleep. Dubazana lies beside her the whole night, clutching her arm, lest she kills them by killing herself.

8

When Makhosazana and her brother knock on the door it is still dark. MaZondi, lying awake, gets up and opens it. They enter. MaZondi looks at them but her eyes are dead with guilt and shame. This time her daughter is not crying, but simply enters and throws herself on the bed.

"How are you, my children?" she asks as she bends over her daughter.

"Mama, I wish you had never given birth to me."

"My child, those are very hurtful words." She collapses and kneels by her side.

"You gave birth to this body for it to be assaulted and plundered. Nobody in this world loves me. Even my parents make me a sacrificial goat so that they can survive while I die. The only image in my mind is of a cruel world. I've been invaded physically, emotionally and mentally."

Dubazana, who has sat up on the bed, listens with his mouth open as the children recount the events of the night, which are the same as the previous night's nightmares. His hand repeatedly moves to his eyes.

"Makhosazana's mother, I'm not sure that I'll be able to go to work today."

"I would rather you do go to work today, since it's a Friday and you need to get paid. We need money so that if we escape from this abyss, we can find a room elsewhere and pay."

"What scares me the most is that you may all kill yourselves as soon as I leave," he whispers.

With the hope of finding a home somewhere else, MaZondi assures him that they will look out for one another and that she will watch over Makhosazana and make sure she does not disappear from her sight. They decide to leave the place at night, if possible. Despite his reluctance, Dubazana leaves for work. He copes, and he receives his pay in the afternoon and goes straight home. Although he has brought meat, a family favourite, no one has any appetite. No one is hungry or thirsty, and they eagerly await dusk so that they can at last escape.

First dusk, then darkness. At ten there is still incessant commotion and heavy steps all over the yard, which forces them to change their plans. The alternative is to leave at dawn and take the first taxis before people can recognise their faces. They decide to go to sleep early to make sure they wake early, but they have just dozed off when the door suddenly flies open. When Dubazana tries to get up, the glare of torchlight blinds him.

"My brothers, what is the matter?" he asks, bewildered.

"How can you ask that when you know that you're hogging my girlfriend here!" says one of the men who have packed the room. "Vuka! Wake up! Let's go. You've agreed to be my lover and you took my money." He points at MaZondi, who sits up on the bed, wide-eyed.

"I've never touched your money!" she responds angrily.

"This is exactly what they said where you come from. This is how you operate. But you have met your equal in me. You took my money when I met you on your way to fetch water. It is my hard-earned money and you can't play tricks on me. Wake up!" He grabs her arm and MaZondi is on her feet in seconds.

"My brothers, how about I pay you the money she owes you, as long as you leave her alone?" Dubazana pleads.

"We don't dictate terms on how you spend your money, so don't tell us how we should spend ours. We know what happens to a crook who uses his wife as bait." These are the last words he hears before a red flame flashes in front of him. He drops to the floor and falls into a death-like sleep.

Makhosazana and Nkosana dart off and escape while the thugs carry their mother out, screaming and pleading to deaf ears. Several men chase after Makhosazana, but she stays ahead of them and disappears into the night. She runs all the way to the main road, throwing herself in front of beaming headlights. The driver slams on the brakes, making the car come to an abrupt stop, tyres squealing as the car almost overturns.

"You see, this is exactly what I'm talking about, and the reason you want to imprison me," says Bhekizizwe Zulu, who is in the sleek black car. He sits in the back seat, squeezed between two African men. The front is occupied by a Mr Naidoo and Schutte, popularly known as Siketekete, meaning a lantern, because he is notorious for nocturnal ambushes of his victims. The front passenger and driver curse aloud as Makhosazana darts across the road. When the car screeches to a sudden stop, the thugs chasing her retreat and go back to the Dubazana shack.

Bhekizizwe continues: "The car jerks as if to stop but then suddenly moves on. I thought you served the community. Isn't that what you're employed for and what you get paid for?" He talks angrily to one of the men who, earlier that evening, took him from a shack where he had been hiding.

"Hheyi wena, you leave us alone please! We are not community policemen and we don't account to the public. We belong to a special wing that investigates the acts of terrorists like you who intend to overthrow our government."

"Please stop and let's help that young girl, my brothers! Those thugs will return and kill her. If not them, some other thugs will come across her and rape her."

"You know what, it's a pity that they ran away. Otherwise we would have asked them to kill you for us," snorts the man next to him. "They are lesser scum than you: they are a menace to their fellow people, while you are a threat and enemy to the state." They twist his arm painfully.

"You're making a grave mistake and you'll regret this in the future. You shouldn't break this arm because you'll need it to help you put out the fire that your superiors are kindling, oblivious that they will fail to contain it in the future."

"Thula! You have a big mouth!" They slap him. His mouth bleeding, he turns and scans the dark, pleading with them to make a U-turn and check on the girl.

"That's none of our business. It's the parents who give birth to such despicable offspring who should be bothered."

"What proof do you have or what research have you done to confirm that the girl is, indeed, despicable?"

"This is the research!" He twists his arm, spraining it.

Bhekizizwe groans in pain, and tears flow silently as if from a tap.

"My brothers, the time is coming when the people you set alight will also incinerate you in return and in the end you will all burn together in one big fire. My point is that a government that employs firebrands becomes a government of a fire-spitting nation."

Siketekete suggests, "If only you could cross floors, become part of us and abandon all your foolish actions, you could live like a king."

"Don't you understand? It's ridiculous that you call yourselves state security police while you imprison those who are striving for the welfare and stability that will ensure the safety of the country. It is futile and self-destructive for the state to solve problems through the barrel of a gun and handcuffs. Since millions of people are homeless, you guys should know that every squatter camp, filthy shack and seedy street where they scramble for a temporary abode has become a breeding ground for a national catastrophe. In that disaster, there is, amongst other things, squalor and illiteracy. If you want to destroy a nation instantly, create a fatal bomb with poverty and ignorance as your main ingredients. You will be devoid of a government, just as you already are. You'll preach till you froth at the mouth, telling people about the national economy, but the masses won't understand you since they won't know anything about the economy, destitute as they are. And how can you mention national pride when people have been stripped of their dignity? When ignorance is rife, the nation is shackled by its catastrophic lack of understanding," says Bhekizizwe.

"There's a lot of truth in what this man is saying. Don't touch him again," says the man seated to his right.

"Oh, has he also contaminated you with that propaganda about poverty that he goes around preaching, misleading the multitudes in the process?" asks Siketekete.

"It's true what he says. And in the dark, in which we're groping, I can see some rays of sunshine. My mind is ..." the man rubs his forehead, "my mind has opened up ... Indeed, isn't it time for oppression to be replaced by progressive and forward-thinking attitudes? Perhaps the saddest part is that you and I are two of the many prisoners of ignorance in this country."

The one seated to Bhekizizwe's left utters a faint sigh. "You too, Ngidi, are betraying us?"

"Ximba, we'll move faster towards democracy once we get rid of a government that causes confusion and divisions."

They talk as the car speeds on the highway towards the city. It soon reaches the city and weaves through the streets until it comes to a stop in front of a tall building. Bhekizizwe cannot believe his eyes when Ngidi is unexpectedly handcuffed and locked up.

When Makhosazana stumbles and falls onto the road, she watches in horror as the Special Branch car swerves from side to side, trying to avoid hitting her. She scrambles to her feet and runs into the dark, then trips on what feels like a mound in the tall grass. She falls on top of it. But it is the still-warm body of a portly man who has recently been mugged on his way from work and stabbed to death. Startled, she screams, "Maye! Maye! Oh my God!" Smeared with blood, she tries to calm herself. There is no time to dwell on anything, and she runs until she finds herself inside the yard of a house in the nearby township. Knocking will land her in worse jeopardy, she thinks, so she tiptoes to the back, and, peeping around the corner, she sees a dustbin. Desperate with the desire to simply vanish, she lifts the lid, jumps inside and closes it. The smell is atrocious but somehow it makes her feel safer, makes her feel that this is what she is part of: the trash in this world. Yes, the bin is a befitting shelter for her.

She feels the dead man's blood drying on her face and her thoughts return to the mayhem she left at home when she fled for her life. The prospect of becoming an orphan brings tears to her eyes, and, shivering, she ponders the fate of her family after her father was beaten up and her mother faced the same brutality that she had just managed to escape. Every now and then she lifts the lid slightly, hoping to see signs of dawn, but closes it each time against the darkness outside.

It is dawn when Dubazana regains consciousness. He feels blind and numb, and his head is heavy, muddled and throbbing. He is so disoriented that he does not recognise his surroundings. He has good reason to be in such a state. Everything has changed in his room since he was knocked unconscious with a heavy knobkierie. Vacantly he stares and, as if in a dream, sees a body on the floor next to a flickering candle, about to blow out at any moment.

Slowly, reluctantly, his mind begins to clear, but the scene in the room still confounds him. The room is empty and devoid of any furniture. Has he been abducted, robbed and dumped in a shack elsewhere? Shaking his head, blinking repeatedly he sees an unused candle on the floor, staggers to his feet, lights the fresh candle and takes a closer look at the body. Fortunately, it still has some signs of life. It is his wife, her face swollen beyond recognition, and there are wounds all over her body. The monsters have kicked her around, injured and raped her, probably right here. The children are nowhere to be seen. What happened to them, he wonders tiredly.

9

On Sunday morning, parents brave the sharp sun and arrive in numbers for a meeting called by Mr Donda, the principal of Mzuzwana. Donda is a light-skinned man of medium height, in his forties. He stands in front of a table behind which the school committee, comprising the chairperson, his deputy and other members, sit. The parents, sitting on benches, listen attentively, admiring his blue blazer, grey pants, white starched shirt and neck tie.

While tiptoeing in his black shiny shoes and adjusting his glasses in their shiny gold frame, he spreads his hands: "Of course, teaching has become impossible. You parents know the truth, but you still point fingers at me, complaining that my teachers are to blame for the poor results. Tell me, then!" He spreads his hands again. "What do you expect me to do if each class has, on average, a hundred pupils who have to sit on the floor and kneel when they do their schoolwork? And then, besides the plethora of problems that plague our education system, of which you are aware, what must we do about the plight of our homeless children? I am referring to children who sleep in the same room as their parents, who have to rent in other people's houses? This includes children who have homes: four-roomed matchbox township houses, in which the parents, their children, daughters-in-law and their husbands and grandchildren are all packed like sardines. Places where people sleep on each other's backs, and where doing homework is impossible."

Donda continues: "What must we, as teachers, do if we are entrusted with the success of children who share a tiny room in the slums where they have to fight for a droplet of drinking water; where violence and killing have become a pastime for our pupils? What must we do when pupils who have been soldiers at night arrive at school without their homework and fall asleep at their desks during classes?"

He removes his glasses, steps nervously towards the window, and takes out a handkerchief to wipe the tears from his eyes. Although it is a sunny morning, there is a fog outside emanating from smoke that has uncertain origins. He puts his glasses back on and takes the floor again. "What must we do if we teach pupils from townships where bottle stores and beer halls have mushroomed in every section? To this day, libraries remain a distant dream. In conditions like these, conditions that distress parents and drive them to booze, fighting and sharing alcohol with their kids, what are we expected to do? I am asking you, parents!"

They are silent, staring at him and clearing their throats but without responding. "I am asking you, parents, what are we as teachers supposed to do when we teach pupils born in single-sex male hostels; since they live and sleep where men and female strangers sleep together; where there is drinking, singing, dancing and brawling all night? Are these conditions conducive to success in life?

"This is a reality. Teachers are entrusted with the daunting task of building a future nation. I don't have objections to that. But my question is: how can we build such a nation if we teach pupils who are either cohabiting, pregnant or already have a child or two? If we ask them why they live with their boyfriends, they respond by asking where are they supposed to stay if their parents don't have homes or if they come from a matchbox house that doesn't even provide enough room for a couple.

"In a political environment like this, where pupils have been turned into weapons, how can you teach a nation about being human, since they have become human weapons made for killing? My question is, in a time when the youth are recruited to violent camps where they are exploited and raped, with some falling pregnant and some getting venereal infections, what do you expect? Children are violated in camps, hostels, rented rooms, in the filthy places where they live and in overflowing houses. These children have lost hope in life and anything beneficial that you teach them simply enters through one ear and flies out the other.

"Some of the pupils have killed. Some of them have killed violently, setting people alight. When you teach them, they stare at you with inflamed eyes that seem to spit fire. Some are on drugs. What do you expect us to do?

"What can we do when these pupils fail exams, then shoot their teachers dead, just as it happened in this school earlier this year, and in many other schools?" He takes his glasses off again and rubs his eyes. "When I realised that teaching these pupils has been ineffective, I approached social workers to come and address these disturbed children. But I can tell you that I was deeply disturbed by their report; in it, they said they themselves are confused by the confusion that permeates all our schools. Since then it's become clear to me that I am also confused, and my teachers and the social workers are also confused in the same way that the children are confused, because we are all products of the same environment.

"The most disturbing part, the part that's almost driven me insane, is that when some pupils told their parents that I'd brought social workers to the school, the parents reported me to the authorities. The authorities contend that I'm trying to poison and convince a healthy community about non-existent sufferings. I am certain that I will be imprisoned any time now." These words seem to startle him anew. He shakes his head, glances through the window and checks his wristwatch as if he is under some great pressure. "My point is that the government policies have splintered the backbone of black people's lives in this country. When something wrong happens to the backbone, the next step is incapacitation. Nonetheless, should I be taken away now, may I bid farewell to the parents of the beloved pupils whom I adore, despite being fed all the muck that I have referred to."

He looks at the parents and tears unexpectedly flow from underneath his glasses. He paces the floor as if possessed. Then he turns towards a green chalkboard on the wall where lines from a poem are written in chalk:

These people are miserable
Said a bird, perched on a prison roof.

"To avoid going to jail, I must skew these words and say:

These people are well off
Said a parrot, sitting in a fat cat's house."

He grabs some chalk and writes the parrot's words underneath those of the other bird.

"If the situation is like this, where does it leave us, fellow brothers?"

The talk finds a place in the parents' hearts. You can hear a pin drop; some are sniffing, while others are wiping their eyes. But some have their eyes fixed on the floor in shame, their consciences gnawing at them and reminding them that they are awaiting their pay cheques for spying on Donda.

Donda glances at his watch and cannot remain on his seat. He rises to his feet and paces the floor as if his gut is warning him about impending danger.

"Hhayi, no," he says, resting his arms on his belly, "if I think about imprisonment, my bowels loosen. Let me rush to the toilet. Should anyone want to see me, tell them to wait and don't disturb me." He does not use the door though, but suddenly jumps through the window, holding his stomach all the while. He enters the teachers' toilet at full speed, his coat tails flying in the air, and locks himself inside. Some parents find his athletic prowess amusing and smile understandingly.

As if on cue, a sleek, shiny car slinks through the gate and then suddenly disappears from view. Soon after, two men emerge: a giant and a midget, sporting black hats and black suits with matching shoes and dark sunglasses. They have been sneaking against the walls but increase their pace on approaching the hall. They enter the hall and ask to see Donda, the principal.

"Poor him, he has a runny tummy and had to rush to the toilet," says a light-skinned woman sitting in the front row, dressed to kill and wearing stylish, expensive glasses.

"When did he go?" asks the giant, who has not taken off his hat as good manners dictate.

"A short while ago."

It's the midget's turn: "He sees us and develops a runny tummy. Hawu, where is the toilet?"

Somebody points it out and the midget leads the way. They stand in front of the toilet for five minutes, then ten, then twenty without Donda coming out. They knock. No answer. They kick the door open, but, as if they have met a mamba inside, they fly out, looking around outside the toilet and then they run back again. They even look in the water cistern, banging on it, but Donda fails to materialise. Livid, they enter the hall again. "Where is Donda? We can't find him."

The whole hall points at the toilet.

"That damn dog!" The giant reads the words on the chalkboard and fumes. "He is busy misleading everybody. Who says that people are suffering?"

"It is cheeky of him to quote from this poem because he's fully aware that it's been banned." The midget grabs a duster, jumping up and down several times to wipe off the offending words. He leaves the parrot's words, at which he points, announcing, "This is the truth!"

The whole hall erupts, "Do us a favour then and replace the school door that you've broken."

"That's none of our business. We are the authorities. And what's worse, the dog ran away!" They leave to fetch others from the car and then comb the whole school yard for any sign of Donda, even going through some chalk-boxes. All in vain! Tyres scream as their car speeds away to his house, his in-laws and relatives. It emerges later that they leave empty-handed.

After this display, the parents leave the school grounds down-spirited, wondering what has become of Donda. Some rush to church as the church bells have started ringing, summoning them to service.

Meanwhile, with each passing minute, the cars taking turns to transport Donda bring him closer to the border of a country where he will board a plane heading to foreign lands.

"Yesterday, I went to the slum area, to a branch that has been established by a church member who lives there. I was excited that the house was overflowing, with some seated on the floor and people even outside the house. I became worried, though, when I led them in song and only a handful joined in. My spirits dampened when I started preaching, beseeching the congregation to repent because the Kingdom of Heaven is near, and so is Judgement Day and the throwing of sinners into eternal fire.

"That was when the house began rumbling, with a man in old, tattered clothes disrupting me with a question: 'Is it possible for a starving slave to have proper faith while he watches the rich feast and feed their dogs with the leftovers? If starvation forces the hungry to steal, does that draw them away from the Kingdom of Heaven?'" Reverend Mbambo recounts this story as he stands on the church pulpit in Mlazi. The house is full, and amongst the audience is a tall, hefty white pastor from the Dutch Reformed Church, a certain Fanie Pienaar.

The Reverend Mbambo, who is of medium height with neatly trimmed whiskers, continues, "The prisons that we call townships are human dumping sites. They are an abyss where people burn in flames of misery; there is abject poverty and stark destitution. It is where a person kills to live and to survive the claws and nails of death. In the kraals, where people are shepherded into loyal submission, there is filth, congestion, poverty, disease and a myriad of miseries. Yes, there are vast lands but no place for the majority. The minority has the lion's share.

"In a situation like this, how can I preach to the congregation in parables and allusions to Sodom and Gomorrah when the masses already languish there? How do I mention Babylon when they already burn there? How will I preach to people to correct their ways and avoid perishing by fire when they are already in flames, long before Judgement Day?

"Please advise me, my countrymen, on how to preach about justice to homeless and landless people? What do I say in my sermons when children sleep in one room with their parents and watch them patch their love with stolen moments of intimacy, without privacy, where they rent rooms in other people's houses? It's true that in such situations, when children leave home to move in with their lovers, the parents cherish the opportunity to have some intimacy. In situations like this, how can my words find fertile ground when I implore the youth to respect their bodies and save themselves for marriage? And when I excommunicate members for premarital pregnancy, on what grounds do I justify that?

"Tell me, my brethren! How do I tell the married not to destroy their homes, when they don't have homes in the first place? And what house rules are their children expected to obey when the parents have to abide by the rules of other people's houses?"

The church is very silent, shrouded in a thick air of sadness. Reverend Pienaar, seated and listening attentively, turns red. It is not because Reverend Mbambo is criticising his race; instead, he is recalling all the hardships he endured as a child. It feels as if the social ills that are being listed have ravaged him too.

"In the olden times," it is Mbambo again, "it is said that wars were rife in the land. Crops in the fields were set alight and livestock was confiscated. Starvation led to cannibalism. It is said that since then, even after normality was regained and there was abundant food and livestock, some had already tasted and enjoyed human flesh and couldn't abandon cannibalism. The same happens here. People have become cannibals. Since they have become so used to it, even after the nation has seen the light, some will continue to consume others and benefit from other people's plight.

"In a situation like this, my people, the work of God is impossible to carry out. You can see that for yourselves." He spreads his hands. "It is difficult to embrace the Kingdom of God when the rulers of worldly kingdoms rule with an iron hand."

Some people now take to the floor and share their testimonies, and the service begins to resemble a revival meeting. "Mfundisi! Reverend!" says a man in a suit and wearing glasses. "I am a personnel officer at work. Daily I handle many cases of people who arrive at work disheartened. They don't have homes. Their wives and children are abducted, taken to the veld and raped. With such disillusioned manpower, the economy of the country disintegrates. In a situation like this, working becomes a challenge, Mfundisi."

Another giant of a man gets up: "Mfundisi, I am a policeman by profession. In a social environment like this, it's impossible to work when my responsibility as a policeman is not to ensure safety and security but to arrest the hungry and the unemployed and to dump them like trash into ditches in the form of homelands. It is impossible to work, Mfundisi, if my job is to force people to obey the laws of oppression. It is impossible, Mfundisi, when on the one hand, the law encourages crime and on the other, there are policemen who kill those who oppose the criminality of the law. What are we supposed to do, my brothers and sisters?" He sits down, disconsolate.

Another woman stands up and begins to sing. She is light skinned and dressed in a gold-flowered dress. It is moist behind her dark glasses, "Mfundisi, my name is Bathandekile Dlomo. I work as a nurse and I am responsible for family planning. Mfundisi, this work is undoable. How can you do your work and educate people on family planning when the authorities are flooding us with foreigners who enrich themselves at our expense; living in posh houses while the indigenous people are left destitute? Although we appreciate the dangers of overpopulation, how can you advise people on family planning, considering the government policies?" She starts a song and sits down.

"Reverend!" booms Reverend Fanie Pienaar as he ascends the pulpit and stands next to Mbambo. "We hardly know each other. We often bump into each other in town and exchange hurried greetings. It is through hearsay that I thought that blacks live comfortable lives in townships. Little did I know that the nation is subjected to so much anguish. I will therefore go back to my fellow whites in the city with the question: what does the Scripture say about doing unto others as you would want them to do unto you? The Lord's Church that belongs to both blacks and whites should understand that a human being belongs to God. You alienate yourself from God if you discriminate, enslave, cripple and traumatise others physically and emotionally. I plead with you, dear brethren, to forgive those who impose such laws for they don't know what they are doing. Once the fog of ignorance clears from their minds they will be mortified and scramble for shrubs to cover their nudity when they realise that they have been walking around naked all these years."

"Indeed, brethren," Mbambo responds, "there are some who dump blacks in the townships and tell them that the sky is the limit. Unfortunately, the township sky is indiscernible because of the smoke. What I appreciate most in you, my black brothers, is your bravery. How my heart overflows with joy when I see my people walking tall, proud of who they are. How much joy I feel when our youth embrace themselves and strive for progress and prosperity! Be steadfast in doing good, my people, but be warned: because when all this darkness is over, a bright light will emerge and blind people into confusion and cause them to kill one another all over again. But the vigilant, who have discarded their shackles, will enjoy the fruit of their toils."

Soon after the service, the congregation disperses and people form groups outside, applauding the sermon that bordered on provoking the government. It is then that the two men in black, who were seen earlier in the day at the Mzuzwana parents' meeting, disappear into a small room that serves as the priest's office. They have a bone to pick with the man of God. After a while they emerge with Mbambo, his black robes fluttering wildly, steering him towards their car. Tailing them sheepishly is Reverend Pienaar who keeps saying, "If you arrest him, arrest me as well."

"We can't arrest you, you are white and only whites can arrest you because we don't have permission to do so. Our duty is to arrest our own people only!"

"Truth is life and lies result in death! So I don't mind if I am arrested for the truth because it means that I have been arrested for a life-giving cause. May that life be an everlasting one!" Reverend Mbambo shouts as he is bundled into the car, where he sits in the middle, flanked by the two men.

While the congregation is still numbed by fear and shock, the car rapidly drives away, blowing up thick dust on those gathered outside. Reverend Pienaar summons the congregation to an impromptu briefing, after which they burst into song and prayer for Mbambo. Some cry and some cannot even speak as they walk home in solemn silence. Others amble sluggishly to their cars, most of which are parked in the shade of trees.

Thabizolo Thabekhulu, clad in a blue suit, also walks to his car unhurriedly, as if he has a deep respect for the ground. He is lean, tall and light in complexion, forty years old, with receding hair, signalling imminent balding. He carries a Bible in one hand and with the other holds that of his wife, Zamaswazi Dlamini, who is thirty-seven years old and light skinned. She has a slender, trim figure and wears a skirt and coat that are the same colour as her husband's suit. They are walking to their new Toyota Cressida that also matches the colour of their clothes. Thabekhulu is about to open the door for his wife when he sees a couple who sit leaning against the car with their daughter and son between them. Puzzled, Thabekhulu greets them politely.

"My brother," Dubazana rises to his feet. He is dusty and his mouth is white and dry from hunger. He rubs his hands and politely says, "What will become of us if you leave us here?" Thabekhulu looks silently at this young man and his family, all of whom have sorrow and misery written across their faces.

"Yini? What's the matter?"

"My brother, as we stand in front of you, we have suffered so much in this world that we have lost all hope that anybody cares and loves us. We decided to come to this holy place in desperation. Perhaps we could meet a person with ubuntu who, on hearing our story, would sympathise and offer a helping hand." He recounts the events that they have recently been through in the slums. They escaped at dawn and the only possessions they have are the clothes on their bodies. They have not eaten all day. They ask for a slice of bread that they can share among themselves and a shelter in which to squat until Dubazana has saved enough to buy them clothes and find a room to rent.

"Oh my Lord, but who do we leave you with, since the reverend has been arrested?" asks MaDlamini as she ponders the plight of a family that stares at her with sullen, grief-stricken and hungry eyes. She and her husband excuse themselves, step a few metres away and consult with each other, their discussion guided by the conscience that emanates from the Bibles they hold in their hands.

10

Thabekhulu's car weaves its way through the slopes from the church and heads to their home on the outskirts of E-section in Mlazi township. Their home is one of the houses perched above the valley, overlooking the Mlazi River. The back seat of the car, where the four Dubazana family members sit squashed, has caved in. The Dubazanas sit in silence, each of them lost in their own misery and pain. The air is filled with sweet, soothing music at low volume. The car is shiny, spotless and smells nice, befitting its decent, perfectly groomed owners. It eventually stops in front of the gates of an impressive house with a green fence, yellow walls and red roof tiles, clearly recently renovated and extended.

Thabekhulu gets out, opens the big garage door, then comes back to the car to drive into the garage where they all get out. He closes the gate and the couple lead the Dubazanas to the front entrance. MaDlamini opens the main door through which they enter an expansive, expensively furnished dining room with a long eight-seater table and room divider. On the wall a big clock glitters like gold. Timidly the Dubazanas trail behind, scared even to walk on the thick carpet. Huge and beautiful homes like this one are associated with whites, and they have never been inside one. They tiptoe behind the couple who lead them along to the lounge.

"Take a seat, guys, and make yourselves at home," says Thabekhulu, pointing at the leather couches. They sink into the softness and comfort of the couches, and their brittle spirits are immediately soothed. Thabekhulu sits down on an adjacent two-seater couch, while his wife is off to the bedrooms.

"Please sit back and relax while Thabethule's mother and I make arrangements for your stay."

"We really appreciate your generosity, Thabekhulu," says Dubazana, despite feeling uncomfortable and out of place in the expensive surroundings. He is aware that he has not washed in a long time and, with all that he has been through, must be filthy and stinking. Thabekhulu walks to a large imbuia room divider that fills the whole wall, switches on an expensive hi-fi stereo and soul-soothing music fills the room. Then he goes off to join his wife.

Wordlessly the Dubazanas sit, avoiding each other's eyes and breathing in the luxurious atmosphere that pervades the house. They stare at the varnished wooden ceiling and admire the expertly designed decorations. They see exquisite lamps of various sizes and shapes strategically positioned all over the living room, some hanging from the ceiling and some clinging to the greenish walls. On the walls hang pictures of the couple's wedding day and photographs, presumably of their children: a son and a daughter. The other pictures are decorative. MaZondi's eyes are fixed on one with the couple seated in a chair, holding a bowl from which they both scoop food.

After a while, Thabekhulu returns and asks to have a word with Dubazana, who immediately follows him into the sitting room through a red curtain.

"With regard to the tragedy that you said has befallen your family, I wonder if it is okay with you if your wife and children take a bath before reporting the matter to the police and consulting a doctor?"

"My brother," says Dubazana as he whisks off a fly that looks very out of place in the house, "I would be inflicting more pain on them if I were to let them go in this condition. Secondly, I feel that taking them to the police, who will bombard them with questions, will just increase the pain in their hearts, particularly since we've taken a long time to report the matter. I'd be grateful if you could just arrange a bath for them, which they'll appreciate deeply."

After a brief consultation between the Thabekhulus, MaDlamini asks MaZondi to go to the bathroom. In tears, MaZondi rises and follows MaDlamini sheepishly. She is shown the bathroom and the clothes that MaDlamini has put out for her to change into after the bath. She locks herself in the bathroom and admires the interior. There is a shower, mirrors on the wall and a cupboard in which all the necessities for bathing are stored. Everything is spotless: you could eat off the floor. She slowly undresses, then immerses herself in the foamy bathtub and begins to wash. She scrubs herself vigorously and repeatedly before climbing out to dry herself. Still, there is no relief and relaxation in her body. Nothing. Instead, she feels filthy and repulsive. The image of what happened to her is engraved in her mind. She is angry.

She sprays herself with perfumes, brushes her teeth and, holding back tears with her eyelids, walks timidly back to the lounge. Dubazana also goes to the bathroom and baths; he is wearing some of Thabekhulu's clothes when he returns to the couch. Makhosazana also leaves for the bathroom and returns angry, clad in clothes belonging to Thabisile, the Thabekhulus' daughter. The last to go is Nkosana, who emerges floundering in oversized clothes belonging to the son, Thabethule.

MaDlamini, who has been busy in the kitchen, soon brings a tray laden with cool drinks and biscuits and puts it on the coffee table in front of them. Thabekhulu cannot believe his eyes when he sees the alacrity with which the Dubazanas pour and gulp down the drinks; their thirsty and parched throats have not swallowed water, or any liquid for that matter, in a long time. But they chew the biscuits as if they are gritty. Food has lost its taste in their mouths.

"Dubazana, I really feel sorry for you both," says Thabekhulu, disrupting the silence that permeates the room. "The scourge of homelessness has a stranglehold on so many in this country."

"That's true, indeed, Thabekhulu," Dubazana nods, casting his eyes down like a timid child. "One has suffered so much in this world, squatting in one place after another and getting punch-drunk from the blows of hardship. When you rent rooms, you move from witch to sorcerer until you lose count."

"I agree, Dubazana. In most cases, people rent out rooms out of financial desperation. So they get jealous when a tenant acquires desirable things. That's when conflicts and confrontations begin. I know that very well, Dubazana. You may not believe it, but we also started there. In some houses, by the time you move out, half your possessions have been stolen. And if you happen to have a beautiful wife, poor you," he claps his hands once and looks away, "you're in deep trouble. And also, if you're a handsome man, you become a hunted person."

"And the sad part, Thabekhulu, is that they hunt you down, but they don't even love you. Their intention is to plunder whatever possessions you have and to discard you when your usefulness expires."

"What else can they do, Dubazana, except fleece you? People are desperate in townships."

MaDlamini bows next to her husband and invites them all to the dining room where a laid table and the aroma of delicious food are waiting. Thabekhulu and his wife pull out their chairs and sit next to each other at the side of the table, while the Dubazanas hesitate, unsure about the appropriate sitting arrangements. Then they sit down, the daughter next to the mother and the son next to the father. Thabekhulu says grace and they start eating.

As the Dubazanas ponder the feast in front of them, not sure where to start, the Thabekhulus chat softly to each other like lovers. They dish up for each other from bowls of food spread across the table and eat. They split pieces of meat between them and at times take turns feeding each other, now and then stealing glances at the Dubazanas. MaZondi dishes up for her children and husband but it is only Nkosana who seems to have an appetite and does not hold back. The others eat sullenly, chew the food reluctantly and swallow as if they have sore throats. They soon put the food aside and only feast with their eyes.

After the meal Dubazana says, "Thank you very much, Thabekhulu, what you have done for us, my brother, while we didn't even know each other, leaves me speechless. Only the Almighty can thank you on my behalf."

"What can one say, my brother? As the saying goes, helping a person is like saving for a future need. You help a person today and they reciprocate the favour tomorrow."

They go back to the lounge where the Dubazanas remain while Thabekhulu and his wife help each other to clear, wash and dry the dishes, holding hands and kissing in between. They eventually finish the dishes and rejoin the Dubazanas.

"I really feel sad about the burdens that you have to contend with," says Thabekhulu. "We don't rent out rooms in this house, but the way you have explained your plight makes us sympathise with you. Of course, we have children too, but at the moment they are away at school in Ladysmith."

"I hear you, Thabekhulu."

"I've discussed the matter with my twin here, and we'll accommodate you temporarily while you find your own place."

"Thabekhulu! Siwela! I really don't know how to thank you," Dubazana exclaims jubilantly, reciting Thabekhulu's clan praises. The Dubazanas are shown their bedroom. Since the whole house has been renovated recently, the airy bedroom has not been furnished yet, but it is spotless, freshly painted and decorated with attractive curtains.

"Don't worry about a bed: we'll lend you the children's one."

"But, Thabekhulu, why do *you* worry about the bed? We can comfortably sleep on the floor. There is even a carpet on the floor, so no need to worry."

Thabekhulu shakes his head, "No one deserves a low-class life. Circumstances have forced you to suffer, but you deserve more than that."

MaZondi, who keeps thanking the couple, takes Makhosazana's hand and follows MaDlamini out. The males busy themselves with moving the bed and a wardrobe into the bedroom that the Dubazanas will now be using.

Despite their surroundings, there is the noise of traffic during the night, and it escalates at dawn. A passing train wails like an infant as it snakes its way through Zwelethu, Mnyandu and Lindokuhle stations. The buses roar and taxis rouse the workers from sleep with their noisy honking, summoning them to various places of work. At half past three, the wall clock rings like a church bell, singing a wake-up call for the Thabekhulus. They wake, and soon the sounds of pots and dishes fill the kitchen. The couple are helping each other to get ready and start the day. Thabekhulu drinks his tea while his car purrs softly in the garage, warming up the engine. As soon as he is done, he gets into the car and drives off, leaving his wife yawning and heading back to bed.

The sounds of Thabekhulu waking up and preparing for work rouse the Dubazanas from their sleep. The couple immediately open their eyes wide in panic and confusion. They are totally disoriented. The Thabekhulus' footsteps moving around the house instantly remind them of those of the criminals who tormented them in the slums. The light that they left on when they fell asleep also adds to the confusion. Dubazana last slept in a house with electricity years ago when he worked as a house-hand in the whites-only suburbs. MaZondi has never slept in one.

The sleeping arrangement has caused conflict. Dubazana has spent the night sleeping on the carpet. Nkosana has also slept on the floor, behind the bed. MaZondi shared the bed with Makhosazana. Then suddenly and unexpectedly, MaZondi started crying. Dubazana heard the muffled sobbing and turned his back as if MaZondi was sleeping right next to him on the floor. He felt too weak to attend to his wife's grief, not realising how much she needed his comforting words and her cheeks needed his hands to wipe the burning water away. He and his wife were not on speaking terms when they went to sleep, and as the new day begins, Dubazana cannot face the situation. What causes him the greatest heartache is that he feels degraded as a man. His mind fixates on how his wife was violated instead of approaching the problem from a black man's perspective: the awareness that a wife is a home and fort personified, not only to her husband, but also to the ancestors of the family and the nation at large.

"Dubazana, what are we going to do now?"

"About what, MaZondi?"

His wife looks at him. "You know how much I love you. I'm asking you not to distance yourself from me while I'm going through this emotional and physical pain. Instead, hold me closely. When you drift away as you're doing right now, my soul feels cold, naked. Please clothe it." Crumbling, she pours tears on him and says, "I wonder if I am still worthy to live. My soul is battered and my body sore."

Still disoriented and sad, Dubazana sits up in despair against the wall. He tries to speak but his voice stalls, throttles ...

"I would like to hear from you, father of my children, as the head of the family, how you envisage rescuing your wife and children from this horrific mess?"

At last they begin to discuss the matter thoroughly. First, they do not have the money to report the matter to the police and seek medical help. Even if they had the money, how could they summon the energy to brave the unsympathetic interrogations by the police, the trauma of being referred to hospital for treatment and, possibly, the insults and sniggers from nurses? There is also a possibility that the case will end up in a court of law where there may be journalists splashing her name all over the newspapers. Disclosing the names of the perpetrators to the police would be an open death invitation and Thabekhulu's house would be set alight. They decide to accept their fate, painful as it is, and not to report the matter to the police.

MaDlamini rises early and starts cleaning the house, kneeling to polish the floors. She finishes, baths in a hurry, takes a metal box, puts it on her head and embarks on her daily trip to the meat market.

Soon it is time for the children to go to school. They have been absent from school for a long time and have lost count of the number of days. Dubazana does not know how to handle the situation. Eventually, he asks, "Sweetheart, don't you think they should go to school and show face to avoid expulsion?"

"I don't think showing face will help, since schooling is not only about faces and physical presence, but demands mental participation as well. After the recent events I feel they're not mentally and emotionally ready for school yet." And so the Dubazanas remain in the house, silent and avoiding each other's eyes. At about eleven MaDlamini returns with her load. She calls out to MaZondi as soon as she enters.

"MaZondi! Lend me a hand, my sister!" Numb to her surroundings, MaZondi opens her eyes wide in panic. When the voice gets closer she recognises it, then shuffles to the kitchen and helps to offload the box of meat. The box is indeed heavy and as soon as it is on the floor, MaDlamini staggers to the sitting room, throws herself on the sofa and moans, "Oh my Lord! This is torture!"

MaZondi can be heard asking in a faint voice, "Such a big load, MaDlamini! What's inside?"

"It's offal and intestines, my sister. We will sell the lot." She pants heavily and wipes the perspiration with her head cloth.

"And you returned so early? Were you able to get meat that easily? I have heard that it's often normal to come back empty-handed."

"That's so true, MaZondi. I have an advantage in that my husband works at the factory. He's the senior foreman."

"I envy you, my sister. At least you're making some financial contribution to your family instead of idling around."

"My belief, MaZondi, is that a sign of maturity is to realise that a family is not built separately by a husband or a wife. Instead, it's a collective effort that results in a strong, self-sufficient family." MaDlamini goes back to the kitchen and opens the box, upon which uninvited flies settle. She wipes the table, spreads the meat on it and asks MaZondi to help her. She cuts the meat into pieces according to size and price. She thanks MaZondi and warms up some leftover food she has left in the fridge. She eats in haste and goes out, carrying the box. It looks heavy, as though laden with lead. She heads for the men's hostel near Mnyandu station where she plies her trade.

"MaZondi, I think I should walk to work and stop moaning about the lack of bus fare. You can see that in this house everybody has to put in an effort. How long are we going to live as beggars? I'm sure that at work I can find someone to lend me money, albeit with interest."

Dubazana takes a bath and goes to work, still clad in Thabekhulu's clothes. He wobbles along as if his feet are sore. It feels as if the people who stripped his family of their dignity can see him as he walks and are mocking him and laughing at his stupidity. Fortunately, he meets some of his colleagues on the way who are willing to lend him his bus fare.

MaZondi returns to bed with her children and, for a while, sleep rescues them from their hunger pangs. At one in the afternoon there is a knock on the door which MaZondi does not hear at first. She only stirs from her sleep when the knock becomes louder. She runs to the door. There stands Thabekhulu dressed in blue pants and an expensive brown jacket that looks supple and comfortable. He looks at her with soft eyes, smiling warmly: "Poor you, it looks like I have disturbed your sleep, my sister." He closes the door behind him.

"I'm very sorry about delaying opening it for you. I didn't know that you knock off early from work."

"I knock off at noon because I start early in the morning." He takes off his jacket and throws it on the couch, takes out an expensive handkerchief and wipes his face, regaining his usual attractive glow.

"It must have been a lonely day for you," he says as he takes a seat. "Why didn't you turn on the radio?"

"I was afraid to do so, Thabekhulu."

Thabekhulu smiles, "There's no need to be afraid, just feel free and be at home here. Treat me as your sibling. Do the same for my wife because, since you are staying with us now, we regard you as our siblings and family."

"Thank you, my brother. I appreciate it," MaZondi responds weakly. Thabekhulu looks at her and finds her face to be cold and surly. Her eyes are blinking like lightning. They look pregnant with torrents of tears. He cuts his talk short and lets MaZondi retire to her bedroom to battle with the emptiness she feels inside. He makes himself a cup of tea and sits in forlorn silence, sipping it slowly. When he is done, he takes the newspaper he has bought on his way home and reads till he feels drowsy. He moves to the bedroom to rest and keeps glancing at his watch, calculating the hours that remain before his wife will finish her business. At four, he rises to his feet and washes his face before knocking at MaZondi's bedroom to tell her that he is going to fetch his wife. He gets into his car and drives away.

They return at five and MaDlamini goes straight to the bathroom, runs a hot bath with soothing bubbles and slides in. Her husband, who is next to her already, takes a cloth and soap, and, as usual, washes her back and patiently starts rubbing her with scented oil all over her body.

After a long while, they come out of the bedroom and go to the kitchen. While one switches on the kettle, the other takes out the cups and places them on the table. They chat and laugh happily as they do this. When the tea is ready, Thabekhulu takes out the KFC goodies that he has bought as a surprise for his wife. They eat from one plate and sip their tea, and then they help each other clear the table and wash the dishes. They then walk hand in hand to the sitting room. MaDlamini gives him the novel she has been reading during the day and her husband gives her the newspaper he has been reading in the afternoon.

After a while, they leave the sitting room and Thabekhulu goes out to water the lawn while MaDlamini busies herself in the house preparing supper for the Dubazanas. When she is done they change into their casual clothes and drive to town where they park the car and stroll hand in hand on the beach. Refreshed, they return home at night to cuddle up in bed and share ideas and highlights from their readings until they fall asleep in each other's arms.

Meanwhile, it is as though the bedroom where the Dubazanas sleep teems with bedbugs that make MaZondi and her children turn and toss uncomfortably. They battle to sleep, since haunting thoughts do not leave them alone. Even the clothes they are wearing seem burdensome. They have slept in them and worn them during the day and are now sleeping in them again. They are too embarrassed to approach the Thabekhulus for new clothes.

Dubazana arrives at eleven and knocks on the bedroom window. His wife staggers to open the door for him. She is startled to see a strange Dubazana at the door. He is wearing a dirty overall and heavyweight work shoes, all tattered. He has his changing clothes under his arm. To him, coming out of the darkness of the night into this bedroom is like plunging into a pool of misery. In this bedroom, the possibility of a cure for the problems that now beset their marriage is rapidly disappearing. Instead of drawing them closer to mutually vent their pain and comfort each other, the bedroom that now serves as a home for the family offers no opportunity for intimacy and bonding.

Three months pass and the situation continues to deteriorate. They have eventually summoned enough courage to seek help from the police and medical practitioners where, as they expected, they were flooded with questions and had to undergo various blood tests. MaZondi tests negative for HIV. Unfortunately, test results indicate that Makhosazana, who is now pregnant, is HIV-positive. There are suggestions that abortion is the best solution under the circumstances. Makhosazana blatantly refuses: "Please, I may not give my soul the right to kill when I am myself a walking dead," she says.

"Pity my child whose life has been ruined, the opportunity to enjoy her youth and virginity taken from her." While MaZondi has agonised in solidarity with her daughter, Dubazana begs them to stay calm: the Thabekhulus are not supposed to know about the matter, lest they evict the Dubazanas from their home.

11

Despite their seemingly improved circumstances, the Dubazana family are like walking corpses, their souls crushed. MaZondi is consumed with self-pity and has lost whatever is left of her confidence. She feels neglected and unloved. The HIV issue has terrified her, and she is still not sure if she has escaped infection. She empathises deeply with her daughter, feeling not only infected like her but also that she is carrying a foetus whose father is unknown. There are times when she looks at her daughter – who no longer goes to school and whose body is becoming shapeless – and wishes that she was dead. The quiet one, Nkosana, also cannot cope with the fact that painful things have been done to him; he has become a loner at school and is always withdrawn. When at home, Dubazana looks at the three of them silently and feels at a loss to find answers to all the questions that keep him awake at night. It is his silence that exacerbates MaZondi's anxiety and the feeling that she is neglected and unloved.

As time passes, Thabekhulu senses that MaZondi is suffering and feels great pity for her. When he arrives at noon from work, MaZondi opens the door for him and stares at him with sickly, gloomy eyes. Her body is withering away rapidly, just like that of her daughter. Thabekhulu has wondered why the daughter has stopped going to school but cannot summon the courage to ask MaZondi about it.

A while later he finds himself discussing the matter with his wife in their bedroom. "MaDlamini, have you also noticed that the Dubazanas are persistently morose and grief-stricken?"

"Of course. In fact, they have never cheered up since they arrived here. But it's easy to understand. They have been through so much!" MaDlamini whispers in agreement.

"I feel that we should help them cope with their predicament."

"But how do we go about helping them?"

"By simply talking to them. You know what, when you're troubled by problems, having someone to talk to is a welcome distraction. So I suggest we take them out of their bedroom and sit with them in the lounge. While I am trying to heal Dubazana's mind, you will deal with his wife."

"I wish you knew how much I have tried to warm up to her, but she just slips back into her cocoon."

"That's typical of a person who has too many devils to fight."

But the efforts by the Thabekhulus to bond with the Dubazanas prove futile. It seems as if the latter have programmed themselves to lock themselves in their bedroom and have no intention of venturing out to socialise. Beyond exchanging polite pleasantries, engaging them in a conversation seems to cause them pain; and when they do sit with the Thabekhulus, they never open up or even allude to the raw nightmares they are battling.

But it so happens that one day Thabekhulu arrives from work as usual and the door is opened by MaZondi, who stands again as if engulfed by depression and wounding. Thabekhulu enters, closes the door behind him and gives her a lingering look.

"MaZondi, please sit down and confide in me. What is this pain that won't go away and is breaking your heart?"

"I will tell you some other day, my brother," she responds and her eyes become wet.

"Suffering alone won't solve the problem. You're inviting a heart attack if you isolate yourself, but you may find a remedy in something as simple as talking to another person. I beg you to please sit down, my sister." He patiently pleads until she relents. Soon they sit on the couches, facing each other, as Thabekhulu patiently engages her in conversation, prodding her heart gently to elicit whatever secret she is wrestling with.

MaZondi, groomed into safeguarding her family's dirty linen, skirts evasively around the matter.

"I can't tell you my problems because we'll be in trouble, or even face eviction, should the news reach MaDlamini's ears. So, I would rather we suffer in silence."

"I won't tell her if you don't want her to know about it," Thabekhulu promises in a sad voice, his eyes glued to MaZondi's pathetic figure. His assurance seems to win MaZondi's trust and she begins, bit by bit, to bare her soul. Tears stream down her face, "I plead with you to keep this between the two of us because if you tell your wife that my daughter has this disease there won't be a place for us here."

"I stand by my promise to keep this a secret," he says, giving her a handkerchief to wipe her tears.

"Let me not get you into trouble, my brother. I am scared that you may be infected if I use your handkerchief."

"Hhayi, no, the disease can't be transmitted through tears. Besides, to me you look healthy and pure."

"I wish my husband felt the same way. He can't even touch me; not even with his pinkie."

That shocks Thabekhulu and he asks in surprise, "Did you also test positive?"

"Lutho, not at all; but he couldn't accept the results. His attitude has really wrecked my self-esteem and I've lost all self-confidence. Who can help enlighten Dubazana and advise him on how to handle this?"

"MaZondi, I wish I could take you to my pastor. Unfortunately, he got arrested and is still in custody. However, I'll approach Dubazana and try to discuss the matter with him."

"And who will you say you heard this from?" she asks in panic.

"My wife and I will ask you to join us in the lounge, then I will broach the topic on how couples should treat each other. The issue of HIV will automatically slip into our conversation. MaDlamini and Dubazana will participate without knowing that the two of us have discussed this."

"Eviction is what scares me most."

"But perhaps you will find healing in sharing these ideas with Thabethule's mother."

"It's also possible that she will feel that we'll contaminate her with all the bugs and lice – in the form of problems – that we have brought with us from the shacks. As we've agreed, if you don't mind keeping us here despite our HIV infection, let the secret remain between the two of us."

After this conversation, MaZondi regrets disclosing her family secret. Thabekhulu, on the other hand, sits in his bedroom worrying about the Dubazanas. He is aware of the turbulent times that rock marriages, making it difficult for couples to treat each other with respect, love and tolerance. This has also happened to him and his wife in the past, and for him the most painful period in a marriage is when spouses ignore each other when they need each other most.

He cannot fall asleep and wonders how they can intervene in the couple's challenges. He recalls that he and his wife devoted themselves to the church only after a fellow worshipper had visited them a few months earlier while he and his wife were not on speaking terms. The brother sat them down and explained patiently that their family was in darkness because they had distanced themselves from the Light of all marriages, who created humankind through marriage. So, if the Dubazanas are reluctant to attend church, Thabekhulu takes it as his own responsibility to revive in them the positive spirit that should permeate a marriage.

From that moment onwards, he regularly makes time to sit and talk in the lounge with Dubazana whenever they knock off early from work. In the evenings, MaDlamini often invites MaZondi to the lounge and the four of them sit and discuss marriage-related topics.

"Good people, marriages don't only get into trouble after tying the knot. Things often start going wrong while people are dating," elaborates Thabekhulu innocently one evening when they are all sitting in the lounge, watching television.

His wife is curious. "How do things go wrong while couples are dating?"

"What I mean is that the first wrong step is taken when a person opens their mouth and tells somebody that they love them without any idea of what love means. Dubazana, there are people who are joined in marriage and think they love each other while in fact they don't."

"Yes, but I don't think there is a person who can approach another, declare his love, propose, pay lobola and in addition to that, contend with all the expenses that culminate in a wedding, if he is not really in love."

"Unfortunately, the majority are such individuals, Dubazana. If I were to ask you: what do you *mean* when you approach a woman and tell her you love her, and what does she mean when she accepts your proposal, what would you say?"

Dubazana remains silent, pondering the question. He has, on numerous occasions, felt in love and has declared his love to many a woman, but he has never given any serious thought to exactly what he meant when he said that he loved somebody, other than being attracted by their beauty.

"Please answer me, Dubazana. It is also good that both of us are married. What did we mean when we said we loved them? They are also going to tell us what they meant when they accepted our love."

"What I meant was that I loved her because she could help me build a family for the Dubazanas, collectively."

"I like that answer, Dubazana, because a wife belongs to the whole family. But my question is, even before we talk marriage, what do you *mean* when you approach a woman and declare your love for her?"

"Well, perhaps our intentions are not the same. But I've stated my side, what do you think, my brother?"

"As for me, Dubazana, I believe you approach a woman and ask her to accept you." He looks at their wives and asks them, "What did you mean when you accepted our love?"

MaZondi and MaDlamini look at each other. MaZondi smiles softly for the first time since their arrival at the Thabekhulus.

"Tell us, MaZondi, when you blushed – butterflies and all – and accepted Dubazana's proposal, what is it that you meant to tell him?"

MaZondi blushes once again. "I meant to tell him that out of the many suitors who, like him, waxed lyrical about how much they loved me, he was the only one in my life that I was asking to love me. And since that day I haven't asked for any other thing from Dubazana except that he shows through his actions that he loves me." She looks at him lingeringly with her soft brown eyes.

"Wow, MaZondi, there's complete truth in that: actions must show love. And you, MaDlamini, what did you mean when you said that you accepted my love?"

"I share the same sentiments as MaZondi, father of Thabethule. It is said that where there's love, there's also a way. There is only one thing I ask of you, my husband: love. If there's love, my life's resolve will be to weed out anything that interferes with our love, and to water our love generously so that it bears fruit abundantly."

These words find a spot in Thabekhulu's heart and delight him. Smiling from ear to ear, he looks at Dubazana and asks, "Dubazana, can you hear what our wives ask from us?"

With a defeated voice, Dubazana consents. Thabekhulu continues: "They say 'I am accepting you and expect you, as you say you love me, to love me in return and to show it.' But Dubazana, it's unfortunate that in our times, right from the beginning of a relationship, often the person who is supposed to show love becomes evasive. The next thing you hear is that they are courting someone else without having made any effort to show love to their previous lover. In other words, they ask for love while they have no idea what love is.

"The act of accepting and loving goes a very long way, Dubazana. Even the Bible attests to this when it says, 'Husbands, love your wives; wives, honour your husbands.' I interpret honouring as an act of acceptance, because you accept a person unconditionally when you love and respect them. Most marriages collapse through failure to honour these two requests. You find that one party reaches out with open arms, expecting to be loved in return, only to be shunned and given a cold shoulder."

"Exactly. It is mutual acceptance and love that result in a couple deciding to take their relationship further and get married," agrees MaDlamini. "But it makes me wonder about what it actually means to be married to each other. My friends, this is a question that my husband and I once asked each other when we were also lost in the fog of being in a marriage but had no clue about what marriage meant. I'm convinced that there are many couples who reach the stage of divorce without having sat down and asked themselves what it is that they are divorcing each other from.

"In our quest to find answers about marriage, we realised that marriage is not necessarily about our physical bodies – which we always trust someone else will find attractive if we divorce. We found that there's a special spirit that permeates families and homes and which every marriage should breathe in order to survive healthily. It is this spirit that we feel is vital and surpasses everything else: across nations, cultures, throughout the world. Without this spirit – this air – we can't live, my friends. We know that even the Creator blew the air or spirit of life into man's nostrils after creating him. We love a person because of the spirit of love and peace they possess."

"If we ponder the different roles that the life-spirit plays," Thabekhulu intervenes to assist his wife, "we find them quite amazing. Sometimes you take a book and read it and the mood that breezes through it inspires you and makes you fall in love with its author, whom you don't even know in person. The same goes for singers that you love through the mood that emanates from their music, and you become their ardent fan though you haven't even seen them on television, let alone met them in person. Likewise, marriage is governed by its own special spirit. It is that spirit that makes couples marry; neither for beauty nor for wealth. It is that spirit that makes a young man sing happily as he takes all his cattle to pay lobola for the woman he loves. This spirit should be integral to a marriage. How many times have you heard of a husband arriving home and becoming restless when he finds that his wife is not home yet and that the house feels cold, devoid of the warmth that emanates from the spirit of marriage? Divorces were unheard of in ancient Zulu marriages simply because it was appreciated that the spirit of marriage can't be divorced from the shadows – the souls, the personalities – of the married couples. Even when a person is divorced or widowed, the spirit that they are somebody's former spouse doesn't dissipate. May we then, from this evening onwards, sleep with this holy spirit holding us together."

MaZondi feels the furnace that has been blazing in her soul beginning to abate. Her voice is calm: "I really thank you for inviting us to this conversation. By simply talking, one feels the burden of pain that one carries around lighten slightly. I feel that our sitting here as married couples, sharing our opinions, may help mend the cracks in a marriage on the brink of collapse. What touched me the most was the point about the spirit that should dwell in married life. It reminded me of what my husband once said when we were knee-deep in problems and he had to restrain me from committing suicide. He defeated me, however, when he said to me, 'We may not have a tangible house, but we have a firm home with you around us.'"

"Wow, that is how a real man speaks. A man becomes complete through his wife," Thabekhulu echoes the sentiment.

When they all retire to sleep, the Dubazanas, to their surprise, are shown another of the bedrooms and told to use it until the Thabekhulu children return for the school holidays. They enter a spotless, airy room with a huge bed adorned with brand new bedding linen that still smells of the fresh perfumes of the shop from which it was bought. They take a bath and MaZondi climbs into bed, while Dubazana sits on it, miserable, his cheeks buried in his hands. His wife, who has not been taciturn in the conversation with the Thabekhulus and has felt the embers of love and happiness rekindling, tries in vain to resuscitate the jovial mood, saying, "The Thabekhulus are really good intermediaries in a discussion. Moreover, they have really valuable suggestions that they've gathered from their own experiences when their marriage went through storms."

Dubazana simply ignores her. It is a long time before he speaks: "Of course, it's not unusual to be big-mouthed about a tragedy that you've never experienced first-hand, and when you have no idea of the agony that someone who has been through that incident is enduring."

Immediately MaZondi slips back into brooding, her hopes crumbling. The bedroom and its beauty suddenly become lifeless and suffocating. The couple remain in silence, as if they are mourning the death of their spouses. MaZondi cannot fall asleep and sunrise finds her deflated, longing to be cuddled and loved.

As the days pass – the tension between the couple still stifling the air – the situation regresses to its former pattern: when Thabekhulu arrives from work, MaZondi opens the door and greets him with a gloomy face. Thabekhulu is painstakingly amicable and gentle when he chats and jokes with her, and so MaZondi warms up, gradually finding a friend and a confidant in him. His sense of humour always puts a bright smile on her face and she finds herself looking forward to his knock when he arrives from work, and she dreads Dubazana's arrival with his signature tilted head and a hand permanently supporting his cheek. Through his humour, Thabekhulu assures her that he will help her win the battle to regain her husband's love and favour.

The evening conversations continue while the couples sit together, watch television and have animated discussions.

"You sometimes hear people, who don't even know what married life is, eloquently dissecting marriage issues. Marriage is, in fact, not child's play. Let me remind you, my friends, that we have also made foolish mistakes in our marriage. There was a testing time that once entangled us, when we felt the spirit of love in our marriage turn into an unbearable incinerator."

"Thabekhulu, when I look at you two it wouldn't occur to me that you've also been through such turmoil," intimates a frowning Dubazana. "Tell us: what happened?"

From a bowl laden with fruit in front of them, Thabekhulu picks an apple, slices it in half and gives his wife the other half. Dubazana, who already has a partially eaten apple in his hand while his wife munches away at an orange she has peeled unassisted, watches Thabekhulu's action with envy.

"What caused a rift between us, Dubazana, is that we'd become strangers and hardly recognised each other. There we were, married, but we'd never sat down and soul-searchingly analysed what marriage meant to us and what belonging to each other entailed."

MaZondi, who is patiently chewing her orange and gently wiping its juice trickling from her mouth, listens eagerly. "Did you find answers?"

"Let my wife comment on that," says Thabekhulu, beaming at his wife.

"The answers we found, my sister, were amazing. We looked at each other and found that each was like a planet that has to be traversed – explored continually – for the rest of one's days on earth. We realised that since true humanity and joy are only achieved through treading carefully and respectfully on earth, we also had to conquer our battles by mutual love and respect. You show love and appreciation to the planet on which you live by building, ploughing and watering it and then harvesting what you've planted. We also found that you don't only love each other during happy times but also support each other in times of sorrow."

"Just as my wife has pointed out," Thabekhulu smiles tenderly at her, "as soon as it dawned on us that handling your spouse with cold hands is like pouring ice on yourself, we were healed and revived. Since then, my friends, we've been aware that we need each other. We learnt and understood what it means to be of one flesh, each forming a piece of the other. Perhaps since your arrival you've noticed that we share whatever we do. Even when I buy a newspaper, we share the reading of it, and when she has read a certain book she shares with me passages from what she's read. This sharing has made us always aware of one another."

"In our case, we no longer say 'what is mine is mine, what is yours is yours.' Whatever we have belongs to us and is for the family," interjects MaDlamini.

The conversation continues for quite a while until they go to their separate bedrooms and separate actions. While the Thabekhulus are smiling pleasantly in their bedroom, MaZondi is weeping sorrowfully in the other one.

Another remedy that the Thabekhulus think could help the Dubazanas' marriage is to take them out one Saturday for a trip around the city. They discuss it, and Dubazana welcomes the idea, but on condition that he has a chance to buy some clothes to wear on the excursion. Thus one Saturday, the four of them get into the car, smartly dressed, city bound. Music plays softly in the car as it weaves its way through the township. The songs are romantic, making the couple in the front caress each other's hands fondly. MaZondi feels the music soothing her soul; she draws closer to her husband and clasps his hand, which goes limp and frigid.

"Township life is a mystery, shrouded in fog and smoke. In Johannesburg's townships, you can understand it: people use braziers and coal stoves, hence the smoky air. Here in Durban, you see smoke all over the place and wonder where it comes from and what it is that burns so endlessly every day," quips Thabekhulu on seeing a thick black cloud of smoke that envelopes the hill towards which they are driving. It looks as though a house is burning somewhere nearby.

"I'm not surprised at all. There's mayhem in the country," comments Dubazana.

The car drives along, past all the potholes on the sloping road from Mlazi, until it reaches the smooth, flat road that leads to the city. When they reach the city centre, they park in one of the tall parkade buildings. The Thabekhulus walk around hand in hand as the couples embark on a window-shopping spree. The Dubazanas begin to feel old sparks rekindling and take one others' hands, albeit timidly. Of course, they are not familiar with such a public display of affection nor with taking leisurely walks on safe city streets.

"My friends, we're fortunate to be couples who are able to stroll the streets romantically at this time on a weekend. Some couples are already blind from drunkenness. Besides that, you'd be surprised by the responses you'd get if you were to ask some husbands about the last time they kissed their wives. Some last kissed their wives on their wedding day when the cameraman coerced them to pose for wedding photos."

They laugh at Thabekhulu's remarks, but the joke does not sit well with Dubazana, and it pierces his heart. He suspects that the three are colluding against him and that the joke is on him. So it is with relief that he hears them change the subject as they stroll further towards the city hall. The entrance area is bright with the beauty and splendour of the shrubs, flowers and meticulously trimmed lawn. They enter the hall and sit down on some chairs. A live performance by the Blue Cranes, a local group of veteran singers who have toured overseas, is on. The sweet melody of the voices and musical instruments captivates them, caressing their hearts with love and peace. To hear his wife whisper softly and call him "Sithandwa, sweetheart" while they exchange comments about the band has a strangely healing effect on Dubazana. For a while, his mind erases the miseries of the township and focuses on the activities in the hall. They are still enjoying themselves when the performance comes to an end. They take a leisurely walk back to the car and drive back to Mlazi, where there is gloom and shacks, and where no one can be brave enough to take a stroll with his lover on the streets, wearing gold necklaces or laughing with gold teeth.

"We really appreciate that you took us out for a trip and showed us a different world, populated by different people. I've been preoccupied with our misery for so long and had forgotten that just a short distance away in the city, another world exists. The disparities are glaring: light and darkness, progress and regression."

"We're also grateful, Dubazana, if you enjoyed the excursion. As you've just mentioned, there are people who are in darkness; but there are also people who we must ensure we always honour with our hearts and actions."

"But do you think honouring people is still feasible in our chaotic, distressing times?"

"In the midst of that chaos, we still have our heroes. You really have a true partner in a person who is willing to die where you have fallen. We are fortunate to have women who have loved us throughout the painful times of oppression and discrimination. It would be inhumane not to honour them for not deserting us during times of starvation; squatting with us in the makeshift houses called shacks. How can we not honour them when they've loved us as full-blooded men even when life's circumstances belittled us? We honour and praise them for not being enticed or distracted by the glamour and glitter around them. They bore us children and raised them amidst the grime and gloom. Dubazana, you can attest that they have been molested, plundered, but they still retained the faithfulness and essence of African wifehood. What is amazing about our oppression-era wives is that despite being immersed in misery, it is very rare that they kill their husbands. And even now, to MaDlamini, MaZondi and all of you wives who loved us during oppressive times, I take my hat off and salute you!" he enthuses as he stops the car in front of his house.

12

Makhosazana's frequent visits to the hospital and its department of social welfare have resulted in the social worker from the hospital regularly visiting the Dubazana family. Apart from her love for her work, the young woman shares the same clan name as the Dubazanas and feels obliged to help out. Duduzile Mwelase is a notably beautiful, tall young woman. Her gait exudes confidence and accentuates her waist that is tight as a wasp's. The Dubazanas treasure her and feel that her presence in their lives goes beyond her responsibility for their comfort and wellbeing.

The last month of the year sees Duduzile, true to her name – Comforter – succeed in consoling Makhosazana, who slowly begins to regain her dignity. Of course, Makhosazana has no reason to despise and blame herself, since *she* has not wronged anybody. She begins to realise that isolating herself and hiding away is to die without helping anyone else in life. She vows to go back to school the following year so that she can communicate with other young people in different schools. She wants her message ultimately to reach those who see nothing wrong in fighting their battles by using children as weapons. Can they explain to her how this can resolve the current crisis? She wants to use her condition to pave a way forward for the destitute and those who are ill-treated for being homeless. Their plight needs to reach the ears of those in power. And by the time schools close for the year she prays daily that a cure for the killer virus will be found while she is still alive.

As Christmas draws closer, everybody seems to be in a travelling mood: some head for the countryside and others visit the cities. The Thabekhulu children arrive and the Dubazanas have to share one room again.

Even though these are days of sadness, most people enjoy the festivities of Christmas. But people like the Dubazanas do not even know what the day means. They listen absently, even when sounds marking the beginning of the new year fill the air. They do not expect any difference between the dying year and the new one.

When the festivities are over, people go back to work and school. The Thabekhulus send their children back to Ladysmith where they are at school. The following weekend, when the Dubazanas are alone, they are visited by Duduzile. When she sees her, MaZondi confides that the actions of love between Thabekhulu and his wife have brought back images to her of the old days which have now disappeared from her husband's mind.

"According to our religion as black people, my brother," Duduzile later tells Dubazana, "a woman is like a homestead's main house where the ancestors are spoken to and their wishes fulfilled so that the homestead survives and doesn't collapse. The ancestors are not spoken to by someone who has a ragged heart. And in Christianity, marriage is regarded as holy and the body of the couple is the Holy Communion to them. One does not partake of the Holy Communion if one's heart still harbours suspicions." Duduzile heaps wisdom on Dubazana, but it elicits no response from him, as he half-listens to what he regards as a time-wasting sermon.

While the efforts of Duduzile and the Thabekhulus help to lift Makhosazana and her mother from the problems they have been through, Dubazana's mind cannot wipe out past events. His suspicions frustrate and depress him. In the many homes that he has been in and out of with his wife, there were always false accusations that MaZondi was seducing landlords for financial gain. It was like that even at the Mlangenis: they were adamant that she was trying to seduce Qumbisa. Even among the shack-dwellers, Dubazana had heard, before they hit him with a knobkierie, that his wife was a girlfriend of one of the attackers and had taken his money that day. The lies he has picked up as he went in and out are now confusing him, threatening to make him lose what he has for something that is not there.

"What I am saying, my dear brother and sister, is that for married people to reject each other is like killing one another. If you – who are the home – are dead, the children also cease to exist and whatever you've been trying to build is destroyed. The saddest part is that if you allow a crack in the marriage, you eventually create a chasm between you. Let this sulking at one another stop," Duduzile counsels further.

Her parents buy Makhosazana a new school uniform and she goes back to Mzuzwana where she often talks at length about her illness and how she contracted it. Her mother tends to stay alone in the house, talking to herself. Her main interest now is Thabekhulu's early return during the day and the way he helps her through her sadness by talking happily to her, which makes her happy, unlike Dubazana's return. He remains ill-humoured. And Thabekhulu's heart has developed a soft spot for MaZondi. Something about her worries him, making him feel sorry for and sympathetic to her. He has tried in vain to help her by giving advice to Dubazana. He has no idea how to wipe away the tears that MaZondi pours on him every time she opens the door on his return from work. Indeed, one could say that a storm is silently brewing in their hearts. With each day that passes, they are increasingly on one another's minds.

At noon on a Thursday, soon after Dubazana has left for an afternoon shift at work, Thabekhulu arrives home and knocks as usual. MaZondi opens the door and greets him with her usual sad and worried look. On this day she does not linger about but quickly retreats to the bedroom that she and Dubazana reoccupied after the school holidays.

With a newspaper casually tucked under his arm, Thabekhulu proceeds to his bedroom, throws the newspaper down and takes off his clothes. He hurries to the en suite bathroom, opens the cabinet where he keeps his shaver, and stands in front of the mirror while he meticulously applies shaving cream to his chin and cheeks. He then starts shaving. When he is satisfied with his clean-shaven face, he runs a bath. The warm water has a soothing effect, making him stay longer, rubbing every smudge of dirt from his body. At last he gets out, wipes himself dry and sprays some cologne. To his smoothly shaven face, he generously applies aftershave lotion; it smells so good that he cannot get enough of its aroma. He steps back into the bedroom, takes his time to dress and neatly comb his hair, then he takes his newspaper and heads for the couch to read it.

Something catches his eye as he walks past the bedroom that the Dubazanas occupy and makes him come to an abrupt stop, mouth open. The door is ajar and there is MaZondi, scratching her back by rubbing it against the edge of the wardrobe. He has to extend a helping hand ...

His hand quivers as his soft fingers delicately trace her back. She pushes it away; it pauses for a few seconds but soon resumes its journey and lingers when she gently squeezes it as their eyes close simultaneously ...

A bolt of thunder has struck MaZondi and Thabekhulu, numbing them in its wake. In their separate bedrooms they lie, each feeling the wind of regret blowing over them. The truth that a marriage belongs to God, because it is like His soul's eye, is now dawning on them. The eye of a marriage does not get drowsy, neither does it sleep or die. It pierces the conscience with its glaring rays. When a married person commits an error, it feels as though the innocent spouse is watching from somewhere. Even if they have divorced, or their spouse has died, the one who is left behind and strolls about with a new lover feels the eye of the soul staring disapprovingly. That is why, in African tradition, whoever joins the family of the deceased spouse has to be introduced to the ancestors for approval.

Thabekhulu is like someone who has gone to bed drunk. His mind is slowly regaining consciousness and beginning to see the trouble he has caused by letting his flesh and mind fail him. He keeps asking himself what has happened, because even during the days of hardship between him and his wife he never felt love for a third person. But here he is, and today he has fallen after being locked inside his house with the wife of a man who is haunted by homelessness. His conscience ravages him. Besides his thoughts about his wife, he feels that the integrity that MaZondi thought he possesses has vanished. How will he ever be able to advise her about fidelity in marriage? And he has belittled his wife in the eyes of another woman. The moment MaDlamini prides herself on her marriage, MaZondi will know this, and may cynically and silently mock her. And how is he going to look Dubazana in the eye, let alone his own wife! And even as he twists and turns around all these things, the eye of his marriage seems to glare at him, particularly from the wedding photographs on his bedroom wall, from where his wife's eyes gaze unblinkingly at him. His lips shiver as he utters a short prayer, begging for forgiveness.

In the other bedroom, MaZondi lies flat on her stomach, her face buried in her hands that rest on the pillow. Her battered soul is crumbling. The calamity that has struck her and Thabekhulu is like a thunderbolt tearing through the trust and generosity MaDlamini has bestowed on the Dubazana family. Tears flood her eyes.

It thunders and hits her. That eye of marriage stares at her too. It is as if Dubazana has seen, and is glaring at her now as she weeps. When she thinks about Thabekhulu, she feels how her dignity has vanished. She never wants to see him again. If she could have her way, she would move that very day and rent elsewhere.

The clock on the wall chimes like a church bell, confirming the passing of an hour. A few minutes past four, Thabekhulu shame-facedly passes MaZondi's room, asking her to look after the place, as he is leaving to fetch his wife. The fact that he is fetching her scares MaZondi.

That day MaDlamini does not see MaZondi at all, as she has locked herself in the room. Dubazana comes back and finds her teary. The words that she hungers for more than anything, that would comfort her, are that Dubazana still loves her.

In the days that follow, her conscience incessantly gnaws at her. She does not know how to ask forgiveness from MaDlamini, whom she cannot look in the eye. Even when the four of them sit in the sitting room talking, guilt clouds both her and Thabekhulu's eyes. Their guilt is exacerbated by MaDlamini and Dubazana clearly feeling more relaxed than the two of them when they are talking. They laugh out loud, having no guilt to worry about. Even their laughter is now like punishment to the guilty parties.

MaZondi finally gathers the courage to ask MaDlamini if she and Dubazana can accompany the couple to church. At first Dubazana is very much against this decision. What annoys him most about church sermons is that they all insist that people will be equal in heaven, in spite of the segregation practised by the very same people who brought this European religion. But MaDlamini patiently pleads with him, and he relents, albeit reluctantly. For him, church is strange because he grew up on farms where young men chanted with the guidance of a lead singer instead of a pastor; there was also no church or singing in the prisons where hard labour was the order of the day.

But this very same Dubazana who enters the church reluctantly, heavy-kneed, comes out feeling stronger and reassured. His hungry soul has been served with reviving spiritual food. He feels his conscience and his sense of love and peace revitalised. From that day, on every Sunday when he enters this building, he feels himself born again when he comes out, and his heart, which was so clotted and laden with grudges, feels cleaner and less burdened.

It soon becomes clear to him that the role of church services is to guide lost souls to the right path, and to soften stony, discriminatory hearts. His mind gradually clears, his short temper subsides and his heart becomes aware of the warmth of peace.

While the spark of light is flickering in Dubazana, his wife loses her zest for the church and eventually stops going. Their habit of being together as two couples on the sofas also comes to an end as Dubazana's wife is almost always in bed. It seems to him that she cries the whole day when he is at work and the whole night when he is home from work. While Dubazana feels well in spirit since he started going to church, MaZondi's soul withers away. So eventually Dubazana loses his enthusiasm, and the services are only attended by Thabekhulu and his wife, sometimes accompanied by Makhosazana and Nkosana.

"I've tried in vain to find out from MaZondi why she's now reluctant to go to church and to sit with us in the evenings. I don't understand, because she's the one who asked to come with us," comments MaDlamini one evening when she is with her husband in their bedroom.

"What do you think has happened, Thabethule's father?"

"I wish I could give you answers. But, as you know, all families have challenges, and you can't understand other people's problems." That is all Thabekhulu feels he can contribute.

"What does Dubazana say if you ask him?"

"You know him. He keeps to himself."

"I really am confused by all of this. MaZondi seems jumpy and restless. Her eyes have become shifty and if by some chance they meet mine she gets such a scare; sometimes she apologises while I don't even know what she's done wrong."

Thabekhulu coughs a deep, choking cough.

"Is there anyone else with a question?" asks Makhosazana, standing in front of the teachers and students who have filled the hall at Manzolwandle School, where she is visiting. Her mother is there too, sitting in the front row with the teachers, her arms folded. She is watching her child, who has taken on the battle to enlighten her peers about the social conditions that contribute to the spread of diseases, and who is also using the opportunity to raise funds for Aids orphans.

A hand is raised. It belongs to a young woman of about twenty. Makhosazana points at her. "Makhosazana, my sister, we have been touched by the sad story you've told us. There is some confusion though. I have heard that the law allows health workers to arrange abortions for rape pregnancies. What I don't understand is, did the law refuse to help you?" The girl sits down, and then stands up again. "Please don't be offended by my question," she says, and sits down.

"It doesn't offend me, my sister. And what is your name?"

"I am Bongiwe Mbongwa, my sister."

"Firstly, Bongiwe, let me tell you that the law has its terms and conditions. There are stated rules defining what constitutes rape, and that the complainant must report to the police and be referred to health professionals within a certain period after the incident. We live in difficult times, when a person who is raped at home may stay quiet for as long as a year, not reporting her case, because it is taboo to go to the police even if a person has been killed. It is very hard to explain to the police that while you report the matter today, you were raped some months ago; perhaps you have even delivered the baby already.

"But I kept my pregnancy; not necessarily because of those legal procedures. I kept it as proof to the rulers of the land, so they can see for themselves that if you run the country carelessly, people are destroyed by hunger, disease, and crime, inflicting all sorts of pain on each other." She caresses her stomach. It looks as if there are only a few weeks left before she gives birth. Her mother also touches hers and grimaces painfully. She removes her hands and closes her eyes while trying, without success, to wipe her tears dry.

"I am not only talking about the apartheid regime, but also about other systems of government of today and tomorrow that rule through dirty hands, greed and blood – all those who rule by benefiting at the expense of the people whose blood they suck, and whom they rule through the barrel of a gun. With this pregnancy I am speaking out, I am saying that the rulers of today and tomorrow should see for themselves that in a country ruled through violence, citizens become violent too, and believe problems can only be solved through fire and weapons. What is really sad is that there are many who are prepared to commit any evil to fulfil their wishes of being counted as heroes of the struggle. I can still vividly recall how those who raped me praised themselves for being leaders and heroes of the struggle.

"If the rulers rule in such a way that the people they rule over feel like nothing, the people end up behaving like this. For them, life itself becomes nothing, worthless. When life has lost its worth, it means the conscience has died within; a person becomes a walking corpse.

"Another reason for me to go around preaching with this pregnant stomach, is so that people will see for themselves some of the results of creating a landless nation, with citizens who are always on the move, if not on the run. My father's family is a family that has no land; it's a family that constantly comes and goes. Some of those who suffer like us have resorted to selling their bodies in exchange for shelter. Here are the results of being homeless, the results of living in the wilderness, in makeshift dwellings. Religious leaders may preach day and night that people should behave well, but while people don't have homes in which to talk to their ancestors, or to kneel and pray in, those sermons will be a waste of time for a nation that has retained none of the rules of the ancestors, religion or life. This is what happens to a homeless nation." She beats her stomach. "We are like this, not out of choice, but because the conditions of our lives dictate this for us." She beats her stomach repeatedly. Her mother also looks at her own and feels a little pang of fear. She grimaces again, and rubs it like someone in labour.

"How can you expect goodness and justice where a girl shares a bed with her brother, sleeping in the same room with her mother and father in rented rooms or makeshift shacks?"

She starts a hymn, and the hall spontaneously bursts into song, joining her, some faces clearly deeply moved as they sing. The teachers move into action in silent solidarity and move up and down the rows in the hall, collecting money donations.

"Don't cry for me any more. Let those who are still alive be the ones to receive salvation." She holds a bowl in her hand and is now speaking like a priest presiding over the Holy Communion service. Students and teachers kiss and hug her as they donate. With the sadness and singing intensifying, her mother collapses, weeping hysterically. They have to pick her up and hold her like someone who has lost a loved one as she howls out loud, rolling herself on the ground.

"Where are we if things are like this?" says the principal of Manzolwandle, whose maiden name is Manzini – Place-of-waters – as she takes off her glasses and wipes her eyes. "The sharks are doing as they please! We are drowning in the sea, my people! Our ship and all our splendour, the wealth of the nation, are going under. We are under siege and pirates are plundering our shores." The tears that flow uncontrollably become seawater on her face.

13

On a Tuesday after lunch Thabekhulu, who has become wasted in a few days, comes home, walks with leaden feet and knocks at the door. After a while MaZondi opens it and walks unsteadily to the couch where she sits solemnly weeping. Thabekhulu closes the door and sits with her.

"Why, what is wrong that you greet me with tears?"

"Thabekhulu, I think the time has come for me to kill myself. I don't see anything that brings me happiness and comfort, anything worth living for. As we speak, my daughter, Makhosazana, is sick and has been admitted to the hospital. She's pregnant with a grandchild that is dead even before birth. My son, Nkosana, has become a zombie – always quiet, and never plays with his peers. Sometimes I try calling him when he's close by, but he never hears me. It's clear to me that he's lost his mind. At the same time, my husband and I have suffered so much that we have lost our minds too, and forgotten the love that brought us together. Today I am sunk knee-deep in disgrace." She cries louder.

It is a very hot day, yet Thabekhulu feels cold and shivers when he hears her mentioning disgrace. In a sickly voice he asks, "What disgrace have you got into?"

"I told you, Thabekhulu, that I am not feeling well and you gave me the money to go to the doctor. I returned from him a few minutes before you arrived."

Immediately Thabekhulu is anxious. He sits straight up, straining his ears. "What did the doctor say?"

"His words have confirmed my suspicion." She wails.

"Hhawu! Oh no!" Thabekhulu moans aloud. The question he asks next is one of the most stupid things he has ever asked in his life: "Who does he say the father is?"

"He did not say, Thabekhulu. The two of us know the answer."

"Mhh!" Thabekhulu shakes his head. "We are swimming in shame! Does this then mean the destruction of our homes and the loss of trust from the community?"

Thabekhulu's whining revives the pain in MaZondi's soul. She too bemoans their situation: "Today I'm carrying a child that is cursed and shunned before it is born, who will be called a bastard and not even be loved by his father, because he is a home-wrecker. His birth will defame and taint his image in the community. In other words, I am pregnant with the Peace-destroyer and Division-maker."

"You ... you ... you," stammers Thabekhulu, his tongue choking him, making him suddenly develop a stutter that he did not have before.

"And here I am standing in front of you. You are shivering and stuttering because I am a problem you don't know what to do with. I am the temptation that made you stumble; a bane to your family happiness. Nkosi yami, oh my Lord, what is the point of living if I suffer like this?"

Thabekhulu is now sweating and shaking from anxiety. He fears this quake which is threatening to shake the marriage he and MaDlamini have painstakingly worked at for all these years, the mud of disgrace that is now going to deface it beyond recognition. How shattered his wife will be when this abominable secret comes out into the open! How scorching the humiliation! He wonders how people in general, and fellow churchgoers in particular, will look at him and what they will say once they hear about this. And how is he to look at them? What will Dubazana say? Also, how is Thabekhulu going to rescue MaZondi from losing her marriage? If her marriage can't be rescued, what is he to do with her and the baby? Disturbing thoughts flash like lightning through Thabekhulu's mind. For the first time he is heard whistling in the house, defying the tradition that forbids this. Besides, the whistling is tuneless: evoked by a troubled mind rather than an exultant heart. The man is in trouble indeed.

"I feel like a cast-off in my soul, Thabekhulu. It's as if I've infected MaDlamini's hands with scabs, the hands with which she mercifully held me, and those scabs of my miseries will now cling to her whole body. An obvious possibility is that if she hears about this shame she'll leave you, and your family will fall apart. We'll both wander the streets and the scourge of homelessness will grow worse."

Thabekhulu clears his throat as if it is clogged and he is choking, searching for apt words. "My conscience is eating me, MaZondi. She won't be the one to leave. I am the one who will wander the streets."

"Either way she is doomed, and everything will plunge her into an abyss of misery. Even if you move out, your leaving her while she loves you, as I know she does, would be death to her."

Thabekhulu breathes heavily once more. What dismays him is that he did not venture out and invite trouble, but instead it forced itself into his own house, uninvited. The room remains dead quiet as they think about their fate in silence.

"Usually, people hang around you when things are good. But when you are in trouble, they avoid you like the plague."

"Who is avoiding you now, MaZondi?"

"Thabekhulu, do you remember that I told you my husband does not care about me any more? That instead of being the one to comfort me, he ignores me? Now I am in this trouble which was caused by the loneliness that I still feel when I'm with him. And you are now avoiding me. You're distancing yourself from me when I thirst for comfort." She stands up, her voice trembling. "My situation has made me a skunk. No one wants me near them." Slowly and with difficulty she walks to her bedroom.

Thabekhulu remains behind, battered. He recalls the days when MaZondi constantly sobbed because Dubazana was ignoring her. That is where all of this mess took root. Today he feels as if he is now the one carrying the burden of not caring for her. He follows her, his legs weak. He opens the door, enters and finds her slumped on the bed. On both sides of her eyes, rivers of tears flow. Overwhelmed with sadness, he sits beside her and pleads, "Please calm down. I will figure out what to do," dabbing off her tears with his thumb.

"I know that in my condition, Thabekhulu, I am going to smell foul to everybody. In most cases, a finger is easily raised if it points at a woman's mistakes. When my husband looks at me, he'll see a sinner. My in-laws will see a shameless wife. Even at my parents' home, my mother will just dismiss me and my situation. I wish my father was still alive, because he might have at least listened to my side of the story, of how all of this started."

Feeling sorry for her, Thabekhulu pulls her close to him, raises her up and wipes her tears again. He holds her, puts his face to hers and soon both their faces are wet from each other's tears as they kiss.

"My God! I regret the homelessness that put me in all this temptation." She breathes heavily, afraid of what is happening. "I love my husband, and my life is a disappointment without him. And I am sorry, Thabekhulu, that I've been tempted to fall in love with you. I can't help it, because under your wing I feel warm, sheltered and loved. Unfortunately, this shelter is burning with us inside. And, sadly, when the house of marriage burns it collapses on many, and its sparks spread out and ignite other homes."

"What really kills me," whispers Thabekhulu, "is that many people will now have a say in this matter, and they'll view it subjectively, without considering the mitigating causes – causes that might make them punish us less harshly."

Though Thabekhulu and MaZondi comfort each other like this, as soon as they part, each remains alone in their separate rooms, where they once said the spirit of the marriage wind had blown. The truth is that since they made the mistake of committing adultery, they have lost everything that they had in abundance. Even if they now married each other, their home would be weak. In the depths of their hearts they know that their loyalty to their spouses means they cannot really trust each other.

The days pass. MaDlamini and Dubazana, who are not enduring any guilt, gradually become worried and anxious. They are worried because they see that their partners, who are left alone together during the day, are falling to pieces. In vain Thabekhulu brings treats for MaZondi: fried fish and chips, polony and cheese, trying to comfort her, but her heart is beyond comforting. A person dies in two ways – either by going to the grave or by dying while alive through the loss of the dignity that goes with being trustworthy.

In himself, Dubazana can feel a resurrection of the hope and love that has been lost. Despite the disappointments he has encountered in life, he is slowly regaining enthusiasm to rebuild his family. People who have struggled through oppression, but still built beautiful homes, like Thabekhulu for instance, have become an inspiration to him. He needs money to be able to buy land and build. He discusses this with his wife, though she has become evasive and shifty. Over the following weekends, if he is not at work, he can be seen moving up and down the streets selling face cloths and towels he has bought cheaply from a factory shop in town.

His activities break his wife's soul: this is something she approves of and she wants to help him, but her eagerness to help is dampened by what her mind visualises. Her mind perceives her husband's attempts as being like those of a leader who is leading his people through the wilderness and is going to reach the promised land alone, while those he has been leading have been distracted by the desert dust and have lost him.

For his part, Thabekhulu knows that it disheartens MaZondi to be ignored and rejected. He often holds her close to comfort her by being romantic and opening her mouth teasingly to nibble on the things that he has brought. But in his heart he harbours a secret wish that the one he now calls his love will lose what she is carrying, instead of them losing their families.

While confusion is mounting in the minds of the people in Thabekhulu's home, Makhosazana gives birth to a baby boy in hospital and names him Sibonelo, Exemplary-one. Dubazana and his wife often visit her, loving their grandchild, who has features that undeniably resemble theirs closely. They pray and hope that a cure for the HIV pandemic will be found while their daughter and grandson are still alive.

While Makhosazana now holds, watches and kisses the product of brutality, her mother still carries her own bundle of tragedy.

There seems to be a great demand for the items that Dubazana is selling, and this keeps him very busy. His determination to accumulate enough money to build his family a house gives him no chance to rest. One Saturday he arrives home from work, stays a few minutes and leaves carrying bags filled to the brim with towels, face cloths and women's socks. Despite the sun grilling him, he cannot help stopping and admiring the beautiful homes around him and hopes that he and his wife will one day defy the odds and end up owning a similar home. But he cannot gaze endlessly on the pleasant surroundings because sweat keeps obstructing his view, forcing him to close his eyes. He puts down his bags and mops his face with his handkerchief.

By the time he opens his eyes a blue car has stopped next to him. Inside are two men, one black and the other white. They both wear caps, and they look at him with eyes that seem to have been deprived of sleep for many days. They get out of the car, show him their police identity cards and open their hands to show him that they are not armed. They ask him to raise his hands, which he does. Then they rummage through his bags.

"Habe, oh really! You pretend to be selling towels while in fact you sell dagga and drugs!" They show him what they are talking about.

"Hhayi, akukhona okwami! No, that's not mine!" In astonishment, Dubazana holds his head with his hands, his eyes staring incredulously as he looks at the long stems of dagga that have suddenly materialised beneath the towels. Within seconds, the men have handcuffed him. MaZondi receives only a phone call from the Drug Prevention Unit, informing her about the arrest and giving details of the police station where her husband is being kept.

"What I hear about Dubazana being arrested for dagga is puzzling news to me. I have never seen him even carrying its ashes." Tears fall from MaZondi's eyes as she informs Thabekhulu and his wife.

"One day you'll think back and recall that I said a married person could be ruined by the lies of a partner: the one who causes the destruction may wish for forgiveness from the victim partner, but to no avail," MaDlamini says, and leaves them both. Their shocked eyes follow her until she disappears before MaZondi and Thabekhulu look at each other, embarrassed, and silently ask questions with their eyes.

Represented by a lawyer named Bhekizizwe Zulu, Dubazana's case is heard three weeks after his arrest, and then it gets adjourned. MaZondi and Thabekhulu attend and listen attentively. He pleads not guilty to the charge which his lawyer argues was laid on him under ridiculous, blind laws.

"What kind of law is blind?" asks the magistrate.

"If it ignores the oppression of the people, and passes sentences as if dealing with unoppressed people." He explains Dubazana's misery to the best of his knowledge, as he knows it. "Today, my brother is in the holding cells; he's being beaten up, and hardened prisoners are ill-treating him because he's been arrested for the possession of dagga and drugs. He has no idea who planted all of this in his bags in a room that he rents. He even suspects that the owner of the house is setting him up because he fancies the accused's wife. Who knows?" Bhekizizwe gesticulates with exaggeration and then says, "Perhaps a grave awaits him as soon as he is released from prison, to become a feast for ants and maggots. Mind you, it is those who've made the laws that shackle you and me who contribute to the digging of such graves; it is they who allow criminals the freedom to pounce and mistreat innocents. And my brother here is adamant that the house-owner who is snatching his wife has taken advantage of his plight and his homelessness; it's not because he truly loves my brother's wife. And the one who has benefitted from my brother's trouble continues to violate his wife, like the shack-dwellers did before."

MaZondi and Thabekhulu look at each other in astonishment. Shivering with fright, MaZondi whispers, "Is he not saying that Dubazana was set up? Uh ... but who could have set him up?" This elicits no response from Thabekhulu.

The case is heard and adjourned yet again.

"Did you hear what Zulu said?" MaZondi asks as they sit next to each other in the car in the parking area of the magistrate's court. She is agitated, holding her cheek, as she stares at the gigantic police truck that pulls slowly out of the courtyard, taking the accused back to the dark, cold prison cells. The truck itself has gloom written all over it and has no ventilation, which ensures that the passengers crowded in the back are always on the brink of suffocating. Some passengers pretend to be singing in order to muffle the pleading cries of those who are already being harassed and tormented even before the truck reaches the gate.

"I heard the lawyer when he said that Dubazana suspects he was set up."

"The other words that broke my heart in the court are that you don't love me, even though I'm carrying your child; you took advantage of me because I am poor and desperate."

Thabekhulu keeps quiet, his conscience ravaging him.

"The lawyer complained that while we roam the streets freely, Dubazana is locked up, tortured and traumatised by other prisoners." No sooner has MaZondi finished saying this than a man can be heard screaming inside the police van as it eases out of the gate into the main road.

"Perhaps it's Makhosazana's father who's being beaten, my God! How can we save him from this misery, Thabekhulu?" She shifts in her seat and fiddles with the door lock.

Thabekhulu wipes his eyes, shakes his head, and says, "I don't know what to do any more; when I pitied you two and intervened in your plight I never dreamt that things would unfold like this and land us in such a mess. Allegations that I don't love you but have taken advantage of you because you are poor and destitute are a hot cinder in my heart, because I never loved you with the intention of us becoming lovers in the first place. I was trying to rescue you from the pain of your body and your soul. I'm told that when a person drowns, sometimes the rescuer also drowns trying to rescue them. When someone is trying to save a drowning person, the victim clings so desperately to the lifesaver that he suffocates him and they both end up drowning. I know that the world will curse Thabekhulu and forget the reason." He turns the ignition key, and his car, with its sobbing passenger, moves like a hearse from the parking bay, carrying the widow waiting for her husband's body.

The case resumes on the stipulated day. In the late morning MaZondi and Thabekhulu are back in court, dumbfounded and failing to absorb what they hear and see when the prosecutor's questions choke Dubazana. Worse still, today he is defending himself; his lawyer has been arrested for violating the curfew of his house arrest, which stipulated that he be at home from six in the evening till six in the morning. Eventually, and not unexpectedly, the court finds Dubazana guilty. A record of his previous convictions for trying to work without a permit in Durban is read out to him, and this then classifies him, according to the court, as a regular offender.

"Even then, my Lord, I was arrested for contravening some stupid laws; laws that wasted my time by making me a slaving domestic help and gardener for many years, not knowing that I was being deceived and would only receive temporary permits for all my trouble." Today, Dubazana is once again wearing a tattered black T-shirt and shorts that are ragged and dirty, showing parts of his buttocks. The sneakers he wears are black and white, without proper soles. His toes protrude. He speaks with admirable confidence and conviction and is not afraid to criticise the laws that are not supposed to be questioned; he proceeds fearlessly in the face of the security branch detectives who are calling the shots regarding the fate of those who "wrong" the government. At one moment he looks down at the clothes he is wearing and feels overcome with a sense of being a dirty nonentity. Tears filling his eyes, he shakes his head, "Indeed, you killed me a long time ago. It is up to you whether you bury me in prison, or whether you feed me to the vultures, if that is what you like."

"You will have to discuss that with those who deal with complaints about the oppressiveness of the law." The magistrate answers him curtly and wipes his glasses. After making his concluding remarks and comments on the case, he sentences Dubazana to several years in prison. A number of years are suspended but he has to serve two years of hard labour in prison.

While MaZondi exclaims in shock, the police officer grabs Dubazana by the hand and pushes him into the underground cells. He disappears immediately but the air is still filled with his words, complaining that he leaves his children alone in the wilderness to be devoured by poverty and disease. The sentence has been passed, and he does not even have a lawyer to appeal. MaZondi's attempts to see him fail. She is told that she can only see him when he is in prison, as he is still to be investigated that day by some detectives about other cases in which they suspect he is involved.

Indeed, three burly white men arrive: Schutte, Lightning and McIntosh, and a black one whose English name is Lightbody. The three whites are known as Siketekete, Malayitha and Mathoshi (Lantern, He-who-sets-alight and Torches) respectively, because they enter people's homes at night and wreak havoc. They have just testified in Bhekizizwe's case which is still ongoing, so they drill Dubazana with questions in one of the holding cells. They want to know why he has insulted the sacred laws of the country, by insisting in court that these laws are oppressive.

Dubazana and Zulu, whose suspended sentences have been revoked, are on opposite sides of the holding cells. That afternoon they join the other male and female prisoners in song, their voices merging in harmonious melody. And can prisoners sing! They can convert a person even before they themselves have converted. When they sing "Singing consoles the one who is in sorrow" and other religious hymns, Sergeant Vanda, nicknamed Mafutha (Fatty), who usually has no respect whatsoever for the prisoners, holds his head and shakes it. Moving up and down the cells, his own tongue is cleansed by joining the singing. Even though Bhekizizwe is alone in his own cell as a political prisoner, as authorities fear that a mere sneeze from him will infect other prisoners and pollute their minds, his voice can be heard as one of the most melodious ones.

The measly amount of money Dubazana left behind has been spent and finished, and his family is now desperate. It has also become severely uncomfortable to accept handouts from the Thabekhulus. And since Dubazana's arrest, MaDlamini begins to look at MaZondi with suspicious eyes.

With starvation taking its toll on her and the children, MaZondi informs Thabekhulu about their plight one afternoon.

"The only option I see, MaZondi, is to try to get meat for you so you can go around the streets selling it, like MaDlamini does," he responds.

"That's a tall order, though."

"What is wrong? Are you reluctant?"

"I am not reluctant at all; but I'm scared of your wife. Obviously, she will say that I am competing with her for work. Secondly, it will be clear to her that you are the one getting the meat for me, and that will fuel enmity and a quarrel between us."

"Leave that to me. I'll talk to her."

Thabekhulu broaches the matter with his wife, but MaDlamini is livid and will not hear anything of it. She asks why MaZondi wants to be supplied with meat while living in her home, instead of going to her in-laws at Mangweni or her parents' home at Nkumba.

"You should consider, my wife, that they arrived here empty-handed; all they had, had been looted by hooligans at the shacks. We will do this as a gesture to help her buy some clothes to cover their bodies. Even second-hands will do. Then she can go home."

MaDlamini finally relents. "Okay then, as long as it's only a few weeks, and then she leaves us in peace; I'm sure she knows the directions to where she came from. After all, it was explained to them the day they got here that the shelter we'd provide was a *temporary* arrangement. We never said they could always live here with us. And especially now that one of them has set the other up and got him arrested, I am done with them."

MaZondi realises how daunting the task is the first day she leaves Thabekhulu's home with a metal box to collect meat. She feels the sun burning her scalp as she stands in a long, slow-moving queue, waiting for the meat. There are some regulars here who seem to have been exempted from standing in line and they go straight to the counters to collect their meat from the staff. In some cases, the staff will even bring the meat to their acquaintances in the queue and collect the money. Finally she has her turn: after Thabekhulu has brought the meat for his wife, he brings her share too. Ashamed at the prospect of being together with MaDlamini at home while they prepare the meat, she holds her feet so that she only arrives home when she knows MaDlamini has left already.

She cuts the meat, weighs it in her mind, and puts it in the box. She then lifts the heavy load, puts it on her head and leaves. Today she realises that the work is not going to be easy. Even before she starts selling, she is tired. The box she carries on her head is as heavy as stone. The sun burns her without mercy. Oh, and the meandering roads, the hills and ravines of Mlazi! All become a curse before her. She is even wary of other people's homes, but her troubles force her to enter them. Some people buy and others ask to buy on credit. She turns those down, saying her husband does not allow her to grant credit. In some homes she is turned down the moment she greets people at the door. And in some houses she finds men who, after buying, make passes at her.

By midday she is dead tired. It is in the afternoon that the meat is finally all sold. She drags herself to Thabekhulu's home where she finds Makhosazana back from the hospital, sitting in their room with her child, and Nkosana, her brother, mulling over their sorrows. Her body can hardly move as she throws herself onto the bed and stretches her legs. She holds her grandchild and gives the money to Nkosana and his sister to buy food at the shop. They come back with a few items, enough for the evening meal, which they eat. They soon retire to sleep in silence.

The days that follow see MaZondi take to the road, braving the sun, pouring rains and blowing winds, to return to the Thabekhulu home where she and MaDlamini always avoid eye contact. At the same time her husband digs and carries loads to the railway trucks in the scorching sun as part of his hard labour sentence. His sweat runs to the ground, wasted, and cannot translate into putting food on the table for his wife and children. In the extreme heat of the sun, in the fiercely blowing wind and the angry roar of thunder, MaZondi has not forgotten her husband. When she is tired, sitting by herself in the shade, she hears herself say, "Such tragedy has struck us! But if we'd had our own home, things would not have been like this. Had you been here now, I wouldn't be roaming the streets battling the merciless sun and the daunting slopes. May the Lord and the Dubazana ancestors protect you wherever you are. Please remember me always. And when you come back, forgive me, because I am as I am not because of my own will. You know it too." She loves him. The rock that has fallen on her and Thabekhulu fell once only, and has left them with an inerasable scar. Long ago, they both agreed that they loved and cared deeply for their families; they would not have affairs. But now, the foetus growing inside her each day, as if eager to be ushered into a world that does not want it, seems destined to be a curse and a destroyer of love. Preoccupied with this, MaZondi grimaces at the piercing pain in her heart as she feels the baby move in her womb. Tears flow when she thinks that if Dubazana were to see her in this condition, it would mean the end of their marriage.

She no longer receives comfort from Thabekhulu. Even talking to him is rare as she is now spends the days selling, only coming back late, if not at dusk. She thinks that perhaps Thabekhulu is now ashamed to talk to her. When their eyes meet, he looks away. When she considers what happened to her at the shacks and what is happening now, her heart doubts the integrity of men. He acts like a person who has infected her with scabs and then leaves her scratching herself on her own while he is nowhere to be seen.

But on his side, Thabekhulu is also suffering from the wounds to his heart; they do not leave him alone. He is always down, inwardly complaining. His heart is rankled by the secrets and pains that simmer silently and keep him awake at night. His wife frequently pesters him, demanding to know when the Dubazanas are going to pack. But his conscience does not allow him to let them onto the streets. He knows the truth better than anyone in the house does, and better than Dubazana in jail does. He has hinted to MaZondi at the possibility of asking them to go. She pours tears on him, mentioning that her husband's family resent her and blame her for following her husband around, instead of staying with them in the countryside like many wives do. Secondly, when the allegations regarding men who had made passes at her reached home, her in-laws interpreted this as a sign of infidelity on her part, and that she was betraying their son and brother. They did not understand the problems facing men, women and children in the cities and also in the countryside, where they were always on the move, the laws of the country making them nomads. The mere thought of renting a new place sends shivers through her body as she recalls the past in other rented homes and in the shacks. Her old wounds hurt again and flood her with sadness.

Thabekhulu keeps telling his wife that they are going to move today, tomorrow, or the day after tomorrow. MaZondi's growing stomach also constantly threatens a rift. And out of the blue, his wife begins to ask questions that immediately dampen his spirits: "Thabekhulu, we're the ones who revived the love that had faded after the events in the shacks – the events that made them ignore each other. And now MaZondi's pregnant. But who, now, is the father of her child?"

"How can I know, my wife, about the pregnancy of a married woman who was living with her husband all this time?"

"If there is nothing fishy about the pregnancy, then why is it that when her bulge is about to be visible, Dubazana suddenly gets arrested in a suspicious way?"

"I wouldn't know anything about anybody who's been arrested for selling dagga and drugs. They're not familiar ground to me; the meagre knowledge I have about them is through hearsay."

At times it is so quiet that it seems his professed ignorance has succeeded in ending his wife's suspicions. Even so, he feels the change of mood in the house. He feels the familiar spice of love disappearing. They talk less and share their happiness and sadness less. All this haunts Thabekhulu. Losing his wife would be like losing a part of his own body.

"Don't you remember what happened to these people at the shacks, and that they avoided each other because the daughter had tested positive for HIV? Her father was afraid that his wife was also infected and that the virus was just temporarily dormant." This is, of course, one of the questions Thabekhulu thinks of obsessively in their bedroom, which is now devoid of the love-breezes that used to permeate it.

"Yes, I remember," he responds timidly.

"If it so happens that you are the father of the expected child, may I go away so that the diseases you knowingly bring me will kill me in the wilderness, away from here?"

His silence is the only answer.

"Thabekhulu, let this other man's wife return to her in-laws' home, to those whom she was married off to, in the countryside. She knows the way to that place. For how long are you going to keep her here while her husband is away?"

MaDlamini pesters Thabekhulu about MaZondi, who is now heavy with child and hardly ventures outside her room. "Apply your mind, Thabekhulu. Your age implies that you are a mature man now. Firstly, who is going to be responsible for the hospital fees and the transport that will take her when the delivery time comes? And when she has delivered the baby and is discharged from hospital, who is going to support her, the infant, Dubazana's children and grandchild?"

Thabekhulu sympathises with MaZondi. He is concerned about the disgrace that will besmirch her in-laws if she delivers her baby at her husband's home. He is also wary of Dubazana's fury and the hatred he will have for the child when he comes out of jail. His heart bleeds with grief, and tears well in his eyes when he thinks about the abandoned children who live on the streets, exposed to rain and lightning, the sun and life's flames, winds and storms, snow and frost. He has watched some of them scavenging for food in rubbish bins. One day one of them may be his own child, as it is possible that Dubazana will return and reconcile with his wife on condition that she disowns the child that he, Thabekhulu, cannot take in.

"Just look, Thabethule's father, we have worked for years and were about to start a butchery. I've even heard that we may find one here at the hostel. Let them go so that we can be alone, just the two of us, and reclaim the peace and tranquillity we used to enjoy, and focus on progress." Her suggestions elicit no response from Thabekhulu, who has become dumb and numb.

Thabekhulu's failure to force the Dubazanas out opens a door through which the love that once permeated the house slips out. On the chair where love once sat in dignity, hatred now perches. Members of their church also drop by to enquire about the couple's recurring absence from church. Thabekhulu and his wife prevaricate and evasively lock their problems and secrets in their chests. The prayers from fellow church members that pour out during these visits lull their problems, which awaken again as soon as they leave, like a sickness that threatens to kill as soon as the treatment wears off.

The schools close and Thabekhulu's children return. For the first time they arrive at a home that is upside down and in a mess. Their mother and father try to hide this fact, taking them out in the car for excursions, but they can read between the lines that something is amiss.

The chasm between the parents' hearts becomes more obvious as Christmas draws nearer, and MaDlamini catches her husband arriving home with MaZondi during the day, the car overloaded with groceries. She keeps silent as if she is not at home, observing them as they help each other carry the groceries to MaZondi's room. From that day on a stifling breeze of animosity wafts through the house. Christmas passes, leaving in its wake a thick and heavy silence that infiltrates the household. A few hours before New Year they realise that MaZondi, who has locked herself in her room as usual, is in labour. Thabekhulu rushes her to the hospital as her condition intensifies with every minute. By midnight when jolly hooters are ringing all over the place, flames rise from burning tyres and fire crackers, and the firmament becomes kaleidoscopic – red and then blue, and then black with smoke – their son is heard crying, greeting the world with that familiar cry that announces the arrival of a child on earth. Mxolisi has been born. And is he the spitting image of his father!

14

It is said that when people fail to resolve a matter between themselves, it should be put on the table for communal discussion. But unfortunately, it is difficult to discuss a matter that is defeating a woman in her own home.

MaDlamini is deeply disturbed by the suspicions regarding her husband's infidelity. She sees Mxolisi growing up with features that, with each day, are more clearly the image of her husband's. She begins to sense the looming destruction of her home. The worst thing is a photograph of her husband as a young boy, crawling: he looks just like Mxolisi. And the well-meant comments of people who visit them also fuel the fire. As soon as they see the child, perhaps crawling, they express their amazement and ask when she had a baby that looks so much like his father, Thabekhulu. To this she has no coherent response.

Some neighbours, who do not like MaDlamini because they claim she is uppity, come more often to see this wonder. "This is more than looking alike!" they exclaim in amazement. "Are you all relatives in this house?"

This leaves her heartbroken, lying on the bed in tears. "Thabekhulu, do you hear how people express their amazement, and the questions they ask about MaZondi's child when they come here?"

"They are just being stupid; you know that people like to say stupid things."

"Just tell the truth for once, like someone on his deathbed. Why, exactly, does this child look so much like you?"

Thabekhulu immediately becomes restless, "I don't know. As they say a mother knows her child, I have asked the same question of his mother. She just gave me an incredible answer."

"What incredible answer is that?"

Thabekhulu clears his throat, "She said she, too, doesn't know why it is so, but suspects that it is because she craved looking at me when she was pregnant."

"What nonsense is this? If she was craving, why did she not crave peaches and peanuts, instead of you? Well, clearly I have to leave, so that she has the freedom to crave you."

Gradually, the dignity of the family is dragged through the mud. Some of their neighbours, who do not yet have enlightened attitudes towards people with HIV, start to point fingers at the Thabekhulu family. They call it a home of weird activities and spread lies that everyone in the home has the virus. They stop buying the meat that MaZondi sells to neighbours to help support her family. Her business begins to fail; she stays at home and now has to depend on Thabekhulu for financial support.

Church members keep visiting to revive their faith, but they, too, are struck by the sight of a Thabekhulu whose mother is the tenant, crawling in the yard. By the time MaDlamini discloses her secret, the damage to her marriage has become irreparable. Church members fall down and pray, consoling her about the one they call Satan who has ambushed her at the church's gate and waylaid her. They comfort and admonish her to stop worrying about worldly things, but to turn her focus to the heavens.

The speed with which MaDlamini and Thabekhulu are becoming estranged worries MaZondi; they rarely smile and they avoid eye contact, and this is all because of her own family's sufferings that led them to the Thabekhulus. The pain of rejection reopens the wound of loneliness, the loneliness in which she is sinking. She knows the anguish of living in hope of resuscitating a dying marriage, yearning for prayers that will help, and for the ancestors to intervene. One cannot think straight in such a situation! To still have feelings of love but be made to live in a loveless home is like being dumped in a mortuary with dead people while you are still alive. She wants to ask forgiveness from MaDlamini, but fear waves her away.

The love that has escaped from the Thabekhulu house now disappears into oblivion. Instead of love, divorce hovers over the family and remains at the gate like a dog threatening the household. They say a medicine man can't cure his own afflictions, and this is now the case with the Thabekhulus. The deep, wise words they eloquently poured out to heal the Dubazanas' marriage have evaporated. MaDlamini, now feeble, like a sick person, has a broken, fragile heart. She does not know how to react when the two children, Mxolisi and Sibonelo, regularly come to her, the one clumsily swaying in an attempt to perfect his first steps and the other crawling, both vying for her attention. They throw themselves into her arms as soon as they reach her. Sometimes, when she ignores Mxolisi, he climbs on her and looks at her, smiling. Knowing the child has not wronged her, she smiles, blinking back tears.

One Monday morning MaDlamini feels she has exhausted all her ideas about how to handle the problems in her house. She bundles some clothes and toiletries into two bags and, as soon as her husband has left, leaves without a word of goodbye and heads to her parents' home in Chesterville, hoping that her mind can find some peace and respite there. By ten o'clock she is on a bus that is belching and speeding down Booth Road, taking her home. It traverses forests, slopes and knolls that have turned into an open, wild area after the removal of Mkhumbane settlement. She is in a daze and everything outside her window is a blur.

The bus enters Chesterville, and her eyes sweep through the township that she still calls home. It is old, crumbling and littered with shacks that seem to mushroom in every yard as makeshift outbuildings. Any possibility of progress and prosperity is shackled by segregation. There is no hope of building, extending or renovating houses as the township lives in the shadow of a threat by the government to remove it at any time, without notice. The government insists that the indigenous people of this country do not have permission to build in an area that is not reserved for them. What makes this township look even more dilapidated is its proximity to Westville, an affluent white suburb that boasts grand mansions. However, life is turning sour for the fat cats who own them, as the people living in matchbox houses have begun to survive on their rich neighbours, looting their possessions.

MaDlamini rings the bus bell, alights, and walks homewards with slow feet. She does not have any heavy luggage, except the embarrassment of returning home from a failed marriage. She knocks, and it takes a while before a light-skinned, good-looking woman of about thirty opens the door for her.

"Oh, is it you, my sister?" MaDlamini asks, smiling, while she looks at her with disappointed eyes.

"Yes, it's me, your brother's wife."

She goes in and sits down on the sofa, putting her small bundle in front of her, and mops her sweating face. She exchanges greetings with MaMngoma, who is the wife of her first-born brother, Vusumuzi.

"Are you on a break today, MaMngoma?"

"Yes, I have taken some rest from this shop of ours where we have to slave away, even on weekends."

They discuss many topics, the main ones being the problems that prevail in the family. Topping the list is the scarcity of space in the house. MaDlamini's four sisters and two brothers fill the house with their children. Gugulethu and Vusi are the only two of her six siblings who are fully employed, along with their mother. The rest do piece jobs, and can be employed one day and without a job the next day.

"That is what's making me and your brother despair. While we are reasonably well employed, we can't see the fruits of our toil. Instead of taking steps forward, we're falling into a ditch," the wife complains.

Feeling ashamed for adding to their burden, MaDlamini consoles her by promising to talk to her mother and siblings. Her sister-in-law gets up, brews tea and butters bread for her. After tea, she excuses herself and goes outside to wash clothes.

MaDlamini remains alone in the living room, not knowing which room to put her bags in. At last she takes them to her mother's bedroom where, when she looks at its size and the two beds and wardrobe, she realises there is no space for her. She remains by herself, lonely, until the afternoon when her sisters and mother, MaMbonambi, arrive. MaDlamini resembles her mother so much that, as the saying goes, they look as alike as the two thumbs on a snuff box. The women then put their heads together in the bedroom, exchanging stories and consoling each other for their hardships. Some complain about their brother's wife who always whines about supporting their children. Others grumble about their brother Vusi, who they claim is as good-natured as a lamb and has succumbed to his wife's love potions that have softened him. Her mother sheds tears, bemoaning the loss of her husband who left her in misery. She wails without stopping when MaDlamini, her first-born daughter, hints at her troubled marriage, albeit without divulging the whole disgrace that has fallen on it.

"Oh, my child, it never rains, indeed. But where will you run to? Because you've heard your sisters lamenting our plight here. We don't feel welcome here and it's as though we live in the wilderness." Her mother comforts her, and advises that she and her husband be tolerant towards each other, and that when he comes to fetch her she must not say any harsh words.

They cook together, eat and go to bed, but one can hardly set foot in the overcrowded kitchen. MaDlamini only falls asleep towards the morning, her mind teeming with thoughts and images of what is happening at her home. She has harboured some faint hope that when her husband finds her gone, he will feel overwhelmed by guilt, jump into his car and come looking for her. That hope gradually evaporates with the crowing of cocks, heralding yet another morning.

Though Thabekhulu has been told by MaZondi that MaDlamini gathered some belongings and left hurriedly without a word, he has, indeed, been hoping that she will come back. By the time the sun sets, he has repeatedly peered through the window until he tires of it. He has even stood outside, peering about in the dark, all in vain. He goes back to their bedroom, which feels so very cold, sorrow blowing through it. In fact, the whole house is cold, hungry and thirsty for the comfort provided by the wife who was recognised and approved by his ancestors. The way that his wife has left him, after they have lived together all these years, since they were young, makes his heart sob. He sits helplessly on the bed, hearing his heart bearing the truth that he really deeply loves his wife. He feels the urge to get into his car and drive to his in-laws to fetch her, but then he loses it, succumbing to loneliness, hitting his knee, talking to himself, immobile and brooding.

Passing by the room while he talks to himself, MaZondi stops and puts her ear to the door to listen, her heart thudding against her chest. As soon as he is quiet, she knocks softly.

"Ngena, come in." Thabekhulu's voice sounds like that of a terminally ill patient.

She enters, and then bends down in front of Thabekhulu.

"What do you want to say, MaZondi?" he asks, a bit startled.

"No. I am not saying anything, father of Mxo ... Thabekhulu. I just came to ask if that is indeed what happened?"

Thabekhulu turns his eyes upwards, "I don't quite understand what you are saying. What do you mean: is that indeed what happened?"

"No, I just came to congratulate you since you said yourself that it was you who set up my husband. He's serving a jail sentence because you were protecting your home from the whirlwind that is me."

"Did you really hear me say that, Mxolisi's mother?"

"If there is another person with you in this room, then it is he who said it. I thought you were able to stand for the truth. What has happened now?"

Thabekhulu is speechless, straining his ears as though he is frightened by Mxolisi, who has started to wail as if he is being bitten by an insect.

"Let me go and fetch Mxolisi, so that you can explain to me what it is that you courageously stand for, between lies and the truth." She leaves Thabekhulu following her with the eyes of a person whose world has suddenly fallen apart.

MaZondi comes back with the child, sits herself on the chair, holds her child on her lap and feeds him bottled milk. She lowers her eyes, looks hesitantly at the child's father, and then asks politely, "Please tell me, Mxolisi's father, when you set my husband up to be arrested, did you pause to consider my future?"

Thabekhulu keeps quiet and fixes his tired eyes on his fingernails.

"Please open up your heart, my child's father, and tell me who really orchestrated Dubazana's arrest?"

Thabekhulu wipes his eyes, swallows hard. "Now that you've already heard me blurt it out to myself, allow me to say I am sorry, MaZondi, about what happened. I admit that I am the one who planted dagga and drugs in your husband's bags."

"Oh! Oh my God! The sufferings the world piles upon me!" She puts the child carefully on the bed and cries, "Why did you do such a despicable thing, Thabekhulu?"

Thabekhulu takes a deep breath, "I was protecting you and my family from the disgrace that would follow, and from Dubazana's wrath. As Dubazana was already spurning any intimacy between you and him, when would he realise that you were pregnant, and who would you say was responsible?"

"I am not good at lying, Thabekhulu, and besides, it's obvious who the child resembles."

As if he is about to cry, Thabekhulu asks her in an emotional voice, "Then what would people say about me?"

With eyes that flicker with anger amidst tears, MaZondi glares at him, "What are they already saying about *me* right now?"

"I realised that I was going to lose all I treasured: my family and, especially, my dignity. You know that when we first met, you were waiting for us in the church yard. How do you think the congregation would have reacted to the news that I have split two families simultaneously, hitting two objects with one stone, as it were?"

Tears choke MaZondi.

"My intention was to get Dubazana out of the way for a while. Now if he asks you about Mxolisi's father, you can make up a non-existent name and claim that person seduced and lured you into temptation while he was still in jail."

"I can't believe this! In order to salvage your family and your pride, you insist that I collude with you and sink into a marsh, to be a stepping stone for you to walk across to safety?"

"It is safer to quell the fire in one family than allow them both to burn, hoping that we can blow out two fires at the same time. At least you also know, Mxolisi's mother, the saying that a smut slips in even if the eye is wide open. And you know where the speck that besmirched us originated."

"I understand. We have to protect your home with the blood and tears that fall behind prison walls. Indeed, we are the ones who infected you and your family with our afflictions. The truth is, I no longer know what my fate is. In all the places where my husband and I have been in and out, there have always been allegations that I seduce men and tempt them to make passes at me. And at the shacks, when they violated me, they insisted that I was their lover and had pocketed their money. Now I have given birth to a child who is abhorred by the Dubazanas and, even worse, by the Thabekhulus, to whom he belongs. None of the tragedies I've mentioned occurred through my will and intentions. I am simply a victim of circumstances; it is me against the world!"

"As I have said, my sister, you know that the situation is like this not because I was abusing you or taking advantage of you. In fact, I had tried many times to warn Dubazana about the danger of ignoring and neglecting you. It is our mutual caring that ensnared us. Sometimes kindness can be a trap."

"I am sorry, my child's father, about the emotional pain that you have to endure because of me."

"What worries me most is that I don't know where my wife is right now. I have already been disgraced by her leaving. How much greater will my shame be if she shows up with the police to prove that you and I are living together in sin? Now that things have come to this, I think that I should help you out, and we can look for a room where you can take shelter until the storm has settled."

"My child's father, I'd appreciate anything that can help save the home that we found living in peace and love, from a hurricane. When Dubazana comes out, he will decide how he deals with the sinner that I am and the illegitimate child with his dubious origins." She takes her child and reaches for the door.

"You'll hear from me tomorrow when I return from work, regarding where I've found a room."

"We'll appreciate it, as long as you don't throw us out on the street." She leaves him lying on the bed, gazing at the ceiling, thoughts clogging his mind.

In the middle of the night, his wife is awake in Chesterville, and Dubazana, too, cannot sleep. How he misses her! It consumes him, and the thought never leaves him that he is going to be a laughing stock – even to his friends – because he has lost his own wife by attaching himself to another man's wife. He silently revisits all the effort and love his wife has poured into building this home. Does this mean that what has happened to the Dubazana children, being without a home, is going to happen to his own children? He feels like getting up and into the car to go and fetch MaDlamini, but then is discouraged when he realises that he will not convince her to come back if MaZondi and Mxolisi are still around. He is praying for the morning to come sooner, and that his tears will not be in vain when he begs Sithole for accommodation. Sithole is his colleague and he pins his hopes on him to offer MaZondi a room to stay in.

He goes to work in the morning and executes his duties in a daze, his mind failing to register anything. His eyes keep visiting his watch. As soon as he knocks off, he runs to the gate to wait for Sithole.

"Please wait for me, Mondise!" The man he is calling by his clan name and who is about to exit the gate is short, bow-legged and very dark. He has a pointed head with a heavy brow and a small face, bushy and bearded.

"What is it, Thabekhulu?" He looks at him with white eyes and smiles with teeth of the same colour. Sithole is about sixty years old or more, and wears a sky-blue overall and black boots that are so big that they look too heavy for him. He has a stick in one hand and a carrier-bag in the other.

"Hey, I am battling with a crisis, my brother. You may think that I look fine, but things are not okay."

"That is clear, Thabekhulu. One can tell by just looking at you."

Thabekhulu leads him to his car, where they sit and talk. He begs. The humble manner in which Thabekhulu, who is his foreman and commands respect, pleads, softens Sithole's heart and makes him pity him.

"As you know, and you've said it yourself, you approached me because my wife lives in the countryside, but you also know, Thabekhulu, that a room in the township is never empty. I live in the main bedroom and rent out the smaller one as well as the kitchen. Fortunately, though, the dining room, which is rented too, will be vacated on Saturday. Your friend can move in on Sunday if you can assure me that she's not likely to cause trouble in the house; matters that might reach the municipal office and cause my house to be taken away from me. Now tell me, where is the husband of this woman you are begging for so much?"

Thabekhulu relates the story.

"Okay, I understand. If you get a chance, you can both come to view the room."

They get into the car and go to the older section of the township where Sithole lives. They get out and Sithole shows him the room. The house is in a long, train-like building that has many houses in one, joined together without a fence separating neighbours. Despite its unattractiveness, Sithole has tried to clean the yard, so its appearance is relatively decent. Thabekhulu then fetches MaZondi to view the room. Even though her eyes are shocked, as she is now used to a clean house with electricity, she does not say anything and pretends that she is satisfied.

"Well then, I'm leaving it all to you, Thabekhulu, and will see you on Sunday."

MaZondi swallows her tears as the car takes her back to a home that is not her own. She has good reason for her heart sinking in a sense of loss. For the first time she is going to be a tenant without a husband in the house of a man who lives like a bachelor, since his wife lives far away in the countryside.

When five o' clock strikes on Tuesday afternoon, Thabekhulu's car is already roaring along Booth Road. The music playing softly in the car makes him feel emotional, and he is also enjoying the beauty of the land and the setting sun, a deep crimson above the hills. In no time the car stops in front of the Dlaminis' house in Chesterville. MaDlamini, seated in the living room, sees it and her heart leaps, overwhelmed by mixed feelings of shock, happiness and anger.

"We salute you of the Sibalukhulus," he calls respectfully at the door.

"Yes, ngena, come in," says his wife, her eyes sweeping him for a second before she lowers her head and fixes her eyes on the floor.

Thabekhulu stands near the door like a shy, guilty child.

"Sit in any chair you like, Thabekhulu."

Thabekhulu looks at the sofas and chooses the one facing his wife. They greet each other and say they are well.

"I never thought you would come here to look for me, Thabethule's father."

Surprised, Thabekhulu looks at her. "How could you think I was not going to come when you know I have lost a part of me?"

"Oh my, how sad for you to lose a part of you! What did you do to it, or perhaps it just suddenly got mad and ran away for no reason?"

Thabekhulu now has to face his wife's fiery wrath as she admonishes him, pouring out tears and anger about a host of other issues. He endures it calmly, humbles himself, sincerely asks for forgiveness and owns up to all of his mistakes.

"Mother of my family, our forefathers had a saying that we make mistakes even when our eyes are wide open."

"Simply because they are *your* mistakes and you committed them, eyes wide open, the matter is still under discussion. Had the mistakes been mine the matter wouldn't have been considered for discussion."

"Don't even imagine us in such a situation! Sometimes it takes a second to make mistakes, and by the time you realise them, they are beyond correction and your life's in a ditch, aflame. Just as happened to MaZondi and me. Sometimes the scars are more permanent on the sinner and perpetrator than they are on the victim."

With eyes now red with tears, MaDlamini asks, "Thabekhulu, how can it happen that Dubazana and I, the victims, are now the laughing stock of the community? I am a displaced wanderer, while he is subjected to the atrocities of jail. I really stabbed myself with my own spear when I accepted the Dubazanas into my home."

"As I've said, we who have sinned are left with permanent scars. When the one who is wronged has forgiven, they know they have come to terms with the matter. The sinner, besides losing integrity, must live with uncertainty that they have truly been forgiven. If you were to forgive me now, even if I love you very much and would do every good thing I can for you, I will always worry and doubt that when you forgave me, you truly did. Queen of the family, please find it in your heart to forgive me; don't discard me but spare me for the future. If our family falls apart, what will happen to the children?"

After Thabekhulu has cajoled and pleaded for a long time, just as he did when he courted her, his wife's heart softens and relents. As he anticipated, she stipulates a strict condition that she will not set foot in the home while MaZondi and Mxolisi are still there.

"She has also realised that she has to vacate the place. She's looked for a room and found one where they said she can move in this coming Sunday."

"Hhayi, no, she doesn't have to rush; I can stay for years in the wilderness waiting for her to leave. Let's see what happens on Sunday then."

"Meanwhile, I'll check if she can leave before that."

"And before we can hope to have a healthy relationship, we'll need to get tested for those diseases that are killing people like flies."

That does not sit well with Thabekhulu. It stabs his heart like a sharp knife. He hears the words and breathes heavily. His voice sounds tired. "Ngiyavuma, I agree. As I've said, the one who has sinned in marriage feels empty and ashamed: the emptiness of being tested for venereal diseases like a young playboy when you are already married!"

"It is like that in marriage. And the weakness of one partner weakens and bewitches the whole family."

Later, Thabekhulu's in-laws arrive home, exchange pleasantries with him and begin discussions to try and pick up the pieces. It is late at night when Thabekhulu bids them goodnight and steps out of the house with his wife, who walks him out. The couple say their own goodbyes with hugs and kisses. With his heart clotted with the pain of parting, he reverses and then waves goodbye as the car roars away with its dazzling rear lights. MaDlamini looks at the crimson tail lights with eyes that swim with tears until the car disappears from sight, swallowed by the night. She remains standing, wiping her cheeks.

15

On a Thursday night, at half-past nine, the train from Johannesburg to Durban slides out of Pietermaritzburg into the darkness of the night. It rolls slowly and gently along the hill, its lights dazzling on its sides, crosses the road to Edendale and glides towards Pentrich station. It passes the station calmly as if to avoid disturbing the neighbouring households, and then snakes along, crossing rivers and ravines, meandering through the bowels of the imposing hills. The passengers in the train are now tired and no longer bother to look outside through the windows. It is no surprise that most are already asleep, having been lulled by the melody of the wheels of this giant metal monster that dances on the rail tracks through the night. The train left Johannesburg the previous day, at dusk. It was delayed the whole day near Matiwane's Kop where there was an accident involving a derailed goods train.

Pietermaritzburg is no longer visible, and the train is swallowed by the night as it passes Mlazi River, Camperdown and Cato Ridge. In the passage of one of the carriages Dubazana stands; his head clean-shaven to a shine. He is wearing clothes and shoes that look as if they may belong to a prisoner. As the train passes Georgedale and Hammarsdale, facing the boulders of Cliffdale, he stands as if in a trance, gazing at the darkness. He watches the head of the train, its horns pointing upwards like those of a mad horned viper, searching for uThungulu, the coastline. He stands there, lonely and self-conscious, giving the few people with him in the compartment some space, and freeing them from staring at him, pop-eyed, watching him like a lost soul, distrusting him. They are holding on tightly to their luggage, not sure about its safety while he is hovering around.

When the train reaches Ntshongweni, moving through one tunnel to the next, leaving each of them clinking, Dubazana feels a sudden rush of goosebumps and is filled with such a fervent longing that he wants to cry. He cannot suppress his feelings any more and mutters to himself, addressing the train like an imbongi: "Oh, there you go, skirter of the hills! I wonder if I will ever ride you again in the company of my family, with the peace of mind of a secure job and financial means! When will you take me again and plod along the mountains so that I can see my parents and tell them about the events that have happened to me over the years? Oh my mother, daughter of Nkabinde, I wonder if you even know that right now I am groping through the night, shrouded in the acrid smell of jail?" He stares into the darkness with moist eyes. "I wonder if my children and their mother are still alive and how the journey with the virus has been for Makhosazana and my grandchild. Will I find my wife and children at Thabekhulu's, since I got no responses to the letters I wrote them? If only she knew how much I love her, how much I miss her, as this train dances with me until its rumble is echoed by the hills!" He asks himself these questions as the Mariannhill station glows with red lights behind the train, the tall grass dazzling as the enormous viper speeds through.

While he questions and answers himself, his wife is fast asleep in the room where he has left her. In her arms lies the baby whom Dubazana does not know, but who has been named Mxolisi, One-who-seeks-forgiveness, because it is through him that MaZondi will ask Dubazana to forgive her. His wife is tired, having spent the whole day at the hospital where she took Makhosazana and the grandchild who had both suddenly fallen ill. They were eventually admitted to the hospital. Nkosana, who is ignored generally around the house, lies flat on the bed, snoring loudly. The one who cannot fall asleep is Thabekhulu, whose mind is preoccupied with his wife. He is counting the days that remain before MaZondi leaves, after which MaDlamini will return home. He really misses his wife tonight, so much so that he is using her pinafore as a pillow, hoping her scent will lull him into a deep sleep. Sleep defies him, though, as he feels a constant pang of fear, whose cause he cannot explain, and he shivers.

The railway line rattles through valleys and Dubazana is still gazing at the night, lost in thought. Ah! A nostalgic recollection washes over him. It is indeed on this train that he arrived in Durban from the countryside for the first time. It is the same train he has boarded on many occasions as a prisoner, deported for being in Durban without a permit. The train has also taken him, in handcuffs, when he was escorted to serve time in Emazambaneni prison. Today he is back from serving a sentence for the drugs he has neither seen nor touched in his whole life. Even now, as the train reduces speed, wailing through Rossburgh station, the bright Durban lights beckoning a distance away, Dubazana wonders aloud as to what the impenetrable darkness holds in store for him and what valleys he will be roaming by the next sunrise.

Towards midnight, the train screeches to its final stop at Durban station. He gets off, not expecting to find one to Mlazi, but before he even catches his breath at the waiting area, the last train appears. Commuters jump in and by midnight it has snaked its way to Mlazi.

At Zwelethu station, Zwelisha Dubazana gets off and, indeed, is greeted by a place that is a world apart from the glitter of the city where he boarded the train. A world set aside for blacks only: a train of shapeless conjoined houses where hordes of people sleep in congestion and do not have space even to turn. Such deplorable conditions defy the laws of humanity, health, righteousness and tradition. Since there are neither buses nor taxis in sight, he sets off on foot, resigning himself to the possibility of being mugged in this neighbourhood that teems with gangsters.

It is eerie outside. The clouds in the sky turn to bloodcurdling images, strange shapes hanging in the firmament. When he crosses the Mfongosi River the moon stares at him now and then from beneath the clouds looming over the hills. The wind suddenly begins to blow angrily, making him walk with swinging strides. He skirts through the maze of matchbox houses until he reaches Thabekhulu's home and emits a sigh of relief when he realises that the small gate is not locked. His heart throbs loudly with apprehension as he quietly tiptoes around the house, wondering whether he is going to find his wife and children still there, and if so, how will they be? Afraid of announcing his arrival to someone at this time of the night – the time of danger and witchcraft – he stands against the room where he had been sheltered before his arrest and knocks timidly on the window.

MaZondi, in her deep sleep, hears the faint knock as if from a distance and in a dream. At first it sounds like droplets of rain trickling down the window pane. She wakes, her eyes wide open, as the knock persists. She jumps to her feet, fearing to even ask who it is. She grabs the child in haste, flies to Thabekhulu's bedroom and storms inside without knocking. He has also heard the knock and his ears strain anxiously.

"Why, what's the matter?" he asks in fright.

"Someone is knocking at my window," she whispers.

Thabekhulu whispers back, "Who is it?"

"I was too afraid to ask."

The finger taps at the window again, a little louder now. Thabekhulu looks at the watch on his wrist and mutters, "Well, it can't be Dubazana at this time of night. Let us hear." He leads her as they go to her room and asks in a firm voice, "Ngubani? Who is it?"

"Yimina, it's me, Dubazana, my brother." The voice that responds is weary and defeated.

"Hawu Nkosi yami! Oh my Lord, oh my mother! Dubazana is here! I am dead today! In whose house am I going to hide?" MaZondi runs from the room and paces the passage, shivering, and decides that if Thabekhulu opens the kitchen door at the back, she is going to run out of the front door.

"It's okay then, Dubazana. Go to the front door, I will open for you," Thabekhulu says, after parting the curtain slightly to confirm that it is indeed Dubazana.

"What am I going to say about Mxolisi?" she asks in a daze as they collide in the passage.

"If he asks you, be evasive, give him incomprehensible answers."

"What do you mean: incomprehensible answers?"

"I told you that you should say his father is some man you don't know, who lied to you, and you didn't see him again," he says, leaving her behind while he heads for the door.

"I don't know how to lie, Thabekhulu, so how am I going to do it?" She shivers alone in the passage, suddenly deciding that the best option is to leave the child in Thabekhulu's bedroom for safety and first go and greet her husband innocently. As she comes out of Thabekhulu's room, her eyes fall on those of her husband, who has just sat down on the sofa in the living room. She trips and almost falls. Feeling faint and gasping for breath, she walks shakily along the passage to the living room. Dubazana's eyes are fixed on her, flooding her with guilt and scaring her away from him. She finds herself sitting next to Thabekhulu on the same sofa, both of them facing Dubazana who sits on the opposite sofa. Seeing this, Dubazana is utterly confused.

"We greet you, Dubazana," Thabekhulu says with shifty eyes. Dubazana blinks, and feeling intimidated by the walls that now look strange, is humiliated by the spectacle on the opposite sofa: two people also blinking their eyes while weakly returning his greeting. They enquire about one another's health and all say they are well. Just then the room reverberates with a sharp scream from the baby in Thabekhulu's room. Thabekhulu and MaZondi exchange quick glances, their minds in turmoil.

"It seems that MaDlamini is fast asleep and can't hear her baby crying," comments Dubazana. "Wake her up, Thabekhulu, the child shouldn't cry like this."

The two simultaneously look at him with eyes that speak volumes about their helplessness.

The baby continues screaming and his mother keeps ignoring him, wondering how long it will last. It is only when his crying becomes interspersed with bouts of choking that MaZondi jumps to her feet and runs to Thabekhulu's room. She finds the child gagging with his eyes popping, snatches him and runs back to the living room directly to his father, "Oh my God, my child's father, my child is choking to death here!" she says fanning him. "Wake up, my boy! Wake up, Thabekhulu!" She sings his clan praises to him.

While the mother tries to resuscitate her son, beads of sweat trickling down her face, Dubazana feels himself seething, his face damp with sweat. He tries to mop his face with his hands but the sweat persistently drips down it, blinding him. The baby's eyes regain their colour and he blinks them at his mother, smiling at her before crying again.

"Don't cry, baby." The child's mother sits next to Thabekhulu, retrieves her breast and suckles the child.

Thabekhulu wishes for a pit to hide in. Dubazana rubs his eyes in consternation, wipes them, opens them wide and stares at the drama unfolding in front of him as if he is dreaming. Dumbfounded, he asks, "Is this real or am I lost? Am I at the Thabekhulus where I was a tenant when I got arrested and where I left the love of my heart, my wife?"

Thabekhulu and MaZondi both drop their eyes in shame.

"I am asking, folks, and beg for an answer. If I am in the home to which I am referring, may I please see my wife, who I haven't seen in ages and have missed very much?"

Dubazana throws a fierce look that blinds Thabekhulu like lightning, causing him to stare at the floor mumbling, "You are indeed at the Thabekhulus. This is the wife you have missed." He points at her with his head.

"Thabekhulu, I heard but couldn't grasp that she called you the father of the child, whom she affectionately showered with the Thabekhulu clan's praises. Thabekhulu, I can see, but my eyes seem to deceive me by suggesting that it is really my wife who is suckling your child." His eyes glow like flames and with tears in them he barks, "Are you the father?"

"Ask his mother."

"I am asking because I saw her fetching him from your bedroom."

"She was holding him when she flew into my bedroom, startled by your knocking in the middle of the night."

"MaZondi, wife of Dubazana, mother of Makhosazana and Nkosana, whose child is it that you are suckling?"

The air is thick with tension in the house as they all scowl at each other. Tears run onto the child MaZondi is feeding.

"Don't flood me with tears, MaZondi. All I asked was: whose child it is that you are suckling?"

MaZondi swallows nothing, and stammers, "He is ... he belongs ... Please forgive me, Dubazana." More rivulets follow.

"How can you expect to be forgiven when you have not even spoken the truth? Answer me, I asked you a question!"

The answer is silence.

"Perhaps I erred in asking you about our private family matters in the living room, and, worse, in front of the landlord. Let us go and talk about this in our room ... I mean the one Thabekhulu is helping us with." He rises. MaZondi, seated and without any strength to rise, looks at Thabekhulu. As if they have arranged this beforehand, MaZondi and Thabekhulu softly cough repeatedly and simultaneously. Dubazana is extremely annoyed by this, thinking that they are communicating through some covert code. He finds himself snatching the child from his wife's arms, like a hawk snatching a chick from the wings of a hen.

MaZondi screams and gesticulates in desperation, "Dubazana, I admit I did wrong, but please, do not kill my child!"

Dubazana glares at her with fiery eyes and snarls, "Cough out the truth then to ensure I spare the child!" He stares at the baby, who looks back at him, oblivious of the battlefield around him.

"I did tell you, Dubazana, that it is my own."

"The father?" He looks at Mxolisi again, and suspects what many have suspected. "Is it Thabekhulu here?"

She sees her husband's eyes suddenly like those of a lion pouncing on its victim, and hears herself admitting, "Yes, Dubazana, it is as you've seen for yourself."

Dubazana scrutinises the child again. The child smiles at him as he had smiled at MaDlamini.

Unexpectedly, he utters: "No, God's innocent creature, how can I fight with you when you haven't wronged anyone?" Dubazana smiles back at Mxolisi before giving him back to his mother.

Deeply touched and relieved, MaZondi thanks Dubazana as she takes the child, hoping she is strong enough to remain standing and holding him.

The realisation that his family has disintegrated makes Dubazana feel weak at the knees and he collapses back onto the sofa.

"Now I understand clearly what triggered my arrest."

"It pains me too, Dubazana, that my taking you in and you two ignoring each other resulted in *me* swimming in tears. Today I am disgraced; I feel ashamed and racked by scandal," Thabekhulu explains, his eyes misty with remorse.

"I admit that mistake, Thabekhulu. When I was alone in the pit, the prison, into which you threw me, I also took stock and realised my own selfishness: I should have embraced my wife as a part of me after the incident at the shacks. My wife, may you forgive me my error of judgement," he pleads. "I wonder if you can find it in your heart to forgive me."

"A person who seeks forgiveness should be forgiven. I forgive you wholeheartedly."

"I honestly appreciate your forgiveness. My fault, however, didn't mean that you could orchestrate my arrest out of your love for each other, burying me alive, subjecting me to unspeakable atrocities and hard labour on prison farms." His fiery voice is on the verge of crying.

"As you've locked yourselves up here – the two of you and your child – where is your wife?"

Thabekhulu is lost for words. He stammers, "Apartheid, Dubazana, created a precipice in your home down which *my* family plunged into an abyss. Your arrival with an ailing marriage infected my own. My wife has left me."

"Then you took the wife of your tenant, a destitute, and helped yourself for free to the loot."

MaZondi, still hushing the child on her lap and simultaneously looking for an opportunity to escape if the need arises, does not know who to placate as the war of words between the two men intensifies. As the altercation escalates with no party relenting, the harsh words exchanged ignite sparks and the grenade explodes. The prospect of seeing himself dethroned and expelled from a fort in the form of his wife – to whom he has run for refuge from life's whirlwinds – clouds Dubazana's mind. He pounces on Thabekhulu, head-butting him like a ram in battle, as if using his fists would merely waste time. Thabekhulu's teeth rattle and he bites his tongue as he spins dizzily and collapses on the floor. Dubazana is suddenly all over him, pounding his stomach with punches as if he is kneading dough.

"Please, Dubazana, don't kill the poor person who took us in when we were homeless." Agitated, MaZondi takes the child, puts him on his father's bed and runs back to find the men still wrestling fiercely. She pounces on her husband, lunges for his eyes and squashes them. Reeling with pain, her husband bellows, "You too, MaZondi, my wife, are betraying me?"

"I am not betraying you, Makhosazana's father. I beg you: restrain yourself! Don't kill Mxolisi's father in his own house because of *our* problems." She is panting heavily as she shouts loudly, not even aware of what she is saying.

Dubazana feels his eyes burning as if they are going to explode, lets go of Thabekhulu and gropes for his wife. As swift as lightning, Thabekhulu jumps to his feet, shivering with anger. He too, for a minute, loses sight of what has happened and led to all this chaos. All he thinks of is his manhood, refusing to be humiliated by being beaten in front of a woman. In a split second Dubazana is underneath him again. Thabekhulu throttles him as he bites his bleeding lip. MaZondi, startled by her husband's amazing strength, and unaware that he is writhing to free himself from Thabekhulu's grip on his throat, charges at him too, helping Thabekhulu by pressing Dubazana down with her knee on his stomach.

"I am going to kill you, Dubazana, if you think you can insult me in my own house," Thabekhulu hisses through his teeth, allowing him to breathe a little.

"Hhawu, oh my! Even you too, MaZondi, my dear wife, betray me while I love you so much?" Dubazana chokes, his words sounding as if they come from a punctured throat.

The words find a place in MaZondi's heart and she pleads, "Please let him be now, Mxolisi's father. He no longer has the strength to fight back."

"If you both forgive me, my wife, I too will forgive you. I ..." Dubazana's voice is becoming a whisper as he stretches out and then lies down flat.

"I no longer trust him!" mutters Thabekhulu, huffing heavily and tightening his grip on Dubazana's throat.

"No, stop it, he has lost it now. He won't be able to fight back. Let go of him."

As if breathing his last, Dubazana writhes and goes silent.

"Myeke! Let go of him, Thabekhulu, I left my maiden home to marry this man!" She rises and pulls Thabekhulu by the ears. Like a man putting a stone on a hole with a mamba inside it, Thabekhulu slowly lets go of Dubazana, who is gazing at him with rapidly receding eyes. Thabekhulu stares at him in panic, springs up, then suddenly kneels and looks at him, startled, and smacks him lightly on the cheeks, asking, "What are you doing, Dubazana?"

"What is he doing?" MaZondi comes closer and gazes at her husband with eyes as wide as an owl's. She shakes him, "Dubazana! Dubazana! Hawu, Mkhululi wami, my Saviour! What is happening to me?" She falls to her knees next to him. Indeed,

Zwelisha Dubazana's eyes, at which his mother MaNkabinde had gazed lovingly just after his birth are fading; this morning, with the moon a dangling crescent over the mountains, MaZondi sees them blink for the last time and then disappear into eternal oblivion.

"Makhosazana's father! Nkosana's father! What is happening? Have you just fainted? Give me water, Mxolisi's father, to pour on his face, so that he can regain consciousness. What will I say to my mother, who is so fond of her son-in-law?"

Thabekhulu is so frightened that his heart almost stops. He fetches cold water from the fridge in a jug. They also put ice cubes on his forehead and chest. Dubazana does not stir. All their attempts are in vain. There is no truth other than the one that stares back at them: Zwelisha is gone. Like his name suggests, he has gone to a new land, to his ancestors.

"Makhosazana's father! Wake up, father of my children. Wake up, please, my beloved. Vuka!" She is kneeling beside him, pleading, "Who do you expect me to belong to, knowing that I love you, that I am yours and you are mine?" She wipes his face, lowers her head and kisses him. When she starts to cry, Thabekhulu grabs her, closes his hand over her mouth and whispers, "Be strong, Mxolisi's mother. It was just a mistake. I couldn't control my hand. I sincerely did not mean to kill him. I was just trying to defend myself."

"But why did you keep strangling him even when he had said he would forgive us if we forgave him?"

"Please don't cry. We need a plan of action. If either Nkosana or our neighbours hear you screaming, we'll land in jail. Please, be quiet." He wipes his own tears with his fingers. MaZondi breathes heavily, trying to suppress her sobs. Stupefied and in a daze, Thabekhulu lifts her up and sits her on the sofa, then sits next to her, drawing her head onto his lap, gently patting her chest and feeling her wildly beating heart. "We are jail material now. We made one little mistake and now we are undisputed candidates for the hangman's noose. No doubt about it. Dubazana is dead; I am worthless and deserve to die, but your death would create orphans with no caretaker."

"I haven't lost hope, Thabekhulu, I still believe that Dubazana has just fainted and will regain consciousness in due course."

Dubazana is still sprawled on the floor, motionless. If he were to rise and laugh with them again, that would be an improbable miracle. MaZondi, who has become a widow overnight, still rests her head on Thabekhulu's lap while the murdered one glares at her with unblinking eyes. Thabekhulu whispers weakly, "MaZondi, make him respectable by closing his eyes."

"But Thabekhulu, why should I close his eyes? Why should I?"

"I'm sorry, MaZondi, but I think he is gone."

"Where has he gone to?" She slips from the sofa and crawls towards Dubazana, sprawls out over him and runs her fingers across his face. He is becoming cold. Monotonously she moans as if there is no end to it.

"Moaning won't help us now, MaZondi. Please accept the situation and close his eyes."

"Oh, my dear Dubazana, this day has made me feel the most terrible pain for you! I wonder why I don't die right now and lie next to you." When Dubazana becomes wet from the torrent of tears falling on his face, his wife puts her hands on his eyelids. Her quivering fingers finally close all his life's chapters.

The widow rises to her feet and sways to the chair. As they hear the door in Nkosana's room open, MaZondi and Thabekhulu exchange quick glances in alarm. They simultaneously rail at him as he emerges from the room, heading for the toilet, "Go back, you!"

With extreme lethargy and in exaggerated slow motion, he retreats to the room and cautiously closes the door, his eyes fixed on them.

"It's likely this child did see," MaZondi says, breathing heavily, her mind visualising clear images of both of them hanging to death in Pretoria where prisoners are executed.

"Even if he's not certain that his father is dead, he's going to be suspicious because of your tears. Wipe them dry if you want to survive this and be around for your children," he admonishes her. She hurriedly wipes them but they persist.

"What if we turn off the lights in the house and let this boy of yours go to the toilet and then lock him in when he's back?"

They agree. Thabekhulu drags Dubazana to the dining room and then proceeds to the room in which Nkosana sleeps. He peeps inside and tells him that he can go to the toilet. And, indeed, Nkosana, who is sitting on the bed, his hand on his cheek, stands up, goes out, and walks to the toilet. He returns to the room where, as soon as he is in, the doors are locked.

"Sunrise is approaching. Let's not waste time," Thabekhulu whispers as he goes back to the room of dramas. "Take a shawl and cover him quickly, then we'll decide what to do with him."

MaZondi staggers to the room, grabs two shawls and returns, panting heavily. She covers her husband with one, and throws the other over her shoulders as a sign of respect for the deceased. Thabekhulu turns off the remaining light and sits close to MaZondi, and they conspire in hushed voices.

"There is no better plan to protect ourselves than to carry him on our backs and take him to a forest somewhere. We'll hang him so that it will look like he hanged himself before he arrived here from prison. That could work because he has no wounds. If he is found soon, before he is decomposed, the District Surgeon may not discover the truth because, after all, he did choke to death. He would just be guessing. What do you think?"

"What can I think? I have never killed a person in my life."

"That makes two of us. This is the first time. And I am not even sure if this plan I have will not trip us." It worries him that they have killed. It is dead quiet, and they are even scared by the movement of the leaves that waft outside. "There is no other way. Let me look for a cord and you can help me carry the body."

"How can I help you, because if I leave the child here he will scream like crazy? Also, it's not right to take him with me to the car and expose him to a corpse at his age."

"There's no other way. Today he will be in a car with a corpse. Besides, I don't trust you any more. If I leave you alone here, you will cry and invite inquisitive ears and land me in trouble. I would rather the child cries in the car with us." The bloodlust that one acquires after killing starts to show itself: his fiery eyes look like those of a madman. He stomps out to the garage and returns with a cord of wire. He has to switch on the light where the corpse is so that he can tie it with the wire.

"Please help me to put him in the car now."

MaZondi's shawl falls to the floor, as if in response to the task at hand, as she grabs Dubazana's legs while Thabekhulu lifts him by the shoulders. A cock crows outside, startling them and making them drop the body simultaneously.

"*Nx*, it is just a cock-crow! Give me a hand," curses Thabekhulu. They carry him out in a daze, their eyes blinded by anxiety. How heavy the body of a dead man is while it is still warm! They stagger with him to the garage and heave him into the car boot. They cautiously close the boot and hurry back to Thabekhulu's bedroom where MaZondi takes the child. She tries and fails a few times to put him on her back but he keeps slipping, almost falling to the ground. She decides to throw a shawl over him and bundles him in her arms. Then she and Thabekhulu scuttle out. Thabekhulu starts the car, his hands shaking. It stealthily glides onto the road just as the moon sinks and disappears beyond the mountains. At first Thabekhulu drives slowly, but as soon as they are away from their neighbours, he starts to move swiftly through the dark. MaZondi, who does not know Mlazi that well, and has never explored the township at night, is clueless about the direction the car takes. They end up moving out of the township, travelling through an area that is in pitch darkness, without electricity and with no sign of a lit candle. The car slows down and then veers off onto a dirt road and faces what looks like a huge black mountain. They stop near a river that glitters as it journeys down to the sea.

"Let's carry him and drop him off in the forest."

"Oh my God! Is this the forest? Are we not going to be bitten by venomous snakes?"

"They'd help to free us from the burning coals we're carrying in our hearts. Let's be quick, lest morning comes before we're done." He puts on his coat, takes a torch from the car and puts it in his coat pocket.

"Who will stay with the child in the car?"

"If we close the windows, I don't think anyone will hear him, even if he cries."

They get out of the car and lift the body. Thabekhulu breathes heavily as he tries to carry the large corpse. Off they go, with MaZondi constantly tripping over nothing, then rising, only to trip again and fall. They continue until they reach the thick forest when suddenly a light appears in front of them. Their hearts almost stop from fear. They mutter a sigh of relief when they realise that the light is just a firefly that twinkles in the dark. Dog-tired, they let the body fall.

"Hu!" Thabekhulu sighs again, takes the torch from his coat and points it at the trees. "Hold the torch for me." He gives the torch to MaZondi, raises the body and leans it against the tree. He climbs into the tree, perches on a stout branch and then asks her to help him when he pulls it up.

And indeed, he raises it. It lifts slowly while Thabekhulu grimaces, grinding his teeth as he pulls. But then the body slips and pushes MaZondi to the ground. As she falls down, it lands on her.

"Hawu Nkosi yami! What have I done, Dubazana?"

"Stop whining! You'll get us arrested," Thabekhulu barks and jumps down, livid. He again raises the body which now lies face-down on top of its wife who pushes it aside. They catch their breaths for a moment and try to work out how to execute the daunting task. MaZondi has to pull from the top of the branch. They resume the pushing and pulling, panting and groaning until there is some distance between the body and the ground. "Now you can tie it," instructs Thabekhulu.

MaZondi ties the cord and the body dangles. She climbs down to Thabekhulu, who helps her and then climbs up himself to tie the body in a manner that he hopes will not make the police suspicious. Satisfied, he too gets down and then they both lift their faces and stare at the body that dangles and sways gently, like a coat on a coat hanger on the washing line. In MaZondi's mind flash the words Dubazana spoke earlier when she helped Thabekhulu pin him to the floor: "Hawu, you too, MaZondi, are betraying me? You whom I love so much?" Her tears stream uncontrollably.

"What I'm not sure of is whether a person who has committed suicide closes their eyes or just leaves them open," Thabekhulu comments pensively, "but it looks like they pop out; after all, who would close them when the person dies?" He climbs up again and tries unsuccessfully to open them. "*Nx*," he mumbles in frustration and climbs down. He now takes the torch and scrutinises the ground in the light to make sure they do not leave any incriminating evidence behind that may lead the police to them. Satisfied, he looks at Mxolisi's mother, "Let's go now."

"Please, hang me too, Thabekhulu. I cannot leave my husband hanging alone in the darkness and the cold," she bursts out.

"MaZondi!" He hugs her. "Let's go home to discuss this and then maybe we will come back to fetch him tomorrow night."

He takes her hand and leads her away. As they walk, MaZondi keeps repeating that she wishes she could die too. "Can a lion show up here to devour me?" But it does not happen. There is only the firefly escorting them, flashing around them until they get to the car; then it moves back towards the tree from which the body hangs.

In the car, Thabekhulu scoops up the child and gives him to his mother. He starts the car and heads for the glittering lights of his home, leaving Dubazana in the darkness where blue flies will be all over him as soon as morning arrives.

"Oh God, what will I tell my children if they ask me where their father went to?" she asks as the car approaches and comes to a stop at the gate. "I entered these gates with him. Today, with my own hands, I buried my love on a tree." She pours out a torrent of tears.

16

The fear that MaZondi may become hysterical or commit suicide compels Thabekhulu to enter her bedroom. This morning MaZondi sits on the bed with her feet stretched out, her head leaning against the headboard, in tears. Thabekhulu sits next to her, holding her close. He is trying to console her, begging her not to dwell on what has happened. He feels her body shiver uncontrollably.

"Don't touch me!" She pushes his hand away.

"What have I done? Do you now loathe me that much, MaZondi?"

"Please don't touch me. As I sit here it feels like the eye that watches over all marriages is staring at me. I sit here in fear and feel as if Dubazana is sitting somewhere in this room, looking at us." Her body quivers even more.

"Let us please move to my bedroom then, to erase his image from your mind."

Though she is reluctant, he remains patiently persuasive. And her fears make her succumb and agree. He holds her gently by the hand and leads her to his bedroom where he sits her on the bed and reclines her against some pillows for comfort. He creeps closer and tries to console her, but once again, she shoves his hand away.

"What is the matter now? Are you still troubled by Dubazana's eye, even here?" he asks with a tone of deep concern.

"As I've already said, as I sit in this room, I still feel as if he is watching me. While I hear Dubazana's voice echoing in my head, crying, promising us forgiveness if we forgive him, it's as though MaDlamini's eye is glaring at me as well."

"I really don't know what else I can do for you now, MaZondi. I've exhausted all my efforts. Your tears are like shackles that imprison me; I'd prefer death to a life like this. My heart aches with pain, and *I* need a consoler next to *me*. And who else can be my consoler but a woman who loves me? But you push me away if I come close to you. I don't know who you want my soul and feelings to belong to."

Sleep eventually gets the better of MaZondi and she dozes off. Thabekhulu's cuddling and leaning against her makes him, too, fall into a deep sleep. They are still in dreamland when dawn approaches. At eight in the morning Thabekhulu is jolted from his sleep, startled.

"Argh, work!" he moans. Alarmed, MaZondi gets out of bed.

Now it is Thabekhulu's turn to experience what Dubazana felt earlier when he was worried about leaving his wife in their shack lest she commit suicide. He decides to skip work and attend to MaZondi's heartbreak.

"I'm disturbed by the fact that your son opened the door and saw his father lying on the floor," he says. "Perhaps he's aware of what happened and will tell his sister when she arrives. Try to assess how much he knows. If he acts inquisitive, tell him that the person he saw lying on the floor was a drunken visitor who had spent time with me and drank more than he could handle."

"Oh, the mistake we've made, Thabekhulu! We locked him in and forgot that he's supposed to be at school now!" It is only then that they both panic, and Thabekhulu rummages through his pockets for the key and opens the door for him.

Nkosana is sitting upright in the bed, his arms folded. Thabekhulu senses the hardening of the boy's heart as Nkosana looks at him with the fiery eyes of a wounded tiger. When the boy later walks out of the room, he glances at Thabekhulu's bedroom through the door that is ajar, and throws an accusing look at his mother who is still seated on the bed. He takes a quick bath, dresses hurriedly and leaves without asking for food or saying goodbye. Thabekhulu and MaZondi remain behind in silence, consumed with guilt.

Thabekhulu spends the whole weekend watching over the widow, nursing and consoling her. When he returns from work on Monday he finds Makhosazana at home with her recovering baby on her lap. As soon as MaZondi enters, she laments that her mother looks sick and emaciated.

"I was wondering why you didn't visit us at the hospital. Now it's clear why you couldn't."

"I wasn't feeling well, my child," she explains in a tired voice, looking at her daughter with baggy, guilty eyes.

"I've been haunted by this bad dream about Dad while I was in hospital. Have you heard from him?"

"Not at all, Makhosazana, my child." She wipes her eyes and starts fanning herself.

"Since Friday I've been dreaming about Dad standing in a dark place with his head bowed, tears in his eyes, and saying, 'Makhosazana, my child, I don't like the place where I am. Please plead with your mother to come and fetch me.'"

"Oh my God! I wonder where Dubazana is and why he isn't keeping in touch." Tears streak down her face, so she excuses herself and goes to the bathroom where she lets them pour freely.

On Tuesday the weather is cool and the sky clear. At midday Makhosazana is sitting outside on the veranda when the postman arrives at the gate and sees her. There is no need to put the mail into the mailbox, so he enters through the gate and gives her the letters. She thanks him and hastens to read the envelopes. Two are just Thabekhulu's household bills. A white one has a red prison-stamp and is addressed to her mother. Her face lights up with joy as she rushes into the house and calls, "Mama! Mama!"

"What is it, my child?" her mother asks from the kitchen.

"We were talking about Dad just yesterday as if we could sense that a letter from him was on its way. Dad's alive! Here's his letter!" She gives it to her mother with a smile.

"Oh my God, it's Dubazana!" She takes the letter and scrutinises the handwriting before opening it. It is from her husband, indeed. She walks slowly to the couch, opens the letter with shaking hands and reads it. At the top is the address of the prison where he has been serving time. The letter was written three weeks earlier. She starts reading, blinking continuously:

MaZondi, my love,

It saddens me that you haven't responded to the numerous letters that I have written to you. Perhaps it is because you don't know how much I love and miss you, or perhaps you do it to punish me for being so selfish and inconsiderate of your feelings after you were violated. I realise my mistakes all the time now whenever I think of you and ponder the pains and joys we have been through. I'm always counting the days and hours, longing for the day when I'll be released and find my way to you, to apologise and ask you to allow me to love you the way a husband is supposed to love his wife.

My soul longs for nothing else but love and peace. As I'm about to be released from jail, my wish is to travel safely until I reach you with your safe hands that will warm up my life. Upon my release, I'll start afresh and remove all the obstacles that may hinder the building of our own happy home where we will live peacefully without any fear of attack or imprisonment. The day is coming when in our marriage we will feel like excited lovers in a new relationship and our dreams will know no bounds.

Please pass my regards to my children: Makhosazana, Nkosana, and my grandchild, Sibonelo. Shelter their souls with love so that they can forget the tragedy that befell them when we were moving from house to house. Tell them I said it doesn't matter how much a person gets stuck in the tribulations of the world; even if it is death, there is only one Lord in whom they can trust, the One who created the world and all that is in it.

Goodbye then, Thuleleni, my one and only! Even if we may be separated physically, we are still one if we are connected spiritually, through which each one of us still lives for the other. I conclude my letter now and am projecting my eyes to that day when it will be as though we are meeting in a new world, shaking hands in forgiveness. Unless he who jailed me chances upon me first and kills me before we meet, in which case our reunion will be in the hands of God!

From the one who holds you in high esteem,
Your husband, Zwelisha

MaZondi spends the rest of the day in anguish, and she gives Thabekhulu the letter as soon as he arrives. What she finds most painful is that her husband has called her a safe haven and shelter that gives warmth to his life. She cannot deny that she had a hand in Dubazana's murder: she pushed him down in the abdomen when Thabekhulu was throttling him. Recalling this brings fresh washes of tears.

The days go by. Whether it is windy, freezing cold or pouring with rain, in MaZondi's heart is a feeling of empathy as if her husband is exposed to all these weather conditions; as if he is still alive and can feel pain. When there is a storm, the thunder rumbles in her thoughts and she feels its lightning deep inside her. By the time ten days have elapsed, their clothes hang loosely on her and Thabekhulu's bodies. They are most frustrated by Dubazana's son, who is hostile towards them even when they try to joke with him. He only gives them the eye of a lion that has a score to settle.

Thabekhulu, who can clearly see that all hope of living together with his estranged wife has been lost, knocks off from work one day and drives to the shops, market and butchery. He buys generously, wanting to make peace with his wife and in-laws. He drives to their home, and as they sit chatting, his wife complains that his eyes look weird, like those of a killer.

"Is Dubazana still alive, though?" she asks lightly.

"We haven't heard anything from jail," he says, but his shifty eyes betray him.

"The truth will emerge, Thabekhulu. I don't believe this fairy-tale you tell me in broad daylight that you haven't fetched me because you are still looking for a place for MaZondi. I suspect that you guys can't think straight on account of Dubazana, whose shadow you carry around wherever you go."

He quickly says his goodbyes, limps to his car and drives home, wondering along the road what further adversities fate has in store for him.

At the end of the third week after Dubazana's hanging, the nearby shack dwellers complain that the wind blowing from the forest above the Mlazi River has a foul stench. They send an alarm to the police, who reluctantly enter the forest to investigate. The one they are looking for is a terrible sight, in an advanced stage of decomposition.

They find a card on Dubazana's body, with details they use to follow the lead that eventually brings them to Thabekhulu's house.

When they report the matter to MaZondi, she behaves hysterically and rolls on the ground crying uncontrollably, bewailing her misfortunes and life's cruelties. They bundle her into the car and drive her to the government mortuary to witness the culmination of the labour in which she has had a hand. What she sees at the mortuary will haunt her to the grave.

On arriving home from work, Thabekhulu is greeted by fervent wailing, and he cannot summon the energy to face the people gathered there. The neighbours and some fellow church-goers who knew about the matter of Mxolisi's birth are murmuring that Thabekhulu must know what has happened. All fingers point accusingly at him.

"I wonder when the parents and relatives of this poor soul will ever get the message, since telegrams take so long in the rural areas?" asks an elderly woman who sits next to MaZondi with a bowed head. In front of them are lit candles placed hastily around the room to signify mourning. The woman is from the Makhathinis, who are their neighbours.

The guilt that gnaws Thabekhulu's insides makes him feign generosity and kindness in an attempt to quell suspicions: "My people, for God's sake, let me extend a helping hand. Though I know I won't be paid, let me offer my car and sacrifice my sleep; I'll go to report to them and bring them back with me so that the parents of this brother end up seeing the bones of their child. This will be the manifestation of my condolences."

"That is very manly of you, Thabekhulu!" Mthimkhulu, a bald-headed neighbour, praises him, appraising him with a suspicious eye. Thabekhulu then takes to the road with remarkable alacrity. No sooner has his car arrived back with the Dubazanas from Mangwaneni than it speeds away to fetch the Zondis from Nkumba. All of them converge at his house, which has women from the immediate neighbourhood busy with pots and keeping the gossip mill running, without bothering to be discreet. When the gossip reaches the ears of the members of the two families, one can smell an imminent fight in the air.

The funeral service for Dubazana is held on Saturday at ten at a church in Mlazi. A convoy of buses is hired, paid for by donations from the members of a human rights organisation. Therefore the church, normally used for religious services, overflows within minutes. It is filled with a mass of clenched fists, the thunderous shouting of slogans and the singing of revolutionary songs interspersed with church hymns. Thabekhulu and MaZondi, who have never imagined Dubazana being honoured with such a dignified funeral – one befitting the elite and the renowned – are newly consumed with shame and guilt, their already whithered souls shrinking even further.

"Thank you, Programme Director!" says Bhekizizwe Zulu calmly. "Most of you assume that this hall is so full today because we are only here to attend Dubazana's funeral. In fact, this funeral represents all the millions of people of this land who have passed on without smelling, even for a second, the sweet aroma of freedom. It represents those who have passed on while being regarded as nomads and strangers in all the corners of the country of their birth – in towns, farms, even in the homesteads that their ancestors left behind. An indigenous person is not considered to have lived their life to the full if they don't own a home where they can freely perform rituals and honour their ancestors in fond remembrance."

And for the benefit of the audience, Bhekizizwe elaborately recounts how he came to know Dubazana, from the time they first met after a meeting at Mbalasi, and on numerous other occasions when life's challenges made their paths cross. "There is a message, though, that this gentleman leaves behind through his death. The message is, even though those in power have tried to bury the monstrous problem that faces this country by locking us up in prisons for years; even though they load us into trucks to dump us in the wilderness to make room for their flourishing suburbs, the time is nigh when shacks will mushroom as an eyesore in cities. Just like an unsightly rash that appears unexpectedly on an arrogant person's fingers, the shacks will spiral out of control and leave turmoil and disillusionment in their wake, leading to chaos that will make Babylon look like child's play." Amidst resounding applause, he descends from the stage and hands over to Reverend Sokhela, who presides over the rest of the service with sacred dexterity.

Dubazana's brothers, Mahambehlala, Mjijeni, Calaliyaphikwa, Msobo and Masobozela, who are all tall and broad-shouldered, carry the coffin out of the hall. On their way out to the hearse, they see Thabekhulu and scowl at him with hate-filled, bloodshot eyes, making him cower away in guilt, misty-eyed. He shifts his eyes away from the coffin and the bulky brothers who are carrying it, but unfortunately suddenly finds himself face to face with his wife. She stands in front of him, tears flowing down her cheeks.

"I'm sorry, my wife," he hears himself say, choking.

"For what?"

He cannot answer.

The crisis intensifies at the graveside. When the Reverend Sokhela has finished with the dust-to-dust ritual and calls upon the deceased's close relatives to say their last goodbyes by throwing handfuls of soil into the grave, Masobozela makes matters worse by looking at the priest with inflamed eyes: "Mfundisi, we appreciate your promises about the wonderful world hereafter. Unfortunately, it seems that we are not going to see that wonderful hereafter, after burying our brother, who died under horrible conditions that defy description. He was killed by people who may be here with us, crying crocodile tears." He looks in MaZondi's direction, points at her and barks: "Wena, you, MaZondi, are going to vomit out the whole truth! As for the man with whom you conspired to carry out this abominable deed, you will have to disclose his identity so all of us can know who he is!"

MaZondi, draped in a blanket as required of a widow, feels her heart sink. Thabekhulu shrinks visibly in his black suit, looks around and thinks of running away. But that would be a big mistake since all eyes are looking at him and MaZondi. Unfortunately for the two of them, their eyes simultaneously, and as if on cue, lock with those of Nkosana, which are flaring with rage. They both blush and drop their eyes.

"Let us leave everything in God's hands!" the priest pleads in an attempt to placate the fuming Masobozela, avoiding his eyes and scanning other burial plots that are already dug up in this cemetery, popularly known as Seventeen.

A spade is extended to MaZondi, and she tries to scoop soil to throw into the grave but is trembling so much that she cannot hold it. All the soil falls off and her empty hand throws nothing into the grave. Thabekhulu has to be pulled away as he almost falls into the grave. Both their heads are spinning dizzily. The rest of the mourners, including MaDlamini, take turns throwing the soil into the grave and turn around tearfully. Then the filling up of the grave with soil starts. As spades of earth thud on top of the coffin, the hearts of Mjijeni, Calaliyaphikwa and other close relatives thud in response.

"Ngeke! No way, Nzima! Ngeke, Khondlo, descendant of Khalalempi! If we were to watch and fold our arms while our brother is buried alone and those who killed him remain behind to enjoy life, it would mean that you gave birth to weakling cowards!" says Mjijeni as he pauses from shovelling the soil and stands, shovel in hand. "Phakathi! Get in here as well, my brother's wife, and feel how it is to be buried!" He grabs MaZondi and drags her into the grave, causing her to slip and land on top of the coffin.

Now there is pandemonium and chaos. Some wail hysterically and cannot believe the scene unfolding in front of them. Some try to plead with the Dubazana brothers who seem to have lost their ears. Meanwhile Thabekhulu stands silently, transfixed, his body numbed by Calaliyaphikwa's piercing eyes.

"You too, get inside!" He points at him and takes long strides towards him.

Thabekhulu cowers and retreats back in fear, without looking around. "Ma-yeh!" he screams as he falls into another open grave into which he has reversed.

After much pleading from the crowd and admonishing from their parents, the Dubazana brothers calm down and reluctantly release MaZondi and Thabekhulu. They are dusty all over, blinking repeatedly and shrouded in guilt and disgrace as they walk away with the crowd's eyes drilling into their backs until they disappear from sight. After their departure, the burial is finalised in silence and without further drama. And thus the mound of Dubazana's grave joins many others that remain as memorials for the dead. The mourners disperse and trickle out of the graveyard. Only MaZondi's mother returns to the Thabekhulus' home as she has to accompany the devastated children back, still reeling in shock and confusion.

17

In the afternoon after the events at the cemetery, the car takes Thabekhulu and MaZondi to Isipingo beach, where he finds a quiet parking spot overlooking the sea. They sit in silence, watching the waves thundering as they break and foam. MaZondi seems to exist only as a bereaved, incessantly weeping being, and this exacerbates Thabekhulu's pain.

After a long silence Thabekhulu clears his throat, looks at MaZondi, and with a trembling voice says, "Even in my dreams, I've never seen myself being as mortified and degraded as this: hiding from people as we're doing, by virtue of me being a murderer. When we all first met, I thought I was just extending a helping hand. Today I'm a killer; I'm on the run and have left what was once my family, which has now also disintegrated." The sounds of the sea continue to roar and spill into the car. Despite the raging waves, the seagulls keep hovering above the sea. The ship that floats in the sea is a hazy blur in the distance.

Restraining herself from screaming hysterically in the car, MaZondi simply continues to cry.

"A mistake you must never make is to blame yourself and think that perhaps we're in this mess because you seduced and tempted me. Not at all. You didn't tempt me. It is just life's circumstances that have brought us here," Thabekhulu says.

"You're better off," MaZondi responds, "because even though your ship is sinking, you still have a partner that you can apologise to and be forgiven by. My situation is hopeless. I'll seek forgiveness from my partner when we meet in the afterlife. At this point, oh my God, I don't know who I belong to!" She closes her eyes.

"I have to take you in and help with caring for your children who are now fatherless because of my mistakes. There's no other way."

"I don't see that such a marriage could succeed because, as you've said, you won't be marrying me out of love but out of remorse and regret. I also don't want your wife to walk on the hot coals of homelessness as I did. Over and above all that, the truth is that we are not in love and have never been in love. Even what we did that time was just a once-off thing.

"Mxolisi's father, please take me back to where I was born. Now. I'd rather they kill me there than be a corpse in your home. You saw for yourself how the Dubazana brothers are. We are going to die now."

When dusk approaches, they are still numbed by the day's events. The conversation they have in the car is incoherent and barely makes sense. Nightfall stirs them back to reality and they slowly and reluctantly drive back to Thabekhulu's home. When they approach the house, Thabekhulu stops the car, switches off the lights, and they both scan the darkness to assess the situation. It is dark outside and there is no sign of any human being around, although the house lights are on. Thabekhulu slowly eases the car into the yard. The homeowner gets out, and timidly, like a secret boyfriend, knocks at his own front door. MaZondi's mother, MaMbhele, answers, and Thabekhulu quietly says his name. She opens the door for him, and as he enters he asks if it is safe. She warns that she cannot guarantee any safety, but as far as she knows, the Dubazana family headed straight home soon after the funeral and did not even bother to make a courtesy call, as tradition requires. The pots still brim with uneaten food that has been prepared for those attending the funeral, but no one has come. He parks the car in the garage and then he and MaZondi walk in to face the harsh realities of their lives.

"I had to release the women who were accompanying me, my children, because I was eager to talk to you," whispers MaMbhele as she sits with Mxolisi on her lap in the lounge. "Please tell me the whole story from the beginning to the end. What is going on?" They tell the story as it is, but deny killing anyone. According to them, Dubazana has hanged himself. MaMbhele listens to them with empathy. They put their heads together and conclude that the best thing is to forfeit sleep. The car has to be on the road early so that MaZondi and the children can be at Nkumba by sunrise.

They pack and load the car in haste and silence. The grief they are going through, but cannot vocalise, can be read from the tears running down the faces of the grandmother, the mother and the grandchildren. Finally the car makes its way towards the Nomandamfu mountains near MaZondi's home, and the Mkhomazi, which, it is said, a mere breeze can cause to overflow, and the Pholela River.

MaZondi has acquired a permanently surly look, and the comments doing the rounds in the community disturb her and give her sleepless nights. Her story is on everyone's lips in the village and has become a regular line when people meet: "MaMbhele's daughter, who committed the unthinkable crime of murdering her husband in Durban ..." She is regarded as a bad influence on the local youth, and must be avoided like a deadly plague. Her energy has dissipated under the weight of hunger and poverty that force her and her children to go to sleep on empty stomachs almost every night.

Dubazana's death and her sudden flight from Mlazi with the children in the middle of the night mean that they cannot attend school for the rest of the year. When the following year finally starts she makes sure that they register at a school. Nkosana reluctantly attends for a couple of months before completely losing interest, and then he just stops going. It feels as though grief is no longer simply chewing MaDlamini, but grinding her with a deep hunger. What oppresses her spirit above all is that Nkosana is always quiet and obstinate. Trying to cheer him up does not help as he simply bites his lips and avoids eye contact with her.

Her mind is always wandering, always in a daze, haunted by Dubazana's shadows that she keeps seeing, day and night. Sleep is kept away by her bad dreams and nightmares, and the image engraved on her mind of her husband sprawled on the ground. The moments when she and Thabekhulu helped each other hang him while he kept slipping are grotesquely vivid in her mind. Most disturbing for her in Nkumba, and also for Thabekhulu on the other side of the mountains by the sea, is the memory of the firefly that followed them when they left the forest, and that hovered over them as they reached the car, until they both swatted it away. To this day, it still hovers over them, day and night, and makes them both gesticulate with their hands, swatting at nothing. She cries in her sleep, pleading with Dubazana to forgive her. She is overcome with hunger, thirst and cravings. She is hungry all the time, but not for food: for love. She thirsts for a comforting voice to water her parched soul that craves consolation. She longs for someone with whom she can share the secrets that burn like a raging fire in her chest. The only person she has is Thabekhulu. She hopes that if they can listen to one another, the furnace in her heart may abate. It is not love that makes her miss him and crave his presence; it is simply because they are partners in crime and, like birds of a feather, have to flock together.

Thabekhulu is drifting in the same boat, haunted by the same nightmares as MaZondi. He wails all night, kicking the air and screaming, "Dubazana, please don't strangle me." He loses sleep and gradually also loses weight because the neighbours keep pointing fingers at him. The home that was once made cosy by the presence of his wife and children, even though the latter were usually away at school, is now cold and empty. He can feel how cold it is when he is left alone in it: when he enters, it feels as if he is entering the mortuary where Dubazana's corpse was kept. When he gets into his bed, though it is expensive and covered with fine linen, it feels as if he is climbing onto a mortuary shelf.

His wife has found work as a saleslady in an upmarket clothing boutique in town, and is renting a room in a house in Mlazi, in a section of the township far from his house. This renting arrangement does not sit well with Thabekhulu, and the fact that his children are crammed into a room with their mother disturbs him. Worse, his children are now afraid of him and refuse to have anything to do with him because of the murder rumours that have spread like wildfire. He did try to find shelter for his soul in MaDlamini's heart, but realised that it had become overgrown with thorns from her many disappointments and heartbreaks. The well of water with which she used to quell the flames in his heart has long dried up. Instead of offering solace, MaDlamini showers him with stinging words, preaching to him about the unforgivable sin of murdering an innocent person. Her threatening words have made him afraid of her, and now he avoids her and keeps his distance, like the sun does in winter.

On a certain Saturday, early in the afternoon, Thabizolo Thabekhulu is sitting by himself in the house watching sport on television when his parents arrive, driving a brand new car. Although he feels like running away when he sees them, they have given him such a fright that he has no strength to rise from the sofa, so he remains glued to his seat. His father, who is tall like his son, bald, light skinned and sturdy, cuts an imposing figure as he towers in the door and knocks authoritatively. The son gets up, rubs his hands timidly and invites them in. His mother, MaMgobhozi, who is younger than her husband, light in complexion and wearing a sky-blue skirt and a matching coat, sits down. She looks at her son and her eyes are soft with tears. When they have exchanged greetings with their son, the parents waste no time, and they flood him with questions. They enquire about his wife and the children, Thabethule and Thabisile. Thabekhulu mumbles some incoherent excuses.

"Mntanami, my child," says his father, "there's nothing that reduces a person to a nonentity more than lies. You know very well how much I emphasised living for the truth in the many lessons that I taught you. All this time, you haven't told me that your marriage has disintegrated, that your wife and children have become homeless and sleep in the wild, while you're hogging this whole house for yourself! This is the behaviour of a scoundrel!" The father looks at his son, sizing him up from head to toe to head. The discussion intensifies and it appears that Thabethule and Thabisile, who have recently completed their matric, have written their grandparents a letter informing them about the disintegration of their family and their living in rented rooms. The grandparents have responded and also written a letter to their daughter-in-law seeking clarity.

"The part that broke my heart," says his mother, opening her handbag and pulling out a letter in MaDlamini's handwriting, "is where it says you have chased away your wife and are now living with a widow who was already cradling our grandchild when her husband died. And there are suspicions that you had a hand in her husband's death. My child, you know how much the people of Ladysmith respect us and expect our children to be exemplary in the community, in line with what your father and I have been preaching. How dare you disgrace us by killing a creature that God loved and made in his image?"

Thabizolo's eyes moisten and he vehemently denies having had a hand in the murder. He elaborates on the matter and explains from start to finish how the Dubazanas came into their lives and ended up living with them. He owns up to the incident that resulted in Mxolisi's birth and emphasises that they had named him Mxolisi because they were regretful and were asking for forgiveness.

The parents, who refuse to hear a word about the marriage falling apart, become restless, get into their car and head for Chesterville to put their heads together with Thabizolo's mother-in-law. No sooner have they returned than they herd their son into the car so he can show them where his wife and children are renting a room.

The car combs through the township, since Thabizolo is not sure of the direction and keeps changing his mind when they think they have reached the destination. He eventually directs them into the badly overgrown yard of a four-roomed house that has not seen paint in a long time. It is one of the houses that face the shacks. Its owner has retired to the countryside, and left it with a son who is renting it out as a whole. The son is always drunk from imbibing home-brewed concoctions and in the evenings his eyes are blind when he retires to the hovel-like shack he built in the yard.

They knock and the dining room door is opened by a woman as thin as a toothpick, shabbily dressed in a fading black skirt and jersey. She asks who they are looking for and then directs them to walk through the dining room she rents as her bedroom and into the smaller room that MaDlamini occupies. They walk through the maze, struggling to find space for their feet. The room teems with grown-up girls who are cradling the grandchildren of the woman and her husband sitting on the bed opposite them. He has beer bottles on the tiny table in front of them. The man scowls at them, his eyes appraising the fashionable clothes they are wearing. The woman leads them through a passage and shows them the door to a room where she knocks, and MaDlamini's face appears.

"Visitors for you!" says the woman irritably, then returns to her own misery.

"Hawu, my God! Mama and Baba, who am I to be visited by you?" MaDlamini looks around the room, but there is no space to sit. There is a bed, and a tiny cupboard next to it. On top of the cupboard lies a Bible. A table stands against the wall, laden with pots, dishes and a Primus stove.

Thabisile gets up to give them space on the bed. They exchange greetings. MaDlamini's response is tears. Her daughter, who has grown into a young woman, light skinned and closely resembling her parents in looks, joins her mother in weeping. This touches a soft nerve in her grandmother and tears also trickle down her face.

"I don't like to see you crying like this, my grandchild. Take the keys and go and sit in the car while we talk here." Her grandfather gives her the keys.

"Bantabami," he says, "it should be obvious to you that you're heading for a catastrophe on account of the kind of life that you're leading. Under these conditions, my daughter-in-law, how do all of you sleep?"

"Oh, Baba, we try and make do," MaDlamini says, rubbing her eyes. "My daughter and I sleep on the bed, my son sleeps on the floor."

"And a son of mine tosses and turns a thousand times all by himself in a house that is supposed to be a home to all of you. Well, today I'm not here to discuss the prevailing accusations and offences. All I can do, daughter-in-law, is request that you join us tomorrow at your house so that we can put our heads together, all of us: your mother and your siblings whom we recently met before coming here. They are also willing to come, and we will fetch them tomorrow for the meeting."

MaDlamini agrees and busies herself with offering them tea and biscuits she brought from town. After they have drunk and are done, they say their goodbyes and release Thabisile from the car.

On their way out they pass through the congested kitchen, which is also rented out. On the small steel-framed bed sits a very dark, short man aged about sixty, with sunken cheeks and bloodshot eyes, as thin as a stick. He is severely short of breath. Next to him sits an eighteen-year-old girl, also very skinny with sunken cheeks and eyes. On her lap is a naked, motionless, five-year-old-boy. MaDlamini explains that she apparently fell pregnant with him at the age of thirteen in the shacks opposite, where she suffered the same fate as Makhosazana. This man – Msulele Mbanjwa – took in the girl-child who was not only pregnant, but also an orphan whose parents had been gunned down in front of her. She has become his live-in partner. What is not clear is where they all contracted the HIV/Aids virus. A sobering truth is that while the virus flows up and down the blood of these three, it is also ravaging Mbanjwa's two wives back at home, and many others who have been incised with the same razor blade of the traditional healer who was trying to heal them.

When the Thabekhulus walk past the three, Thabizolo's father instinctively takes a 20-rand note from his pocket and gives it to Mbanjwa. Mbanjwa does not utter a word. He accepts the money, raises his hands as if in supplication and then resumes his non-stop coughing. After getting into the car, they turn around and leave, still trembling.

"Thabizolo, my child," his father says, eyes fixed on the road, "when you see that child dying with another child and her grandfather, what do you feel as a parent who has a daughter the same age as that one, and renting in the same wilderness with her mother?"

The answer is a cough, swallowing at nothing, coupled with some incoherent mumbling.

The following morning sees the family holding an animated discussion of Thabizolo's case. Thabizolo's and his wife's comments have a sting that is underlain by a love that has become bruised and blotted. It has bruises because Thabizolo is now referring to MaZondi as "Mother of boy" and blots because he has taken a man's life – worse, killing him to snatch his wife away. While Thabizolo denies having done that, he apologises wholeheartedly regarding the child, and he places his hands on his chest for emphasis. Despite the hopelessness of the situation, the parents continue some desperate patching up until MaDlamini softens. She promises to return home in an attempt to rekindle their relationship, provided they are both going to produce evidence in the form of doctors' letters that they are not tainted by the virus.

"This is not just you saying that, my child," muses her father-in-law, "but the dictates of our times and people's lifestyles require it."

They eventually part ways. Thabekhulu's father and mother return to Ladysmith, clinging to the hope that their son's family can be resuscitated despite the doubts they have about their son's HIV status.

Having fully grasped the torture of being a hermit in his own house, Thabekhulu goes to the doctor first thing the next morning for a blood test. He is asked to come back at a later date for the results. He is nervous, but to his jubilant relief, he tests negative.

He returns home in high spirits to quickly freshen up before going to town to show his wife that he is as fit as a fiddle and has proof of a clean bill of health. He stops in front of the house and goes to his bedroom to find something more decent to wear when he hears sounds of movements in the backyard outside. He briskly walks to the kitchen door and opens it. He grimaces as if electrocuted. His eyes pop out wide like an owl's. He is greeted by the sight of MaZondi and her daughter Makhosazana who are sitting on empty cool drink crates, both holding their sons, Mxolisi and Sibonelo. When they see him recoil in shock to see them, they respond by giving him blank, vacant stares.

"Come in, people," Thabekhulu beckons stiffly. Gradually his mind adjusts and a broad smile spreads over his face.

MaZondi and her daughter's once-light faces now have very dark complexions, having been roasted by the harsh rural life and the smoke from cooking with open fires in the absence of electricity. It is unclear whether they are showing their teeth because they are smiling or grimacing. They stir their children from sleep, make them stand and drag them along into the house. While Thabekhulu closes the kitchen door, the four make their way into the lounge. MaZondi enters but suddenly recoils, apprehensive about sitting down. The vivid image of her husband sprawled on the floor looms large in front of her.

"Oh my Lord!" she mumbles, sitting down, embarrassed that her daughter is staring at her, puzzled. Thabekhulu comes in and sits opposite her. They are face to face for the first time since Dubazana's funeral, and they look at each other with glowing eyes that flicker like the firefly haunting them both. He greets them with the calmness of a person greeting a widow for the first time since she has lost her husband. They enquire about one another's health. "There isn't much of a life in us, Thabekhulu. As you see me here, I've brought Makhosazana and her child to the hospital. My grandchild, see how frail he is, is not well at all." Her hand whisks the firefly off.

The news that they are visiting the hospital and that their stay is temporary is a great relief for Thabekhulu, even though it means another delay to the reunion with his family. However, the relief proves short-lived, because as soon as Makhosazana is told she can put the children to bed, her mother starts prodding him with questions.

"Where is MaDlamini, and won't she chase us out if she finds her house filled by us?"

Thabekhulu explains that his wife is not back home yet.

"The thing is, Thabekhulu, now that my family has performed a cleansing ritual for me and I've stayed with my children and watched them starve, I've realised that the only solution is to return to Durban and look for a job. My request to you, my brother, is to help me get a place where I can find shelter. It can be a chicken-run, a pigsty or an outside room, I no longer mind. Please ask around if there's a room to rent." She looks at him timidly. Slowly a tear forms in her eye, later to be joined by others in two wet lines on her face. Thabekhulu looks at her and is consumed with pity.

"And your other son, Nkosana, where did you leave him?" he asks, swatting a firefly.

"We left Nkosana because we no longer saw the need to bring him to Durban; he's become a monster and no longer goes to school." She begins to wail.

Thabekhulu is the only person to whom she can truly and fully pour out her heart for sympathy, because back home when she speaks of her hardships she only receives sarcastic remarks that she is a hypocrite who has murdered her husband. Her heart and soul thirst for empathy, love, care, and solace.

"Don't cry, Mxolisi's mother. I don't like Makhosazana to see you weeping like this. Please get up so that we can get into the car and discuss this away from the children."

"Who is going to watch over Makhosazana while we are gone, since it is not safe here?"

"As I have explained to you, it *is* safe here. Just tell her that we are going to the shop."

"May I first take a bath? I'm sweaty; we've been on the road since dawn."

She gets up, fetches their bags from outside, takes a bath and changes into other clothes, the clothes that Dubazana once bought her. But now she looks pathetic in them because they hang loosely since she has lost weight. Thabekhulu leads the way and she follows him out after she has told Makhosazana that they are going to the shop. He opens the door for her and the car moves smoothly out of the yard, soft music playing in the background. They leave the nosy neighbours watching, staring in amazement, and others moving from house to house spreading the latest gossip, obviously embellishing it.

The car leaves the township and heads for town. It drives along the beach until it ends up in the suburb of Mhlanga and parks in front of the luxurious Cabanas Hotel. The two of them enter a glitzy foyer, then pass through to the restaurant where Thabekhulu shows her where they are going to sit so that they can talk in a relaxed environment. A white lady clad in a crisp waiter's uniform welcomes them warmly and asks them what they would like to eat. Thabekhulu suggests a meal for the gluttonous: the buffet, where one can eat to one's heart's content. Cutlery and condiments are there in front of them, and with diners serving themselves, Thabekhulu and MaZondi are spoilt for choice. They can simply take a plate and help themselves to any and all of the mouth-watering offerings or point at the steaks or cold meat and roasts which are dished out to them in generous portions.

"I ask, MaZondi, that for the time being you just forget everything that has happened in your life and in those of other people that you know, and focus on this place here and its pleasant ambience. Look at how carefree the elderly white couples seem to be. It doesn't mean that, old as they are, they've never encountered any of life's tragedies. Perhaps they have been through worse calamities, and to them bad experiences are not the end of the world but lessons that help them avoid past pitfalls." He says this because she does not seem to be brightening up. "They don't dwell on their painful past mistakes but thrive on their dreams and hopes for the present and the future."

"But Dub ... I mean Thabekhulu, besides my thoughts about what has happened, I've never been to a place like this in my entire life. The only walls I know are the ones in the bundu, and the four-roomed township houses in which we've been tenants and, of course, the shacks. I've never set foot in a place like this, not even for a stolen glance."

Thabekhulu patiently tries to put her mind at ease and overcome the disorientation that overwhelms her. He nurses her along, even through her fear of chewing in front of white people. She is eating shyly and wiping her mouth repeatedly. What makes her feel uneasy is that in the huge restaurant there is not a single black person dining, except for the two of them. The only black people there are staff members such as chefs, their assistants and waiters. She only relaxes when the white people seated next to them leave, and the restaurant has just a trickle of diners at the remaining tables. She even gets up to go and have a second helping.

When they have had their fill, they leave. Thabekhulu parks the car near the beach, where they step out and he leads her by the hand until they are sitting on a rock where they talk as they watch the breaking waves in front of them.

"Mxolisi's mother ..."

"Yebo, Thabekhulu."

"Today I ask that you once again tell me the name that your parents gave you."

MaZondi throws him a glance. "Why?"

"I'll explain to you when you have told me."

"Oh well, okay, even though I'm no longer used to being addressed by it: I'm Thuleleni."

"And I'm Thabizolo."

"I remember it, even though I'll never use it. At home I was taught that you address your baby's father by your first baby's name. Well, because it sounds nice, may I try it just once?" Her head scarf flutters as she waits for a response.

"Say it."

She counts the syllables, saying, "Tha-bi-zo-lo, One-who-rejoiced-yesterday. Your parents named you appropriately and you followed your name."

"Why is that so?"

"Because ever since you met me, the happiness within you and in your household has been a thing of the past."

"If that is so, then you're the one who is going to make the happiness of the past become the happiness of the present and the future."

MaZondi lowers her eyes in shyness and does not know how to respond. She stutters in prevarication, "Oh dear, but you're married, and I even know your wife?"

"A marriage between two people should survive, even after a rough patch. It shouldn't be comatose indefinitely, as is the case with my marriage to MaDlamini."

MaZondi feels a pleasantly cool breeze brushing over her and she melts inside. There on the rock at the beach, they embrace tightly and kiss on the promises of being friends and lovers through love and life's struggles. Even when they get up, they have their arms around each other. The breeze caresses them and gently blows MaZondi's head scarf and skirt.

The car, bursting with the melody of soulful music, takes to the road and heads back to Thabekhulu's house. They are somewhat reserved now, their minds imbibing the music which is interrupted by spasms from their pounding consciences. They reach home and dawdle around, gathering courage for the daunting task of opening the door to MaDlamini's bedroom. Eventually, they both enter the bedroom as Mxolisi's father and Mxolisi's mother and, for the first time, as lovers.

"Whose doctor's note is this?" asks MaZondi, as she stands looking at the piece of paper lying on top of the wardrobe with its huge mirrors.

"It's mine."

"But it looks recent?"

"That's true, I recently went to the doctor for a routine check-up. Well, as you can see, it says I have a clean bill of health and I am HIV-negative."

MaZondi smiles warmly and says, "That's great. As for me, as you know, I did blood tests and the results were also negative."

Thabekhulu jokingly says, "The only virus that we have is the virus of the heart."

The now chronically ailing marriage between Thabekhulu and MaDlamini, and the effort to save it, which is the reason for the doctor's note on the wardrobe, finally collapses.

18

The smoke that has been seething for years, fanned by winds from all directions, eventually erupts into flames that engulf the whole country. The laws keeping the nation trapped in designated areas called reserves unravel. Floods of people swamp the cities, and there is a mushrooming of the makeshift shelters that are people's pathetic dwellings. With hope fading and people harbouring both despair and anger, what spirit of unity there was dissipates and factions develop. The haves and the have-nots become enemies and, in frustration, turn on one another. The prevailing grief and desperation confuse people, making them align themselves with various political formations that have constitutions and procedures that they hardly understand. Inevitably, they clash, and the country is ruled through fire and bloodshed. You have never heard such wailing! The nation is at war, steeped in blood and burning in flames, and the situation is dire; the smell of burning human flesh seems to plead to the Creator for intervention. Hope for the future turns to ashes, and children disintegrate into mobs of mentally scarred youth who will put the future of coming generations in peril. At this point, hope is, on the one hand, placed on the shoulders of those who have gallantly and tirelessly fought against the apartheid system through negotiations and, on the other hand, it is at the mercy of those who are trigger-happy and want to keep the country in flames.

Thabekhulu and MaZondi have thought about the situation, whose impact they feel deep within themselves. They want to apologise to the community for their own misdeeds by serving it. They intend opening a new chapter in their lives: their lives will no longer be their own, but belong to the nation instead.

"Though we have also suffered in the pits of life in the past, we need to remember, and seek forgiveness from Dubazana by working for peace."

MaZondi wipes her eyes endlessly. "Thabekhulu, let us also ask God to give us strength. Let us be one family, in accord with the next generation who are going to be the bridge of peace between the old way of flames and the new one of peace." They fall on their knees and pray.

Despite being part of a community that was born and raised under mind-boggling conditions, they try to keep their promises to start a new life. Now that Thabekhulu has a constant companion in MaZondi, he decides to join a new church whose members do not know him, to avoid the tongue-lashing and gossiping that awaits them at his old church. He becomes a member of a church in the township under the leadership of a Reverend Langa in whom they confide snippets of their life's story. The priest listens attentively and is shocked by yet another example of the atrocities the oppressive system has inflicted on people. When Langa, who has locked himself in the church's office with the couple, swamps them with prying questions, they choose to dilute the truth with lies. Thabekhulu makes the excuse that MaZondi's staying with him is a temporary arrangement because she became a widow while she was a tenant in his house, and it would be cruel to throw her and her children into the streets.

"As I have explained, Mfundisi, we have never been lovers. What happened was a mistake. Meanwhile, her husband had been arrested for selling drugs and sentenced to years in prison. Undoubtedly, he was heartbroken and disappointed with his wife and perhaps on his release he didn't want to arrive at my place and find her cradling that child. And Mfundisi, he committed suicide."

Reverend Langalamalanga Langa, a tall sturdy man of medium age, light in complexion, curly haired and sporting a neatly groomed beard, looks intently at them from behind his spectacles. He removes and wipes them, then puts them on again.

"How did he commit suicide?"

"He was found hanging on a tree, just above Mlazi River."

"Oh my!" groans the priest, placing his hands on his cheeks.

MaZondi's eyes moisten and then she breaks down and weeps.

"My wife," Thabekhulu explains, "finds it annoying that I provide shelter to a widow who is the mother of my child."

"My people, let us not look at what annoys her through *our* eyes, but let us look at it through *her* eyes. Let us say, if what happened to you had been the other way around, if Dubazana had a child with your wife, and Dubazana was a widower and your wife asked you to take him in, would you do it?"

Thabekhulu clears his throat, his eyes shifty.

"What do you have to say?" Langa gently nudges him.

"Well, you know how the saying goes, Mfundisi: 'Two bulls can never rule in one kraal'. A man such as Dubazana should build his own home and not expect another man to build it for him, or to have the wife pleading his case."

"Do you imply that your wife made no contribution towards building your home?"

Thabekhulu blinks repeatedly and swallows, "Mfundisi, why do you not sympathise with me when I have owned up to my guilt?"

"I'm not unsympathetic, my brother, but I want it to be clear to you that the way to the Holy Kingdom of the Lord is straight and does not diverge. There are no obscure shortcuts that lead to it but only straight paths that are in the clear for all to see. Thabekhulu, do you know what it is to enter the Kingdom of Heaven through shortcuts? That is turning to the Lord, abandoning MaDlamini and leaving her destitute while she still loves you and cries out aloud over you in the wilderness." He turns to MaZondi: "Had you been Thabekhulu's wife, would you have allowed him to shelter his child's mother in your house?"

"Mfundisi, the answer beats me; I wouldn't have allowed it."

"That means, according to us earthlings, that the actions of your wife are forgivable, Thabekhulu."

"Of course, Mfundisi, because we can't expect her to accept something that we both agree is intolerable; that we wouldn't tolerate. I love my wife, Mfundisi, and I can't divorce her willingly. She is the one who must file for divorce against me. I have pleaded with her and will continue to do so. All I would like the reverend to understand is that both my heart and MaZondi's crave some shade under which we can find righteousness, peace and forgiveness. We have both searched in vain for it. Our actions – in the hearts of the people who know us – were interpreted as soiling the trees under whose shade we'd found respite. As you see us here, we're despised by the community. As you see us here, we are splattered with insults and are seen as skunks by other people. We accompany each other, not because we are bound together by ways of the flesh, but rather by the weariness of our souls. My soul has a place in this poor woman's heart. She nourishes my soul that hungers for righteousness and she quenches my soul's thirst for forgiveness. The heart that has lost hope, finds it. Her soul is water to me; she is the food and shelter of my soul. All this merges to form the love that brings me closer to God. Her leaving would be the death of me."

"Which means that, if truth be told, had you been married by customary law, you would have taken MaZondi as a second wife?"

"Mfundisi, a regiment of men who are my age is divided into two battalions. The one is for the hunters and the other is for the protectors. The one for the hunters takes a lot of wives because when they see a woman they chase after her and, if she agrees, they marry her and leave her at home, then go back to hunting. My heart is that of a protector and provider. We have ended up in this situation because I was trying to protect her from pain. Even now I'm asking for an opportunity for us to help each other. To answer your question, Mfundisi, if I could follow my wishes, I'd marry her, indeed."

"Well, if you say that you are connected spiritually and not merely living together in sin, then I accept your words."

"What we ask for, Mfundisi," Thabekhulu wipes his eyes, "is to be given an opportunity to worship the Lord and to seek His forgiveness through working for Him and His nation. In my mind I have a revelation, Mfundisi."

"What sort of revelation?"

"A revelation that tells me this: even though the manner in which we met was wrong, if I don't desert her, but, as you have said, we admit the mistake and learn from it, stay together, and ask the Creator for inner peace, we will die peacefully if we die in the warm embrace of His mercy."

The priest looks at them, removes his spectacles and wipes them, "Well, although I'm a shepherd, I'm not a judge of the Lord's flock. If you have personally asked to enter into His House, the Lord Himself says, 'Let the children come to me, don't obstruct them, for the Kingdom of Heaven is for the likes of them.' By dedicating yourselves with your hearts, He will use your hearts to win others over. Perhaps through His power, your good works will reconnect you with your wife, and you will deserve her kindness and forgiveness."

They leave in high spirits, free of the cumbersome burden that has been stifling their souls.

"In the last letter that Dubazana wrote before he passed on, he said, 'My soul craves nothing else in the world except love and peace.' May love and peace be the inheritance that he left behind for our hearts to feast on," says MaZondi as they get into the car and hurry home.

They do not waste time. Their entry into organisations for community upliftment starts with their joining existing ones in the church and establishing new ones with the priest. Funds for the unemployed and impoverished are established. The elderly, some of them destitute, receive handouts in the form of soup and other meals. A church choir is formed, and in time it records gospel songs that become instant hits in the community. The choir's popularity plays a crucial role in the canvassing campaigns that they conduct from church to church, encouraging their members to support the cause. This proves such a success that eventually the funds no longer belong to one church but serve as a pool from which all congregations benefit. What a splendid duo MaZondi and Thabekhulu make when they sing, standing alongside one other, their voices filling the ear with heartrending songs that bring standing ovations and make audiences ask for more!

For a long time, when MaZondi roamed the streets with Dubazana, moving in and out of rented rooms, permit and pass laws restricted her from being employed. Incapacitated as she was, and unable to make a contribution to the wellbeing of her husband and family, she ended up being seen as intellectually inferior. Yet she had been to school in her youth and had passed Standard Nine, an impressive feat. She discusses this with Thabekhulu, and he organises a job for her in a bank where she becomes a tea lady. This removes the mist and the dust that have clogged her mind, and she is encouraged to study privately and get her matric – which she does. Before long, she is sitting among black and white colleagues as a bank teller, serving the long queues of customers who come to bank thousands of rands. Having tasted the sweet nectar of success, she studies further towards a qualification in bank administration.

MaZondi has succeeded despite tough obstacles. Soon after she had started to work, Thabekhulu's parents came to the house and pleaded with their son to break up with her. With tears rolling down his face, their son held firm and reiterated the words he had told the priest. His parents washed their hands of him and stormed away back home.

Another obstacle has been Nkosana, her son: she loses sleep over him and has failed to find a solution. Though he was no longer attending school, she still sent him pocket money through her mother. When she visited her parents' home, he behaved as though she had expelled him from home, and he would only return when she was gone. She did not know how to apologise to him: as soon as she opened her mouth to talk things through, he would give her his back and leave. She has prayed about this. She almost lost her mind over it, and sometimes found herself thinking aloud and talking to herself like a lunatic. The last straw was when she received reports that he had disappeared from home and had been seen boarding a taxi to Pietermaritzburg. Two years have passed without any sign of him, despite many searches.

Nevertheless, the army of peace soldiers trudges on steadfastly. MaZondi and Thabekhulu are now collaborating with other activists, black and white, coloured and Indian, such as Bhekizizwe Zulu, the teacher, Mr Donda, Reverend Mbambo, Reverend Pienaar, and many others. Their battle spreads to centres that feed street children flocking around the city. The reasons for their homelessness are as wide-ranging as the diverse backgrounds of the children themselves. There are those whose parents have been murdered in prisons for fighting the oppressive system imposed by the country's rulers. Others are homeless because the government's laws have caused the loss of people's culture and customs. Some are orphans whose parents were smeared by allegations that they were defectors, sell-outs and spies during the struggle against apartheid.

Of course, some people have paid with their lives for the atrocities they have inflicted on their own people. Others have been killed for their homes, cars or just for being themselves.

Funds are established for victims of other tragedies, for example, the fund spearheaded by Makhosazana for people ravaged by the scourge of Aids, and for the orphans that result from it. With MaZondi's and Thabekhulu's work now succeeding and flourishing, those who have disparaged them are chastened. And those who hoped they would be down and out are disappointed and have to eat humble pie.

Despite their successes in salvaging people in the community from a range of hardships, Thabekhulu has a nagging feeling of sadness in his heart. The renting-life lived by his wife distresses him. Even though she is now renting space in a big house owned by an elderly widow, he feels guilty, because he and MaZondi are monopolising her home. He discusses it several times with MaZondi, who appreciates that it is unacceptable. At work she has successfully applied for a loan to build her own house. But as is usual in the township, she battles to find a site. She then approaches a company of developers that is to start building houses and, of course, sell them at exorbitant prices.

They are discussing this matter on a Saturday evening that is marked by fiercely blowing July winds, when the sting of Thabekhulu's collapsing family pierces him yet again. The phone rings and continues incessantly until he answers. It is his wife calling him in tears and urging him to please hurry over at once.

"Yini, what has happened, MaDlamini?" he asks, out of breath.

"My child is dying! They've stabbed Thabethule! He is sprawled here on the ground. Please hurry and take him to hospital before he dies here!"

"What's the matter … what happened?"

"My child is dying!" The phone cuts out.

In a daze, he looks around for the car keys. Upset, MaZondi asks, "What is happening?"

"My child, Thabethule, has been stabbed! Where are my keys?" He finds them in the pocket of his pants and rushes off.

"Why would they stab my child?" Thabekhulu asks himself as he runs out of the car, leaving the door to slam itself shut. He stops in shock when he hears the wailing and screaming of people who are running about, trying to restrain a young man who is brandishing a blood-dripping bush knife, all the while screaming and quivering with anger, "I want both him and my fiancée dead! I sweated blood to make ends meet and pay lobola for her, meanwhile she has a boyfriend staying in the room with her!"

"They are not lovers, my son!" cries the girl's mother in the dark.

"Who can I trust if my fiancée is locked up with another man in the same house? Even during the day, I sometimes find them together in the house, all smiles. I've told you many times to leave but you refuse because you just can't part with the fiancée of the stupid man that you think I am!"

MaDlamini explains: "As you can hear for yourself, Thabe-khulu, that's why my son has to die. He and the girl are not even lovers. He's dying because he doesn't have a place to call his home." A police van drives by down the street, and on seeing it, the fiancé bolts. "Help me carry Thabethule to the car, and save him," MaDlamini says.

Some who have gathered in the yard help Thabekhulu to lift the boy and put him in the car where he lies on the back seat, his mother holding his head on her lap. He is bleeding severely, with blood flowing down over his spine.

"My poor child, Thabisile, must not remain behind. I'm not leaving without her. Let her get in the car and then we go," says Thabekhulu.

"Drive away, Thabethule's father. Thabisile isn't here. A boy who was armed with a weapon was trying to rape her but was caught by her boyfriend. The boyfriend has taken her to live with him at his home."

"But without having paid a cent for lobola?" Thabekhulu grumbles.

"It became obvious that since we no longer have a home, her boyfriend's home is the safest place for her to hide."

Thabekhulu starts the car with trembling hands and they head for the hospital.

"Now my heart bleeds for my children. You didn't even bother to tell me that my daughter has moved in with a boyfriend. She may easily get pregnant just because the boy finds her an easy picking," fumes Thabekhulu, staring at the road through the darkness.

"This is what happens, Thabekhulu, when a man is preoccupied with saving other men's families while neglecting his own. While he's busy rescuing others, his own family's situation runs out of control. And the Thabisile that you are talking about is already pregnant as we speak and is due any time now."

When Thabethule regains consciousness, he is greeted by life-support machines in hospital, but he will never stand up and walk again: he is crippled and will need a wheelchair to move around.

When MaDlamini realises that her home and family have been destroyed, she chooses to continue moving around, renting with her helpless invalid.

Thabekhulu returns to his house, his soul in bondage. He feels the guilt in his heart; the same heart about which he has remonstrated with the priest until the veins stood out on his face, declaring that it was the heart of a man who was a protector, not a hunter.

19

MaZondi, deeply troubled by all that has befallen her own family, dedicates herself to the church to such an extent that even when she walks alone on the street she can be heard humming a gospel song. And the vibrancy of her faith seems to echo throughout the community and is evident for all to see. Some women have pleaded with her to be part of their prayer group, an invitation that she eventually accepts. Sadly, her acceptance has created a rift that almost causes factions among the women of the church. Some are against her ordainment while she still lives in Thabekhulu's house. The matter has had to be resolved through lengthy, heated discussions.

"Thabekhulu doesn't want to divorce his wife, and the customary law that shuns divorces favours him. He doesn't want to abandon his child to fend for himself in the wilderness, and he'd rather marry MaZondi than do that. But the law of the Europeans doesn't allow him to remarry until he's divorced. Thabekhulu has tried to raise the issue of lobola with the Zondi and Dubazana families but neither family will allow that. MaZondi, then, has become an outcast and is now asking to be accepted into God's family. It's up to you women of faith to decide if you are against the traditional custom and say Thabekhulu must divorce his wife, or whether you say that he and MaZondi must court imprisonment by marrying, despite Thabekhulu's existing European-law marriage. It's up to you: are you saying that they must separate and their child must grow up without a father, or do you permit MaZondi to be at least part of one family with you in the house of God, whose forgiveness abounds for those who seek it?" This is said in the women's meeting, and it is the leader of the women who asks as she repeatedly adjusts her glasses on her light-skinned face.

"Then what will the public say?" ask those not in favour of her being ordained among them.

"The correct answer is that of the Lord whom we serve, who, when there was a case against a woman, wrote on the sand His answer to His accusers and detractors. He recommended that anyone who was without sin among them should cast the first stone. While they left with their hearts having betrayed them, the Lord said to the woman that He didn't find her guilty. He instructed her to go, but not to sin any more. Let us hear from you preachers of the Lord's Word what your take is on the matter."

The majority eventually approve MaZondi's ordainment. Thus she can wear the full uniform of the women's group: a white coat and a black skirt.

Both she and Thabekhulu continue to devote themselves to community work in an attempt to compensate for the emptiness they feel for having failed in their responsibilities to their children. Thabekhulu still nurses his wounds since his son, who had been studying at a Technikon, has become wheelchair-bound. Meanwhile MaZondi is haunted by the disappearance of her son.

On Christmas Day, MaZondi and Thabekhulu take a leisurely stroll on the beach, and there, unexpectedly bump into Nkosana. He is in the company of stray children. The city teems with such children, and even those *with* parents seem like orphans. Nkosana is a teenager now, wearing long pants and sneakers, and his hair is dishevelled and dirty. They greet him and he mumbles a response, his eyes shifty. They ask to speak to him and fortunately he agrees. When he finally looks at them and their glances meet, it is as if their eyes have been poked with awls. In that tiny opportunity he grants them, they plead, almost kneeling, begging him to come home so they can put him through school. Even in Thabekhulu's heart it would be a painful curse if Dubazana's son was sentenced to the dark world of the uneducated, simply because his father has died.

"All we ask of you, mntanami, is that you return to school," cajoles his mother, but she grimaces suddenly in fright and instinctively swats the non-existing firefly, which she no longer sees frequently, flashing though her mind.

"Your mother is advising you well, my son, she's telling you the truth. Education is the only thing that brightens one's future." Thabekhulu whisks the air as he also sees the firefly flying around him. Nkosana just keeps quiet and stares at them in surprise. The sea waves roar, bellow and then thunder on the sand a short distance behind them.

Nkosana eventually agrees to return home. He asks for a moment to say goodbye to his friends.

"It's okay, my son, say goodbye to your friends," says his mother in a soothing voice. "Also tell them that our organisations really love and care for children like them. We hope that some day you'll lead us to them so that we can embrace them with warm and loving arms."

Nkosana steps away and stands with his friend a short distance away, their conversation switching to some coded language. After a while, he returns to his parents and asks them to wait while he fetches his belongings. They nod in approval and the group shuffles away. They wait for what seems an eternity without any sign of him. When they are finally about to give up and leave, he appears, carrying a paper bag in which he has put his meagre rags.

Hunger is written all over his dry, parched mouth. They hurry off into one of the nearby hotels to find a restaurant. While

MaZondi and Thabekhulu eat in a leisurely way, Nkosana gulps down his food hungrily and only takes short breaks to throw them lazy, detached looks.

When they arrive home, Makhosazana jumps around with joyous excitement when she sees her long-lost brother, as though her world is reborn. However, Makhosazana soon realises with shock that he is no longer the Nkosana she knew. When she gives him food, he greedily guzzles it down and even licks his plate clean. She and her mother begin to suspect that perhaps he is taking drugs. By the end of the week they are getting used to his restlessness and his off-tune voice, humming an incoherent song they do not recognise.

By the time the schools reopen and his mother has gone to register him, she has already by chance walked in on him a few times and found him sniffing glue and benzene. Her attempts to admonish him are met with fierce resistance. Her son scowls at her like a wild cat cornered by a black mamba. But he does go to school and limps along with his studies although he is no longer clear as to what his destination and direction are.

Makhosazana's problems, too, do not abate, and keep staring them in the face. They find her one Saturday night slumped on the sofa, watching television with disconsolate eyes as the screen fills with salubrious virgin maidens gracing the Reed Dance Festival. She, on the other hand, is cradling a fatherless child who keeps calling for a father.

"I have a problem, Mama."

Her mother takes a seat next to her, "What's the problem?"

"Mama, my problem is to do with Sibonelo. Especially now that he is chronically ill, he keeps crying, 'Daddy'. I have asked myself endlessly as to where on earth I am going to find this father, whose identity even I don't know, nor whether he deserves the honour of knowing his child."

Her mother is dumbfounded, and her eyes moisten with tears. Her daughter saves her the trouble of responding. "I think it's right that I should find Sibonelo's father – he who flogged me with a thorny weapon – so that I can shake his hand with my warm, forgiving hands. To do that, can you guys help me and come with me in my search? I want us to show him the fruit of their struggle for freedom, which was no longer being waged against apartheid, but instead was an excuse for the most deplorable acts. Perhaps this gesture will help to console others in the shacks who've also been infected with this disease and are neglected, not given medication nor visited by anyone to rekindle their hope."

"You have a point there, mntanami."

"The past is water under the bridge, Mama. Holding grudges never bears fruit that frees one's soul. After a disaster, if freedom and progress are to prevail, the starting point must be reconciliation. In line with my child's name, Sibonelo – Exemplary-one – I'd like to set an example by forgiving his father."

MaZondi and Thabekhulu fully embrace Makhosazana's idea and they put the matter to the priest and the congregation. The proposal is accepted and other churches are informed. So, one sunny Sunday, as dust rises to the sky, multitudes of church members plod along the dirt paths that lead to the shacks where MaZondi once lived.

A revelation shakes them all when they enter. Some of the members living in the neighbouring township, who had, in fact, been involved in the bloody fights over water with their neighbours from the shacks, are clueless about shack life. Some have never even set foot there before. That is why some who see these congested dwellings regard them simply as Babylon or Sodom and Gomorrah. Some church members are gripped by fear, and try to persuade others to retreat to the safety of their church buildings. The priests lead the procession in song and pass the slanting, yardless houses. The shack-dwelling children and parents, some of whom are respectable people, stand leaning against their houses which are variably built from rusty corrugated iron sheets, mud, cardboard boxes that have held sorghum beer, and all sorts of other materials that they could lay their hands on. The place is swarming with army trucks on which soldiers sit, menacingly carrying guns, while others just lean against the trucks, looking gloomy and despairing. Violence rages incessantly in these shacks. People label one another with the tags of feuding political parties, bent on mutual annihilation, and in the mayhem, massacres erupt.

When the congregants assemble for a service under the tree that used to be a jungle court where death sentences were meted out against people; orphans, the offspring of children who had made other children pregnant, cluster there in numbers. Some orphans are fathers of others. None are employed. From mother and child to father, malnutrition has left them with arms and legs as spindly as those of cockroaches.

Some of those who have come are overwhelmed when they see what the regime's oppression has done to people, and they break down in tears. MaZondi and Thabekhulu start a song that leads to a fervent worship and prayer session. The Word of God seems to touch even some of the children's hearts and they walk forward unsteadily to testify. They bare their souls, bemoan their desolation and rattle off the tragic incidents that have brought them here. Some are orphans who were arrested for being struggle activists and who returned home from jail to find that their parents had perished in the political violence. Others have been married off by force. Many have contracted HIV, and even then they have continued to be plundered and raped.

Makhosazana takes to the stage and affirms that she has also been raped, contracted the virus, fallen pregnant and infected her child. She urges the group to show the world love despite the harsh conditions under which they have been raised. She shows them her child and tells them she is there because she wants to show the toddler to the father whom she, as the mother, does not even know. She pleads that those who can recall the incident and know the identity of the child's father should come forward with information. Fortunately, there are, indeed, those who clearly remember and know the perpetrator who so terrorised the youth. There are also others who carry children on their backs, or had children who have died, and they themselves are awaiting death because they have been raped and infected by him.

"Please take us to him so that he can see his child who is brought to him in peace, and not through the violence that he used to bring the child into this world."

Oh, the poor children! Some, carrying their own children, sway weakly along and lead the priests and members of the congregation flanking Makhosazana, who is gently coaxing Sibonelo along as they all walk. The air resonates with their impassioned voices as they sing their hearts out and the ground shakes as they negotiate the tall grasses, thronging their way to the culprit's shack.

They arrive at their destination and someone in the crowd opens the door. It is indeed a shack of horrors. It has four minute rooms, occupied by various dwellers. The first door to be pushed open is entered by the priests, trailing the crowd behind them. The sight greeting them makes their skins crawl with shock. A man who has sticks for legs and eyes buried deep in their sockets – his life is dissipating through his skeleton – leans against the wall. He makes a pathetic attempt to shake off the flies that swarm over his bony face.

"Nangu-ke! Here he is!" say some young men, pointing. They have bloodshot eyes and are immune to the acrid smells here, being quite familiar with living in proximity to death.

"Don't run away, reverends!" What the man means to be a loud plea comes out as a lame whisper. "Could you please finish me off? I've been begging them for a long time to end my life, but they refuse."

"And who could this be, this person of God?" interjects one priest, shivering and fanning his nose with a Bible.

"This is Njayiphume himself."

"Is this what has become of him?" Makhosazana and her mother recoil in shock.

"As you see him, reverends, he was the self-proclaimed leader of the youth that he'd recruited. He forced them to quit school and insisted that he was fighting against oppression. He then turned on them and started terrorising and raping them. A lot of children have kids here as a result of his actions, in collusion with his henchmen. They would stalk them in the dark and forcibly break their virginity before setting them against other youngsters. We eventually turned against his rotten-minded accomplice and necklaced him, sparing this one so that he could witness the consequences of his atrocities," elaborates one young man, appraising his audience with bloodshot eyes.

"But, my children, why watch him die?" enquires the priest solemnly.

"He has Aids as you can see; in fact, he's the fountain from which the disease spread around here."

"Hawu, Creator of heaven and earth!" The priest is sweating profusely. He looks at Njayiphume, "Kwenzenjani mfowethu; what happened, my brother?"

"What they say is true, Mfundisi," he responds in a hoarse voice. "These are all my evil deeds, but I don't want to see them any longer. I've been pleading with people to kill me, but they refuse. I want death, but it doesn't come." He is gripped by shortness of breath. "It wasn't of my own accord that I became like this." He coughs. "I neither know where I was born nor who brought me into this world. All I can recall of my past is being a boy growing up on the streets of Durban, contending with all sorts of abuse, including sexual assault. And then along came a Mr Naidoo who took me off the streets to sell fruit at a stall and in the market, for him and for many others who employed me after him. Even then, I was still harassed and arrested for not having a pass and a special permit. In jail I was locked up with hardened criminals who had a field day abusing me. So the notion that a person can show kindness to a fellow human being is completely foreign to me."

The Reverend Langa faintly shakes his head, and beckons to Makhosazana to come closer with the child. "Do you remember this girl?"

Straining to keep his eyes open, he looks at her indistinctly and acquiesces, "Yebo, yes, I remember them all. This one is from the Dubazana house. I hated her father very much for being kind and docile like a child, unwilling to kill."

"Do you recall what happenend to this child?"

"Yebo, Mfundisi, I'm the one who personally fetched her and her brother from their home. I'm the one who destroyed her future. Let it be her who finishes me off then." Dry, harsh sobs escape him and he tries to wipe his face with his bony hands.

"No, Baba, no, I'm not going to kill you; I have the mercy that you don't possess. I've come here to show you the child born out of your brutality. Even though I now have the disease that is ravaging you, as it does him, I'm saying: here he is, look at him."

With eyes flickering in their sockets, Njayiphume looks at Sibonelo in unfeigned disbelief. "Such a beautiful child is mine; me being the animal that I am?"

"As you have confessed your sins, yes, it is as you say."

"Have you come to arrest me, Mfundisi?"

Makhosazana responds, "We're not here to arrest you, Baba, but to teach you about kindness and forgiveness. Unfortunately, you can't hold your child, seeing how frail you are."

"My daughter, I'd rather you beat me up or arrest me so that I can feel the pain and it will come to pass. The pain of being forgiven sinks too deep into the heart."

"I would be disrespectful if I were to beat up an older person. I forgive you. I want you to know that I don't reciprocate cruelty with cruelty. Ngiyabonga; I thank you."

Njayiphume looks at Sibonelo and holds his hand while pointing at himself, saying, "Sibonelo! Baba, Daddy!"

Smiling, Sibonelo extends his hand, "Ba...ba, baba, baba."

Tears well up in Njayiphume's lifeless eyes. Tapping the floor with his bony hand, he says, "I'm sorry, mntanami. Please ask your parents also to forgive me for setting thugs on them to terrorise them after I'd already wronged them through you."

"Oh, my Lord!" MaZondi goes down on her knees. "From the gruesome deeds that you committed, death spread to my family, and now my husband is dead."

"But do you forgive me, my sister?"

"Though I'm in pain, I forgive you, my brother." The congregants help her rise from the ground and support her as she gets to her feet.

"What is tragic in this world is that, in times of conflict, we treat others with the same acts of cruelty that were meted out to ourselves, and the result is a never-ending cycle of cruelty. Even you, my boys, please forgive him now," pleads the priest.

"Ngeke, Mfundisi! Never! He must die witnessing the consequences of his actions!" The young men remonstrate with fierce firmness.

"But, my children, you shouldn't forget that had the system of governance in the country not been like this, perhaps this man wouldn't have had the motive to inflict vengeance on the community in the way he did. Instead of getting arrested for not having passes and permits, he might have had expert psychological support, had the country been governed the right way. I plead with you to calm down and not to fight fire with fire."

The animated confrontation eventually abates. The soldiers are called upon to summon an ambulance to take away Njayiphume, who is clearly destined for the grave. The crowd disperses back to the township, with no doubts in their minds about the daunting journey that the nation still has to travel to level the mountains of past mistakes, and those still to be committed. Behind them, in the shacks, they have left people staring death in the face, and in front of them, part of the township is burning, engulfed in a thick column of smoke.

Indeed, the whole country is like this, burning, yet hungering for peace and forgiveness, and it is people like Bhekizizwe Zulu who work tirelessly to douse the flames.

"My daughter Makhosazana made a fine example of how peace should spread through our nation," MaZondi tells Thabekhulu as they sit in the lounge that evening. "She's inspired me to seek forgiveness from the woman of this house, MaDlamini. I'm now at the level that I am at the bank because she allowed you to take us in when we were drowning in poverty. But no matter what I do that is good, a feeling of guilt always reminds me of the shackles of conscience that still bind me. It is only her forgiveness that will quell the flames that torture me." She goes quiet and holds her cheek with her hand, pensively. "And the builders are taking their time. I wonder what's causing the delay now? They ought to be finishing the house so that they can give me the keys and I can move out of here for her."

Thabekhulu looks at her with sorrowful and sympathetic eyes. "Your idea is very good, MaZondi. The big question is, how are you going to approach her?"

"I'll adopt the same approach as Makhosazana did, and ask you and the prayer group members to accompany me."

Her requests to be accompanied, and to meet MaDlamini on a Saturday afternoon, are accepted.

On the day set for the appointment the weather is pleasantly bright and cool. MaZondi and the prayer women are singing as they enter a four-roomed house, similar to many others in the township. That the home is gripped by poverty is evident from the yard: one does not enter it through a gate since it has no fence. The grass is so dense and tall that it would hardly be surprising if a mamba suddenly emerged and killed people. The walls have never been plastered and the naked bricks that were once red have faded and turned dull. No one looks after it, and the tenants are always arguing over who should clean the yard. The owners, who got married while they lived at Mkhumbane, only in order to qualify for a house, have since become drunkards who slave for shebeen owners, receiving alcohol as payment.

MaDlamini, who has lost weight drastically, hears the singing and goes out to meet the women. The congregants file into the dining room that serves as a bedroom for her and the children. On that day Thabisile is away at her boyfriend's home, but Thabethule is there in his wheelchair, holding a book he has been reading. MaZondi sees and feels all their grief sinking into the depths of her soul. Her heart feels immersed in guilt and she breaks out and cries even before asking for forgiveness.

Here, just as they did at the shacks, they sing and pray, beseeching God for peace. Even as others take turns standing up to testify, MaZondi remains kneeling in front of MaDlamini, pleading, "Dadewethu, my sister, even if I may not be guilty in the eyes of worldly law, I feel guilty in the eyes of God, your ancestors and yourself. I have explained to the women packed here in this house how my homelessness pushed me to your home, and that you rescued us when we had nothing, physically and spiritually. I'm not going to elaborate further since you know the story from beginning to end. It is because of me that your children are in this situation," she sobs. "In order for my spirit to have peace, I'm asking that you forgive me. I know I wronged you and do not deserve your forgiveness."

The pain rises afresh in MaDlamini. She cries so much that her husband is touched; his hands keep moving to his eyes and he is constantly clearing his nose. The mood in the room is sombre as the women also join in and cry, especially after they see the lanky Thabekhulu's son slouched in a wheelchair.

"At first, MaZondi, I also had feelings of anger towards you and my husband. But later, when I sat down and pondered the matter deeply, digesting your situation, it dawned on me that the two of you might perhaps never have known each other, or we might not have been trapped in the same house, had it not been for the system that deprives and denudes us. I also believe that what happened to me was my destiny, considering how we met. At the church yard, you wouldn't have skipped all the other cars and leant on ours if it wasn't destined."

"Thus your car had bad luck leaning on it."

"You, my sister, also came into my home in terrible shape, after you and your whole family had been through a baptism of fire at the hands of a cruel world. For both of us, homelessness dethroned us from being wives. We became childless even though we had given birth. With these words I'm expressing my forgiveness to you, dadewethu. All we can do now is forgive one another for things we've done unintentionally." She extends her hand and they hug.

"I would also like to apologise to Thabethule, who is like a son to me," says MaZondi, shuffling and crouching until she kneels in front of him. "I'm deeply sorry, mntanami." She says these words as she raises herself to hug him. "If poverty had not pushed me towards your home, I'm sure you wouldn't be like this. To hear you say that you forgive me will heal my spirit."

"Ngiyakuxolela, Mama, I forgive you, though you didn't do anything wrong to me. I also wish for you to forgive."

"Who should I forgive, my son, when I'm the one who has sinned?" she cries.

"Forgive those who did wrong, who deprived you of your right to a decent life and thus pushed you into temptation, and who didn't know what they were doing. We will have found forgiveness if you forgive them."

"I forgive them, mntanami, since the time will come when they will ask for forgiveness from me. We are all together in working to help those who have been spiritually crippled in their wrangles for political power."

"If you have forgiveness, then you have peace. If you have peace, you have won in the struggle for our well-being."

"May I also have at least a droplet from the same chalice of forgiveness?" Thabekhulu asks, abashed.

"Phuza, drink, Thabekhulu!" says his wife.

"Phuza, Baba!" adds his son.

"Thank you, my people." He hugs them.

MaZondi moves back again, and kneels next to MaDlamini, "I'm waiting for the keys to the house that I have bought, my sister. If I could have, I would have long left your home so that you could be free to live there instead of being confined to small rented rooms because of me. If things don't work out soon enough, I'll move to a flat in town, now that they are promising to repeal the laws that were preventing us from living there."

"May Dubazana's spirit, wherever it is, also help you, so you too can experience a life in which you live with your children in a house in the surname of your husband who was arrested trying to build you one."

There is more singing and prayer, then chatting about other general news. Afterwards, they say goodbye and part ways. MaZondi and Thabekhulu feel relieved, as if they have been freed from the chains that have bound and crippled their hearts. They would have slept peacefully this night had it not been for the image of the firefly that leaps out in red and green flames, even on their pillows, when they try to sleep. The firefly is accompanied by Nkosana's red eyes and his humming as he goes about mumbling the lyrics of his song.

20

I saw my father,
A nomadic squatter,
In and out with us
In other people's houses.

They ill-treated him,
Black and white;
Some abused him
Others arrested him.

I saw a man,
In the company of his lover,
Standing over my father,
Who was frothing all over.

When I tried to peep,
They scowled at me
Saying this useless thing
Must go back to the bedroom!

By the time the sun rose,
Father was dangling from a tree:
Murderers, I know you,
I'll avenge him!

Makhosazana hears her brother singing this song for the first time, the song that he has been humming all along. The sun is setting and she is sitting next to Nkosana in the room where he sleeps. He is sad and teary, and his head tilts to the side, slanting like the sun that is slowly setting.

Makhosazana is patiently begging him to tell her the story of who he saw. "Confide in me, mfowethu, and tell me who you saw standing over Daddy's body."

"Dadewethu, my sister," he throws a bloodshot eye at her, "for now I'm not going to expose them. The day I do, will be the day they consume fire and coal."

"No, I won't accept that, my brother. Making people consume fire and coal is murder. I wonder if you're aware that the moment the thought of killing crosses your mind is when you remove your human heart and replace it with an animal's. I don't think I'm wrong in saying that those who commit murder usually don't have good luck. Things never go well in their lives. Even those who are doing well eventually fade away and die."

"All that you're saying, Makhosazana, is your personal belief. It means absolutely nothing to me. When men raped me at the shacks, no one sympathised with me and showed me any of the kindness that you're telling me about. Even on the day that a man and a woman killed my father, no one considered that they were taking away the father that I loved and that they were burying my future. Therefore, I don't have mercy for humanity in general and I don't care whether it is a man or woman. There's only one meal I have in store for them: a plate of coal and fire."

"Hating humankind is tantamount to hating yourself, my brother. Learn from me. You were there when they raped me at the camp; and what's worse, it was men who were older than my own father. Even as my child and I await death, I don't hate men collectively, because I know that not all of them are bad. I believe that a heart full of hatred is always engulfed in flames. It plots destruction as you're plotting it with yours; you intend to make people suffer and feel pain. Didn't you see me rise up with my child to look for his father?"

"The destruction that the world suffers today is caused by people like you, my sister."

"As you call yourself a freedom fighter and have a position of leadership in committees that you regard as responsible for freeing the nation, you're supposed to understand things better and preach that the reason the world is fighting so much is because of hatred, and that we'll never prosper if hatred continues to rule us. All that has been destroyed by hatred will not be rebuilt while people still live in fear of pain and suffering. But the world will be rebuilt if the people share in the spirit of forgiveness."

"The sun will rise and set while we listen to Makhosazana's sermons and tall stories. I have to go to a meeting." Nkosana gets up and walks out across the lounge where Thabekhulu is sitting, and through the kitchen where his mother is. He sings with emphasis the words of the verse that refers to seeing a man and his lover hovering over his father as he lay dead. Thabekhulu slaps his own neck in an attempt to scare away the firefly that flashes its fearsome blue lightning. MaZondi has tears welling from her eyes, her gaze following her son until he walks out before she can raise her hands to whisk the firefly off.

That Wednesday night Thabekhulu does not sleep a wink because of a dream that makes him cry, choking and raising his arm in an attempt to draw attention and get help. He wakes up very tired, down-spirited and not feeling like going to work. He stays at home. "What's the matter with you today, Mxolisi's father?" MaZondi, who is on leave, asks in the morning.

"My body is sore all over and the dream I had last night is weighing heavily on my spirit." He relates it to her.

MaZondi consoles him by saying that the dream might not mean anything bad; perhaps he slept facing upwards. While he drags himself to take a bath, she prepares food for him which he eats half-heartedly and cannot finish.

"If my dreams are like this, I mustn't sleep without seeing MaDlamini first, so that I can plead with her and apologise again if I have a chance to do so."

Indeed, a few minutes before ten o'clock he puts on the blue-and-white striped suit that he and MaDlamini had bought when they went shopping together a long time ago. He bids MaZondi goodbye.

"As it is Thursday, Mxolisi's father, we are meeting at the reverend's place at two with the other women from the group and from there we will visit some houses. If there's anything urgent, you'll find me there."

Just as Thabekhulu is about to leave, the phone rings. He picks it up.

"Mfowethu, my brother," a woman's voice says softly.

"Yebo, dadewethu. Yes, my sister."

"I would like to speak to Thabekhulu himself."

"You're talking to him."

"I'm a woman that you wouldn't recognise even if I described myself in detail. I do know you, although we have never met in person. There's a secret that I would like to share with you. Please don't bother asking me who I am because I won't tell you."

"Yes, I hear you," he answers in a frustrated voice.

"I'm calling out of empathy. I have learnt that in the meeting that was held last night by the youth under the tree at Nozililo, it was decided that you will be fetched from home and be hauled for questioning under the very same tree of lamentations."

"Hu!" Thabekhulu audibly pulls in his breath. "Why do they say they will come for me?"

"They say you also know who you killed. What I'm saying, my brother, is that though I may not know the case date, the sentence is an open secret. If I were you, I'd get lost at once."

Standing some metres away, MaZondi looks at Thabekhulu as he moves his eyes from side to side and instinctively realises that things have suddenly gone terribly wrong.

"What do they say the sentence is?" enquires Thabekhulu, swatting the firefly.

"I heard that it is the usual: the shoe of the car."

"Hawu Nkosi yami! Oh my Lord!" he moans. "Who did you hear this from?"

"As I said, I'm not going to disclose my identity because this was whispered to me by my son who had been at the meeting. If I tell you, I'll be exposed and then the car shoe will be a lover embracing my neck."

"Obviously, that means that I'm as good as dead?"

"Yes, if you do not run away this instant. Let me tell you that you are still alive simply because you are left with a few minutes. Remain well."

"Thank you. Why don't you say 'go well'?"

"If it does happen, I pray that God will forgive your sins and receive your soul with mercy." With those words she puts down the phone, leaving Thabekhulu dizzy, with the receiver in his hand, saying, "Hawu! Hawu! Hawu!" He removes it from his ear and stares at it for a long time. The house goes dead silent as MaZondi watches him with panic in her eyes.

"What is shocking you so much, Thabekhulu?"

"It is the fulfilment of the events in my dream. I'm no more."

He replaces the receiver and recounts the latest news with evasive eyes.

"It's unfortunate that this boy has already gone. If necessary, I'll go to the school and ask Principal Donda for him, face him and tell him please to throw out the evil in his heart. I have no doubt that Nkosana is the instigator and the force behind all this mayhem," MaZondi says.

"Let us admit that we also erred, Mxolisi's mother. We apologised to MaDlamini, but we didn't apologise to Nkosana, a child of my home. I wish I could see him and say how sorry we are."

"Apologise for what?" She pauses and quickly checks if anybody is near, but Makhosazana is not there. She lowers her voice to a whisper, "If you apologise, then you'll have to start by admitting that we killed his father. You can't afford to make such a mistake, Thabekhulu, because that would lead to our arrest. I'd lose my job and leave my children behind as orphans. May we please reveal only to the Creator the secret that we killed Dubazana? Even the trial must be heard by Him instead of Nkosana, who is going to make a mockery of us." She starts crying.

"I don't know, Mxolisi's mother. Usually the body refuses to go to the grave with secrets. That is obviously why I am crying and choking at night."

"Nothing is going to happen to you today, Thabekhulu. If it is Nkosana leading the killers, I'll stop him and my child will listen to me. I am his mother and he can't disobey me."

"If I die without apologising to him, please apologise on my behalf. Where is Mxolisi?"

His mother fetches him where he is playing on the floor. Thabekhulu hugs him and kisses his mother, "I'm leaving. I'll come back shortly to pack what I can and then disappear, if this is not already my last day."

They hug again and walk towards the garage. Thabekhulu gets into the car and reverses out into the yard. He gets out and stands staring at his house, shaking his head, then remembers the urgency and gets back into the car. Just as the car is moving out of the gate, he feels his foot sink on the accelerator as its cable snaps.

"Today everything is going wrong; this is a prelude to the end of the road," he says, getting out of the car and waving the firefly away. However he tries, he cannot fix the cable, so MaZondi helps him to push the car back into the garage and he locks it inside.

Thabekhulu now walks straight towards the taxi rank. MaZondi stands watching him, noticing his tiredness, until he becomes a dot in the distance and disappears. Flapping at her own firefly, she returns inside and collapses face down on the bed, crying into the pillow.

Eleven o'clock finds Thabekhulu ambling in a daze down West Street until he turns into the expensive clothing shop where his wife works. Everywhere there are ladies immaculately kitted out and serving customers, with soft music playing in the background. Thabekhulu tiptoes timidly to his own lady who looks gorgeous and impeccably dressed. As if they have prearranged it, she is also wearing a suit similar to his. While MaDlamini watches her husband from a distance, she is alarmed by the anxiety written all over his face. Standing next to a female mannequin outfitted in a wedding veil alongside an elegantly dressed male mannequin, MaDlamini greets her husband. Their exchange of answers on their state of health reveals that both are emotionally unwell. Although the whirlwinds of life have blown them away from each other, one cannot guess this from the respect and courtesy with which they treat each other.

"Mother of Thabethule and Thabisile, what brings me here is a horrific dream I had last night, and I can't let the sun go down without sharing it with you. I wonder if you could lend me an ear, or does your ear no longer have space to hear my voice?"

"How can it not have a space for you, Thabekhulu, since you know very well that I love you, and that it was this same ear that received the words that changed my surname and made me part of your family?" She looks at the mannequin attired in a wedding veil and the young man next to it, then looks at herself before spreading her eyes to her husband. "Have you ever heard anyone say that they'll never forget certain mountains because that's where their umbilical cord fell?"

"Yes, I always hear them."

"I'm also saying the same to you. I'll never forget the mountains that are you because that's where the cord, which is my youth, fell."

"How sweet those words are and how delightfully they sit in my heart." He bows his head and hugs her. "I'm here to unravel to you my deepest secrets. Is there a place where we can sit and talk in private?"

The manager of the shop, an elderly white lady, in whom MaDlamini has confided her marital problems, is watching them from a distance as they hug. She is happy to see that and approaches them to greet Thabekhulu. She asks to have a word with MaDlamini, and, when they are both a short distance away from Thabekhulu, she gives her an opportunity to go and talk to her husband, hoping it will be a conversation towards their reconciliation. MaDlamini thanks her profusely, takes her bag, throws it over her shoulder and tells Thabekhulu they can go. They stroll out so casually that one of the ladies asks jokingly if they are going out to get married. They smile back languidly and leave the shop, taking West Street towards the beach front, holding each other by the hand. They cross Gardiner Street, pass the city's main post office and walk into the nearby park opposite the picturesque Anglican church building and the old-world city hall.

The scenic park boasts colourful trees and fountains from which water bubbles up as if on the boil. They walk on soft carpet-like grass, past a flock of doves – honorary city citizens – and proceed to a bench in the shade. No sooner has MaDlamini taken her seat than she reclines, resting her head on her husband before asking, "So, what was the dream?"

Thabekhulu hurriedly tells her. "I dreamt I crossed a river to stand alongside Dubazana on its lush green bank. On the other side of the river through which I had waded, I saw a crowd of people standing around my corpse in a coffin that was placed on top of a grave. On that side were people who were crying and rolling on the ground, with you, our children and our parents among them. What broke my heart is that even though I was on the other side, I tried to call out, apologising and telling you the secrets that I had been instructed to reveal, but my voice couldn't reach you although you were not far from me. I was also no longer allowed to swim across and meet you. But the final nail, as if I wasn't already finished off, is the call that I received when I was already dressed and ready to come to you."

His wife sits up and looks at him, surprised. "What was the call about and who was it from?"

"I got a tip-off from a lady who didn't want to tell me her name. She said that at a youth meeting which was held last night, it was determined that I must be summoned to defend myself under the tree at Nozililo."

He looks at his wife, and tears flow down his face. "I want to tell you whilst I'm alive about these secrets that I was instructed to reveal."

"I'm listening, Thabekhulu," she responds in a whisper, her head still resting on his shoulder.

Thabekhulu relates to his wife the story she finds impossible to believe. While he tells it in its terrible detail, his wife starts to cry and rises to her feet, exclaiming aloud in shock, placing her hands on her head.

"Come back, my love. Don't make me lose hope in you, you whom I trust; you are the pillar on which I can lean for strength!" He swats at nothing in the air, and stretches out his arms and draws his wife close. His wife relents and sits down, only to stand up seconds later, as if she has sat down on hot coals. This time she doesn't hold her head, but lowers it and holds her cheek.

"Sit down, MaDlamini! The dream said I must tell the entire truth."

His wife sits and listens attentively before asking, "With your own hands, Thabekhulu?"

"Yebo, yes, mother of my children," he responds timidly. His wife stares up the tree in whose shade they sit, her mouth open with amazement. At that moment the huge clock at the city post office chimes, striking twelve times, and is joined by the bells of the Anglican church chiming their own melody too.

"Together with his wife?" MaDlamini rolls her eyes. Thabe-khulu nods. By the time he finishes the story, his wife is crying and fervently praying, beseeching the Lord to forgive him.

"So, this is what I wanted to reveal to you, my wife, and I wouldn't have liked my heart to stop beating before I told you."

His wife straightens his collar, "Your explanation today has relieved my heart. Now I understand what the bond was that made you cling to MaZondi and abandon me. Since it's clear to me, father of my children, that today is fraught, what with these threats to your life, when I knock off from work I'll fetch the children and come to keep you company. Don't worry about MaZondi, we've made peace and there are no hard feelings between us."

"I'd appreciate that. In fact, had the car not broken down, I would have fetched you myself, especially since Thabethule is in a wheelchair. If it gets fixed, I'll fetch you."

At one o'clock they hug, rise from their seat and walk out of the park, holding hands. They part and Thabekhulu walks away, still in a daze, disappearing into the crowds.

By half past two he enters the church yard, drenched in sweat. Fortunately it is just after a meeting that Reverend Langa has held with the women's prayer group. He asks to see him, with MaZondi present.

When the priest is still outside, MaZondi corners Thabekhulu while they are waiting, kneeling at the altar.

"But, Mxolisi's father, knowing very well that an earthly judge will never forgive us, couldn't you have waited until our case was heard at the Ultimate Court?" "There's no other day, Mxolisi's mother, and this place is also not a place for lies."

The priest returns. The three shut themselves into the church office again and Thabekhulu tells the priest about the dream and the call he has received. He listens with increasing sadness.

"Therefore, Mfundisi, should anything happen, I don't want to be in a situation where I want to come clean only to find that I can't speak any more, hence my decision to come and reveal the truth that we hid from you when we first confessed."

"Yes, I hear you, my brother," the priest nods understandingly but feels embarrassed. He glances at MaZondi and finds her shuffling uncomfortably in her prayer women's uniform.

"I didn't tell you the truth that I'm the one who put Dubazana in jail. I planted drugs among the goods he was selling because I was scared that his wife, when pressed with questions, would disclose that I was the one who had made her pregnant."

The priest clears his throat, "May God forgive your sin, for you have already chosen to repent and dedicate yourselves to Him."

"Mfundisi, I wonder if there is forgiveness for a person with blood on his hands?"

In a soft voice, the priest responds, "I trust that there is forgiveness for the one who repents and apologises while he is still alive. You were stained by the blood of the people you were rescuing from the battle against oppression. It is unusual for someone who is in a battle and for one who rescues people to have clean hands. The person with clean hands is the one who sits with folded arms and locks out wounded people who knock on his doors. You opened your doors to them."

"I appreciate the encouraging words, Mfundisi. I would like you to know today that Dubazana was killed by me, with my own hands."

He opens his hands and looks at them through a veil of tears. "It wasn't intentional. Even his wife had a hand in trying to help me in my attempts at self-defence." He describes the entire episode, and relates how they were caught in the act by Nkosana. This causes MaZondi to jump up with her hand on her cheek. When he reaches the part about carrying Dubazana and hanging him from a tree, MaZondi freezes in astonishment and fixes her eyes on the ceiling, open mouthed. The priest stares at the cross on the wall.

"Now, Mfundisi, this firefly that followed us from the forest has never left us. Every day we see its image with flames, encircling us." He whisks in the air at nothing and MaZondi does the same amidst her tears. "Today its glowing is worse than on the other days."

Kneeling in front of them, the priest puts his hands on them in prayer. When he is finished, they ask if they can cool the fire in their hearts and receive Holy Communion. The priest accepts, and they are served the communion.

"Thabekhulu, would you allow us to visit you today and bring you prayers?"

"How can you even ask? You know the answer, and if you promise, I'll hurry home right now to prepare for you."

"Kulungile-ke, it's fine then. The women have gone to the Msomi home for prayers. I'll fetch them there and we'll squeeze ourselves into the car and come to your home."

Thabekhulu thanks the priest and leaves, carrying the accelerator cable that he has bought in town.

"Mxolisi's father, would you like me to go with you?" MaZondi asks, dabbing away her tears as they stand outside in the church yard.

Thabekhulu smiles warmly, "It's fine if you go with the other women to pray. If the firefly doesn't burst into flames and kill me, we'll find each other at home. If it does burst into flames, we'll meet on the other side of the river that I dreamt of." He holds her by the hand and squeezes it, looks around, lifts it, and kisses it and her cheek.

"When married people ignore each other, it's a thorn in the feelings and lives of those who witness that cruelty." These are MaZondi's last words to Thabekhulu. As she takes hurried strides to catch up with her colleagues at the prayer meeting, Thabekhulu limps away, violently shaking his head, hoping it will help scare away the firefly that is throwing glowing flash-lights from all directions.

21

Thabekhulu alights from the taxi and looks around as if lost. It feels as if lurking eyes glower at him. He stumbles away confusedly and takes one of the roads that lead to his house. He keeps throwing his arms in the air, waving away at something as the firefly circles around him with growing intensity. He is walking past the shopping centre when he hears the droning sound of people singing in the distance. Startled and wide-eyed, he comes to a standstill and listens. The voices are hardly audible. He resumes walking, but at an increased pace now. The singing seems to be getting closer and he starts panicking that he will meet the singers. He stops again, his ears straining. Indeed, a mixture of male and female voices, the voices of youths, gradually become audible, as do the lyrics:

> I saw a man
> In the company of his lover,
> Standing over my father
> Who was frothing all over.

He recognises the song and increases his pace, taking shortcuts, avoiding the main road. He has just left the road when he sees a pupil in school uniform. A few years earlier, coming across a school child used to lift the soul and revive one's hopes for the nation's bright future. But during the days of their chanting, which is forcing Thabekhulu to take unplanned detours, pupils have transformed into fearsome monsters. Anyone who locks horns with them thinks of death instead of survival. And the future that one had hoped will bloom is suddenly discoloured by fumes and flames reeking of burned human flesh, the tears of orphans, and the wasted sweat of a nation that has built houses, and bought furniture and cars that are now consumed by flames.

Thabekhulu has just ascended a hillock and can actually see his home when he is cut short by a throng of youngsters, galloping around and performing all sorts of arrogant physical displays of prowess and a thirst for action. The teenage boys have tied school jerseys around their necks and young girls are hopping in the air:

When I tried to peep,
They scowled at me
Saying this useless thing
Must go back to the bedroom!

They come straight at him, led by Nkosana who is hurtling around in a loose, ankle-length black coat, trailing two boys aged about twelve. The boys have their hands on car tyres that they are gently pushing along.

At school, Nkosana has become a leader of whom it is said that he is leading the youth in their fight against oppression. But his attempt at leadership, his understanding and appreciation of politics, are heavily impeded by his immaturity, his youth, and his pathetic level of education. The fact that at school he has grown into a fearsome monster because of his violent nature – a culmination of the violent episodes he encountered so early in life – also makes him vulnerable to people who prey on young boys like him. They use his weaknesses to achieve their political aims and entice him with money, urging him to fight the oppressive education system by taking pupils out of schools. He now has a clique of fellow pupils who have also grown up being abused, and they will take pupils out of their own school, and do the same in other schools until the streets teem with school uniforms, forming a mosaic of colours that muddles the future. As to who the oppressor that they are fighting is, is unclear. They converge under trees, right there in the township, and try cases of parents who have opposed the disruption of schooling, and label them sell-outs. Indeed, they are sentenced and flogged in public. Some will even be sentenced in absentia and only realise it when their houses, if not they themselves, go up in flames. That is how the people's high court operates at Nozililo – Place of Lamentations – under the umdoni tree.

"Oh my God! Run for your life, poor soul," screams a woman in the yard of a house outside which Thabekhulu stands in confusion and panic. "Oh my God! Run! Run! Poor soul!" She looks the same age as his wife, her light skin in glaring contrast to the black mourning clothes she is wearing. Her husband has recently been shot dead. "I wonder why you're still around; I phoned and warned you to flee!"

But instead of running away, Thabekhulu pauses. He feels faint and dizzy. Everything around him has become blurry while the firefly spits crimson and blue flashes in front of him. He feels as if he is spinning around dazedly, but turns to the woman in the yard.

"Even if I bolt now to escape, if I am meant to die, death will stalk and overpower me anyway, because, my sister, on the day of death, nothing has more power over a person's life than death itself!"

"There's the culprit!" screams a teenage boy in a shrill voice. Thabekhulu's giddiness intensifies as the boys pushing the tyres encircle him. By the time the crowd swarms around him, his mind seems to have fainted and he is oblivious to his surroundings. As the throng of youngsters moves away with him, he feels like a drowning person engulfed by angry waves, drifting away with him at high speed. Dust rises from the crowd as they herd him towards Nozililo, chanting and leaping around until they reach the infamous tree. They make him stand in the open under the tree where the judge of the court sits on a small bench that has emerged from the crowd.

Self-importantly, Nkosana sits on the judge's chair, holding an English newspaper that has infuriated him by criticising what it calls "jungle courts." Two prosecutors in the form of youngsters with faces darkened to a coal-black colour, their eyes bathed in a thirst for blood, wearing grey pants and black T-shirts, sit flanking the judge. Perhaps in a tense situation like this, a daring person with some sense of humour would struggle to suppress a smile if they looked at the dignitaries of the court clad in sandals and sneakers of unidentifiable colour, covered with accumulated dust and mud, grubby toes peeping out as if to greet the assembled court.

The prosecutor asks in a hoarse voice, "I understand you know the offence with which you have been charged?"

"You haven't mentioned it to me, my boys."

"Refrain from saying 'my boys'. This is the court! You should say, 'Lord of the court!'" Mshayazafe (Beat-him-until-he-dies), son of Lindeni (What-are-you-waiting-for?) glares at the judge with fiery eyes.

"I have not been briefed on that, Lord of the court."

"Don't take us for fools; you know very well the accusations against you! You are aware that you colluded with the Judge's mother to kill his father?"

"I plead not guilty."

"This man is cheeky!" grumble some members of the crowd.

"Why do we waste time with the case hearing instead of draping this person with his lover's necklace?"

"Why do you deny the charge, while the Judge's father is dead, and lies buried at the cemetery as we speak?" probes another prosecutor, patiently lighting his cigarette.

"I'm denying that I killed him intentionally. It was in self-defence."

The firefly flickers, and he lifts his hand in a weak gesture.

"If a witness stands up and says that you taunted the deceased, what will you say?"

"I will refute that, since that's not how the incident occurred."

"Are you aware who the witness of this court is?" Again the boy glares at him, narrowing his inflamed eyes, blowing the cigarette smoke into the air.

"No, I have no idea."

The prosecutor glances at the judge. "It is the Lord of the court, whose decisions cannot be challenged. Do you want him to rise and testify?"

"If the Lord did see me, he may rise."

"Are you instructing the Lord of the court to rise? That is very rude of you!" A youngster jumps from the crowd and slaps Thabekhulu so hard that spittle drips from his mouth, making him lick his lips in astonishment.

"Perhaps he looks down upon me since I am wearing sneakers. He forgets that I'd be wearing expensive clothes had he not killed my father," Nkosana's voice has a sob in it, but he quickly begins to sing and chant, repeating the chorus that mentions the man that he saw towering over his father.

"And now you have made the Judge cry!" voices in the crowd bark at him. "Do you admit or deny the charge?"

"He died while I was defending myself, my children. It was not my intention."

"If there was no intention then, why did you remove him from the house, and carry him a long distance until you hung him in a forest overlooking Mlazi River?" He puffs smoke through his nose and mouth.

The question chokes Thabekhulu. He coughs and looks around with timorous eyes. The prosecutor pulls at his cigarette and blows smoke through his nose and mouth again. "And after hanging him you zipped up your mouths and never bothered to report it to the police, and you say the incident wasn't intentional?"

"My children, before the Lord of the court's mother and I reunited with God's congregation, we knelt before God in church and confessed it in the pastor's presence. The incident was not premeditated at all. Bantabami, this matter is very heavy and only adults could understand it if I explained it to them. It's out of reach to a person who hasn't entered into a marital union yet."

"Don't talk bullshit to us! We are not discussing heavenly cases here. We are trying earthly cases concerning the murdering of our fathers!" barks the second prosecutor, livid, and also lighting a cigarette.

The Judge makes sounds of being hurt and breaks out in song, with the others joining in:

When I tried to peep,
They scowled at me
Saying this useless thing
Must go back to the bedroom!

"Do you recall that night, murderer?" Now he is being interrogated by the Judge, whose own tears are welling up.

"I remember it all, my son. Your mother and father know where it all started. Will you please forgive me?" His eyes moisten and he is aware of lights thrown at him by the firefly.

"I am glad you've admitted it with your own mouth." Nkosana returns to his seat and asks the prosecutors what decision they have reached. The prosecutors look at each other. They do not even try to answer, but merely run their fingers across their throats, which is a sign for decapitation, hanging or tyre neck-lacing.

"His lover's necklace around his neck!" screams a girl in the crowd. The Judge shrugs his shoulders: "As you can hear for yourself, the court unanimously finds you guilty of murder. A hand that kills will be killed too. A dog that bites others to death will die through biting too. There is no other sentence that the court deems fit for you except death by necklacing.

"As you killed my father, I see it appropriate and befitting that I avenge him. I normally confine myself to meting out sentences and never necklace offenders personally, but in your case, you will be necklaced by me personally, with my own hands." He licks his lips, then rises to his feet and beckons a boy who is kneeling next to Thabekhulu, holding a tyre.

"Give it to me, my boy, so that we can finish this business before the good-for-nothing policemen arrive!" The boy obliges enthusiastically.

"Hurry up before the car over there arrives. Perhaps it's the police!" warns another voice in the crowd. Nkosana lifts the tyre and gently lowers it onto Thabekhulu's neck, while softly singing, as the crowd joins in:

By the time the sun rose,
Father was dangling from a tree:
Murderers, I know you,
I'll avenge him!

"Mbhaveni! Bath him!" No sooner has Nkosana uttered these words than a scraggy youngster emerges from the crowd with a container of petrol and empties it on Thabekhulu's head, body and the tyre around his neck.

"A cigarette!" shrills another voice. A loose cigarette materialises and is hastily stuck into Thabekhulu's trembling mouth. They give him a match.

"Light it yourself and smoke it!"

Thabekhulu tries to plead, tilting his head so that he can see above the tyre.

"But my child, don't you recall the day that I picked you up, leaning against my car at church, and sheltered you in my home? Please forgive me, ndodana yami, my son."

"Guys, please forgive the poor soul!" A thirteen-year-old girl pleads in tears, her hands on her head in frustration.

"Shut up! Do you want to precede him?" The prosecutor's red eyes glare at her. Some girls, who have been forced to attend the court and are against what is happening, save the crying girl by muzzling her with their hands.

"Smoke the cigarette! Don't play tricks with us!" scream some of the women, their maternal instincts obviously long abandoned.

A frantic Thabekhulu does not even hear a car screeching to a stop, overloaded with members of the prayer group. On seeing the tyre hanging around Thabekhulu's neck, the priest runs from the car with the passengers screaming hysterically all at once. While some members are still helping each other to get out of the car, the priest is already paging through the Bible in front of the youths, pleading, admonishing them.

"Get lost, Reverend!" scream the teenage boys and push him away. "If you are stubborn we'll set your van alight."

"My children, I know Thabekhulu's story very well. He approached the congregation, he knelt before God remorsefully, he explained the matter in detail!"

MaZondi runs towards her son and genuflects, pleading for mercy. All in vain. Instead of taking pity, Nkosana breaks into song and points his finger at her:

"Killers, I know who you are.
I am avenging his death now!"

He pauses and looks at the youngsters. "She is a killer, don't let her escape! Her case has been decided on and the ruling is the same as the one we have applied to him!"

"But how can my son point his finger at me!" MaZondi shouts as she tries to run away, but she falls, then struggles to her feet, only to stumble again seconds later and collapse.

"Kill me instead, my children!" The priest throws himself at them and pandemonium breaks out as he tries to wriggle free, pushing away those who are grabbing him while some trip him, felling him to the ground.

"Kill us, our children! Kill *us*! We wear this uniform as a symbol of our will to die for the truth!" remonstrate the prayer women in defiance of the youngsters.

"Grab the culprit, there he flees!" screams someone who sees that, while they have been focusing on MaZondi, Thabekhulu has run away, tyre and all. Being pelted with stones, his body thudding from the heavy blows, he cannot run any further and stops. They overpower him, force his mouth open and make him drink petrol.

"Strike a match and throw it at him!" shouts a voice among many voices in the crowd.

Thabekhulu's eyes grow wide as a firefly spits out a red, fearsome flame in front of him. Everything goes blurry in his mind. He does not decide on the song, but suddenly finds himself singing:

> When sinners derided me
> Placing a crown on my head,
> Spitting on my face,
> I thought of you all the way.
> Oh, how I wonder if you,
> In return, have thought of me?

The air grows thick with solemnity when the prayer women join him in the singing, some crying hysterically. Some are throwing themselves at the youngsters, offering themselves to be incinerated as well.

The first match that Nkosana and his cronies strike and throw from a distance dies out before doing the job.

"Let the burning begin!" They strike another match. The prayer women cower away. Thabekhulu sees the firefly sputter a last flash, suddenly becoming a ball of flames:

> Right there at the cross
> Crucified and suffering,
> Pierced with nails,
> I thought of you all the way.

Thabekhulu utters these words as he flees, the flames swallowing him, some spitting from his mouth. He goes straight to MaZondi, who is standing at a distance, sobbing.

"Let them be; they will set each other alight!" It is as if they are chasing each other, and it is not clear how Thabekhulu can still see her through the flames engulfing him. MaZondi falls, rising and collapsing yet again. She staggers to her feet once more and tries to run away from the imminent death cornering her from every angle. The prayer women scream hysterically as they see Thabekhulu stretch out his flaming arms, and close in on her.

Oh, how I wonder if you,
In return, have thought of me?

"MaZondi! Here is Dubazana. Please forgi..." he screams as he collapses a few centimetres away from her.

"Indeed, I have thought of you! I won't run away now! I am dying with you!" She falls to the ground too.

"They are not setting each other alight! Grab her!" The youngsters swarm after them. Then, out of the blue, a car screeches to a stop and the driver throws the doors open. MaZondi hurls herself into the car and it speeds away.

"You are the one who protects offenders. We could have caught that woman!" shout the youngsters, venting their anger on the priest as he tries to gather soil to put out the fire on Thabekhulu, who is ablaze on the ground. They push away the prayer women who are also trying to quell the fire, making them fall to the ground. They snatch the Bible the priest is clutching under his arm and fling it into the flames. His mouth falls open.

"Throw in all your school books so that he burns to death quickly, before the stupid police arrive and spoil the fun!"

The children oblige. Even those who are against the deed reluctantly toss their books into the fire, fearing for their lives. Giving up, the priest staggers towards the burning flesh and mumbles a prayer over it.

"My God, what's going on here? I understand it's Thabekhulu who's being necklaced?" says Bhekizizwe Zulu as he runs to the crowd, panting.

"It is him indeed, mfowethu," confirms the priest.

Zulu runs towards the smouldering heap and kneels down sobbing, banging the ground with his hands, "What the hell is going on with our beloved country? My children, when we were beaten up, arrested, some of us getting killed, we didn't sacrifice ourselves in order for you to hijack the law and use it to destroy our country and our nation. We were fighting for rights, justice and freedom; for the making of laws and their application in an appropriate manner. We were striving for people's welfare; not this disaster you are inflicting on the nation. You go around torching the same people for whom we fought and who we supported; people who have never tasted freedom in their lives. You replace oppressive apartheid with fiery annihilation. Lord, we plead for mercy and righteousness in Africa!"

"But bantabami!" It is the deep voice of Donda now in front of the crowd of children, tears welling in his eyes. "What do you expect us to do, we who sneaked across borders, dodging bullets on our way to fight for the rights of the masses who were harnessed to a yoke of thorns, if it is only to find that after all we went through, you harness *us* with a yoke that's aflame with fire? Who do you think will lead us if your hands, that hold our future, drip with the blood of the nation, and are oily with the nation's fat as you roast us alive? Is this a manifestation of love for the Africa of our forefathers? You make a mockery of it to foreigners who now have come to know Africa as a continent where people's lives are cheap! Tell me, bantabami, where does this put us and where are we headed for if things are like this?"

The sun turns red over the hills while they wait for the police. Thabekhulu's ashy remains and charred limbs lie untouched on the ground. Next to the indescribable heap of flesh and bones is MaDlamini, on her knees. She arrived as soon as she heard the news, and is now weeping, broken-hearted. Her sobs are interspersed with consoling Thabisile, who is already heavy with her next child. Thabethule sits forlornly in his wheelchair, his eyes awash. Makhosazana, terrified that Nkosana will come home and set Mxolisi alight as well, flees to Nozililo for protection with the children as soon as she sees an army truck heading there. She stands there weeping, flanked by Sibonelo and Mxolisi, their future suddenly gloomy and hopeless.

Bhekizizwe Zulu expounds: "Without doubt, oppression has created a generation who'll carry lasting damage and lifelong pain; they're disabled and infirm. Unless people are healed physically and emotionally, the imminent freedom that is on everyone's lips will bring nothing but laments for the wasted effort by a nation whose prowess is diminished, like that of a bull whose horns have been removed." He continues. "The people who you see sitting like this in a confused daze are not only the Thabekhulus and the Dubazanas; these people represent the multitudes, the millions who have drowned in the regime's oppressive system. And the crowd of children standing over there and hurling insults at us represents the countless children who've been herded out of schools and have grown up in darkness, doomed to procreate and perpetuate their legacy in darkness."

"The only thing that will intercede," Donda pensively muses, taking weak strides towards the ash, pulling out pages from the burnt exercise books, flapping them and lifting them up for all to see, "is for us to dust off these very books and with the knowledge and wisdom enshrined in them, distance ourselves from the darkness. Through them there is some hope that darkness will lift and that there will be light and discernment beyond. A nation that is ruled in the midst of darkness and incomprehension, decimated by disease and poverty, is in peril. It is also in pain – pain that we hear in the grinding of teeth and wailing – caused by its people killing one another and breeding droves of unwanted children who have no one to support them. One cannot achieve freedom if a nation is built on a volcano."

Reverend Langa also kneels next to the ashes and rummages for shreds of his smouldering Bible. He finds it, shakes off the ash, rises to his feet and shows the pages: "With the words of this Book, and by showing kindness, we can cool people's rage and anger; as long as we don't take sides and don't get locked in political factions, we will be able to move beyond this smoke that is stinging our eyes and choking our lungs, and find mercy and ubuntu."

All the while the prayer women are standing with their heads bowed, holding their hymn books and singing. An army truck idles menacingly in the distance. Soldiers stand on the back of the truck and also look sad and shaken, the barrels of their guns pointing downwards. A short distance away on a nearby hillock, a bell resounds at the Roman Catholic church. It evokes memories in MaDlamini's heart that make her erupt with an ear-splitting bout of wailing. She is recalling that, earlier in the day, as the clock's hands struck the twelfth hour, she and her husband had sat close together, holding hands. The Anglican church bells had chimed, singing for them. Now, Thabekhulu is silent, smouldering. At that very moment, as the hour strikes six, the St. Paul's bells start ringing, resonating through the city of Durban, over its tall buildings and sea waves, singing:

The darkness has passed,
Sunrise will approach;
Hold me with mercy
Like a helpless child.
With my heart I say:
My Lord,
To you, my Lord, I come.

"Another remedy," continues the priest, "lies with the leaders and the nation who will decide whether or not to reconcile and work together; and to invite and accept the Creator of the world and His mercy and His wisdom into their hearts!"

At long last, the police van approaches at full speed and stops, plunging into its own cloud of dust. Like a frail patient, MaZondi is helped out of the van, flanked by the police with long-barrelled guns at the ready. She walks, swaying weakly, and trips over one of the burning shoes that has been ejected, burning, from Thabekhulu.

"But, if things stay as we see them now, we'll continue being dead while alive ..." Bhekizizwe throws a protracted look at the large crowd that has converged to watch. "Where are we in this life?"

In unison, as if on cue and prearranged, the crowd responds, and the voices resonate around the hills: "We are nowhere, our people. AND OUR HOME IS NOWHERE!"

"Ha...wu! Maye, Nkulunkulu wami! Oh dear me, my God!" MaZondi cannot believe what she is seeing and hearing as she stands over Thabekhulu, and she faints and collapses on the ashes of the man who can no longer stand trial in a case for which she too is going to be prosecuted, and found guilty.

"Xola. Forgive me ... forgive us all ... be at peace and resign yourself to this closure, Mwelase!" she whispers, pleading, fondly addressing him by his clan name.

And, far away on the horizon, the sun sinks away into the lurking dusk.

Oh, dear us, my Lord! My beloved child, this destiny was inescapable.

Glossary and notes

baba father
bafana (abafana) boys
bantabami my children
braai barbecue
bundu a wild place, wilderness
dadewethu our sister; my sister
dagga marijuana, cannabis
hawu an expression of surprise
homelands (also known as Bantustans) areas to which the apartheid
    government officially designated black South Africans on the basis of
    their language or ethnic group
imali money
imbongi a performer of traditional praise poems, who performs and
    recites a dramatic form of oral poetry that may include praises, historical
    allusions and criticism
knobkierie a stick with a knob at one end, often used as a weapon
lobola a bride price; traditionally cattle and other livestock paid by a
    bridegroom to the family of his future wife
mfowethu our friend, our brother; my friend, my brother
mfundisi (umfundisi) a preacher, a minister in the Church
Mkhumbane the name given by the residents of a particularly dense
    shack settlement in Cato Manor, Durban. The name came to be used
    more generally to refer to informal shack settlements. Mkhumbane was
    demolished and no longer exists.
mntanami my child
necklace to place a car tyre round a person's neck, douse it with petrol and
    set it alight
ngiyabonga I thank you
Nkosi yami my God, my Lord
panga a bush knife; a machete
pass (also **pass book**) an identity book that black South Africans had to
    carry at all times during the era of apartheid
phakathi inside
phambili forward
phuthu a dry, crumbly type of porridge made of maize-meal
shesha hurry

shisanyama literally "char the meat"; a place where meat is grilled on an open fire, usually for sale

sishweshwe (isishweshwe) a type of printed cotton

sondela, sondelani come closer

struggle, the often refers to the struggle against the apartheid regime

suka go away

thula, thulani be quiet, shut up

ubuntu humaneness, kindness, fellow-feeling; linked to the expression "A person is a person through other people"

umuthi medicine, medicinal charm, or a preparation used to bring luck or influence others

vuka wake up

About the translator

Nakanjani Sibiya

Nakanjani Sibiya was born at Gcotsheni near Eshowe, KwaZulu-Natal, in 1967. He was educated at local schools and at the University of Zululand, and holds a PhD in isiZulu Literature. He worked as an editor of African languages in a Pietermaritzburg publishing house for ten years before joining the Department of Arts and Culture in KwaZulu-Natal where he was responsible for literature development. Sibiya currently lectures in isiZulu at the University of KwaZulu-Natal. He is the author of eight published works of literature in isiZulu, including short story collections, dramas and novels, and has won several prestigious awards, including the JL Dube–Via Afrika Award for Prose, the M-Net Book Prize and the BW Vilakazi–Shuter & Shooter Award. He has translated many other authors' works into isiZulu. This is his first major isiZulu-to-English translation.

To view the translators speaking about the Africa Pulse series, visit
www.youtube.com/oxfordsouthernafrica